School Discourse
Problems

School Discourse Problems

Edited by

Danielle Newberry Ripich, Ph.D.
Department of Communication Sciences
Case Western Reserve University
Cleveland, Ohio

Francesca M. Spinelli, Ph.D.
Indianapolis, Indiana

COLLEGE-HILL PRESS, San Diego, California

College-Hill Press, Inc.
4284 41st Street
San Diego, California 92105

Library of Congress Cataloging in Publication Data
Main entry under title:

Ripich, Danielle Newberry.
  School discourse problems.

  Bibliography: p.
  Includes index. 1. Children—Language—Addresses, essays, lectures.
2. Oral communication—Addresses, essays, lectures. 3. Discourse analysis—
Addresses, essays, lectures. 4. Communicative disorders in children—Addresses,
essays, lectures. I. Spinelli, Francesca M. (Francesca Marie) II. Title.
LB1139.L3R53 1985   372.6   85-12754
ISBN 0-88744-140-8

Printed in the United States of America

jer
4-11-86

To

Frank S. Spinelli   *Forde J. Newberry*
Catherine J. Spinelli   *June Curtin Newberry*

CONTENTS

CONTRIBUTORS

Jan L. Bedrosian, Ph.D., Department of Speech Pathology and Audiology, Kansas State University, Manhattan, Kansas 66502

David Bloome, Ph.D., Division of Developmental Curriculum and Teaching, University of Michigan, Ann Arbor, Michigan 48109

Stephen N. Calculator, Ph.D., Department of Speech Pathology, University of New Hampshire, Durham, New Hampshire 03824

Nancy Creaghead, Ph.D., University of Cincinnati, Cincinnati, Ohio 45221

Sondra L. Dastoli, M.Ed., Kent State University, Kent, Ohio 44242

Mavis Donahue, Ph.D., College of Education, Box 4348, University of Illinois— Chicago Circle, Chicago, Illinois 60680

Penny L. Griffith, Ph.D., Department of Special Education, Kent State University, Kent, Ohio 44242

Aquiles Iglesias, Ph.D., Department of Speech, Temple University, Philadelphia, Pennsylvania 19122

Harold A. Johnson, Ed.D., Kent State University, Kent, Ohio 44242

Gladys P. Knott, Ph.D., College of Education, Kent State University, Kent, Ohio 44242

Susan J. Liljegreen, M.A., University of Iowa, Iowa City, Iowa 52242

Sandra Tattershall, Ph.D., 6421 Dixie Highway, Florence, Kentucky 41042

Brenda Terrell, Ph.D., Department of Communication Sciences, Case Western Reserve University, Cleveland, Ohio 44106

J. Bruce Tomblin, Ph.D., Department of Speech Pathology and Audiology, Wendell Johnson Speech and Hearing Center, University of Iowa, Iowa City, Iowa 52242

PREFACE

This book developed from discussions we had while colleagues at Case Western Reserve University. It seemed to us that a body of information about children's discourse problems was developing; however, this information was not well integrated into the framework of speech-language pathology. Although our backgrounds were diverse, we shared a common view regarding the importance of discourse abilities and children's school performance. For us, this book represents three years of interaction with each other and with researchers in the area of discourse. Represented here are a variety of approaches to the study of discourse. In addition to speech-language pathologists, we invited authors from general education, education of the deaf, and education of children with learning disabilities to share their perspectives. The volume provides a forum for these disciplines, and allows for the cross-fertilization of ideas about the structure and function of discourse in school contexts. The book was constructed with several audiences in mind: school clinicians, graduate students in speech pathology, audiology, education of the deaf, special education, or general education, and teachers who may have children with discourse problems in their classrooms. The book also provides a literature review for researchers and scholars working in the discourse area.

There are at present many unknowns involved in the study of children's discourse in school. However, this book is designed to provide interaction among different disciplines to lead to a fuller and deeper understanding of discourse in school communication.

Danielle N. Ripich
Francesca M. Spinelli

ACKNOWLEDGMENTS

We gratefully acknowledge the work of the contributors. The cooperation of the authors, who represent a variety of backgrounds and disciplines, allowed the development of a new broader perspective of educational discourse rules. Their enthusiasm for the project and willingness to share their ideas generated an exciting working atmosphere.

We thank the people who helped shape our views of education: Eric Sander, John Panagos, Georgia Hambrecht, Louise Cherry Wilkinson, Dee Vetter, and Bob Baldes. We particularly thank the children of Cleveland, Ohio, and Bettendorf, Iowa, who, perhaps, taught us most of all.

A special note of gratitude to Robin Chapman for critical comments. Thanks to Sadanand Singh for his encouragement and interest. We additionally thank Margaret Olson and Cindy Whittemore for their assistance in preparation of the manuscript.

To our families and friends our gratitude is implicit. For loving support we thank Terry, Amy, Michael, Sarah Caroline, Ree, and Sam.

We are grateful for the shared experience of this project. For stimulation of ideas, shaping rough concepts, and everlasting good humor we are grateful to each other. We offer this collection to our colleagues and students in the hope that they will find it a useful tool in the creation of their own work.

PART I

INTRODUCTION

Chapter 1

Discourse and Education

Francesca M. Spinelli
Danielle N. Ripich

The 1960s and 1970s brought about a wealth of knowledge concerning children's acquisition of linguistic structure. The identification and isolation of discreet units of language provided a window for viewing children's individual linguistic systems. It allowed us to create norms and compare specific areas of development as well as to document growth and change.

Bates (1976) suggested that we have paid a price for this focus by losing sight of the ties of language structure to communication and context. Recently, the focus of linguistic concerns has moved outside of individual language systems to larger frameworks of communication events. An emphasis has been placed on examining how the structure and meaning of utterances relate to other utterances in a speech event. This focus on larger "continuous stretch(es) of language is termed discourse" (Crystal, 1980, p. 114). Accompanying the focus on related linguistic context is an interest in nonverbal variables that interact with language use, including situation, participation, and motivation. Consideration of these multiple factors has resulted in viewing communication as a system with the individual's own linguistic ability as only one part that affects and is affected by the larger whole.

More recently, this concern with the larger communicative context has moved to populations exhibiting language deficits and variations. Knowledge about the interaction of language with its context has influenced thinking about language teaching and learning. Consequently, application has been made to the methods and content of language assessment. For example, recent approaches to language assessment have suggested that the content of evaluations focuses on the communication demands of particular environments (Gallagher, 1983). Current assessment procedures consider usual contexts by defining them or conducting assessments in the usual environments or ones similar to them. Similar attitudes are found in approaches to intervention. Teaching language in the context in which it will be used or in a context that parallels the usual context has been advocated (Spinelli and Terrell, 1984).

Clearly, for the school-aged child, who spends much of the day at school, the context of concern is the school setting. During the last decade the field of sociolinguistics has contributed greatly to our knowledge of discourse characteristics in the school setting. Studies of teachers' and students' language interactions have revealed general tutorial styles of instruction (Mehan, 1979) as well as variations. Examinations of classroom contexts have identified frameworks useful for describing larger communicative events (Green and Harker, 1982). The studies have shown consistently that although generalizations can be drawn about school discourse, variations exist (Wilkinson, 1982). These variations are related to a number of factors that may include individual linguistic abilities, background experience, listener expectations, academic level, and contextual characteristics.

The purpose of this volume is to apply current knowledge about classroom research to children exhibiting communication variations and deficits. By understanding the social nature of schools and the range of communicative demands placed on learners, we will have a better understanding of how these children function in the school setting. Furthermore, this knowledge will better enable educators to provide communication assistance that will facilitate academic learning. To accomplish this, the book examines the linguistic knowledge children bring to school based on their backgrounds and disabilities. In addition, language contexts of the school setting as well as those of specialized settings are considered. Based on this knowledge, applications to language assessment and teaching are made.

DISCOURSE DEFINED

Before examining the literature relating to classroom discourse, it will be useful to define a number of terms used in this research. In describing discourse two dimensions can be considered: content and level. Content refers to the knowledge and skills required for understanding and using discourse rules. Level refers to the size of the discourse unit being examined. These dimensions are independent, thus allowing individual content areas of discourse to be considered at multiple levels.

Content Areas for Discourse

Five content areas for discourse can be identified. They are attention, turn-allocation, topic coherence, repair, and role adjustment. For each of these content areas a number of skills are required for the roles of both listener and speaker.

Attentional skills for the listener involve the ability to concentrate on appropriate sources of information (e.g., a speaker) and to provide evidence of this attention. This evidence can be in the form of attention markers such as head nods, vocal acknowledgments, and eye contact, or it can be implied by the appropriate use of other discourse skills such as topic continuation. For a speaker attentional skills involve the ability to obtain and hold the attention of others. An awareness of listener inattention is also required. Speakers may obtain and hold attention through the use of linguistic cues (e.g., saying "Okay, class"), paralinguistic cues (e.g., increasing voice volume), or nonverbal cues (e.g., looking at an intended listener).

Turn-allocation involves a knowledge of the rules used to initiate and coordinate speakers' participation in discourse. Initiation involves the ability to begin a speaking turn as well as to provide opportunity for others to participate. This can be accomplished nonverbally through pause and eye contact as well as verbally through devices such as questioning. Turn-taking skills require that participants recognize turn requests, such as questions.

Topic coherence involves the ability to relate utterances through the use of meaningful and structural ties. The utterances can be tied to those of a previous speaker or to the current speaker's own utterances. Topic continuation involves the ability to maintain a topic, to elaborate on a topic, or to introduce new topics with appropriate topic shifts. In addition to continuity of meaning, utterances can be tied together through the use of structural links termed cohesive devices (Halliday and Hasan, 1976). They include ties such as anaphora, conjunctions, and ellipsis.

The next area of discourse competence, repair, is the ability to recognize, indicate, and clarify unsuccessful utterances. The speaker must be able to recognize that a listener has not understood the intended message, determine the possible reasons for the breakdown, and clarify the message via elaboration, repetition, or paraphrase. The listener's responsibility is to indicate to the speaker that the message has not been understood. A number of verbal and nonverbal means of communicating misunderstanding are available to the listener, such as questions and quizzical expressions.

A final content area of discourse skill is that of role adjustment. A speaker must be able to adjust the form and content of an utterance according to the characteristics of the situation and the listeners. Factors to be considered include the formality of the situation; relative social status of speaker and listener; age, sex, and culture of the communicative participants; and purpose of communication. For example, a speaker may use more direct or informal language with a peer than with an individual of a higher status (Brown and Levinson, 1978).

Discourse rules for each of the five content areas can be identified for individual contexts, including the classroom. Similar contexts may show some rule similarities, yet differences. Competent communicators learn to discriminate and master these contextual variations.

Levels of Discourse

Levels of discourse refers to the size of the linguistic unit analyzed. Chapman (1981) suggests that the lowest level involves a pair of utterances. An utterance and the utterance that precedes or follows it are isolated for analysis. This can include verbal or nonverbal utterances. At higher levels units of utterances increase in size. For example, the notion of contingent query (Garvey, 1977) involves three utterances. This consists of an utterance followed by a request for clarification and a follow-up utterance. The query sequence can be expanded to include the utterance that follows the clarification in order to reenter the conversation (Gallagher, 1981).

Units can increase in size to include several sentences by one or more speakers. Typically the term "text" is used to describe oral or written passages of any length that form a unit (Halliday and Hasan, 1976). One type of structure, narrative or story text structure (Mandler and Johnson, 1977), is often first used at home and in early preacademic and reading activities. Later, various expository text frameworks are used in academic work.

Levels as units of organization have been applied to classroom research by Sinclair and Coulthard (1975). They ranked a series of discourse units in a hierarchical order. At the lowest level are acts. These are single utterances whose function is considered in isolation (e.g., an informative statement). At the next level, moves are combinations of speech acts that serve a more general purpose, such as a follow-up to provide feedback. Exchanges are combinations of moves that form individual steps by which a lesson progresses. An example of an exchange is a question, a response, and appropriate feedback. Transactions are groups of exchanges bounded by shifts in lesson focus. Lessons are composed of a series of transactions and are the highest level of classroom discourse.

The working definition of discourse provided indicates that discourse involves multiple utterances in five content areas and isolates the many ways that discourse can be analyzed. When this view of discourse is applied to a school setting, several questions can be asked.

CLASSROOM DISCOURSE QUESTIONS

The first set of questions involves children's acquisition of discourse rules in the home and classroom and the differences between rules in these two contexts. We can ask what knowledge children possess about discourse rules at the time formal schooling begins. We can also ask what discourse rules characterize the school setting and how they differ from those the child has learned at home. It is likely these rules change as the usual number of participants, the ratio of adults to children, and the purposes of usual communication activities change in the school setting. We can also ask how children adjust to and learn these new rules.

The part of this book entitled Normal Discourse Development focuses on the discourse characteristics of the home and school environments and on understanding how the child masters both sets of discourse rules. From the first months of life, the child is learning discourse rules. Many of the parent-child preverbal and early verbal interactions suggest a discourse structure similar to that of adults (Snow, 1977). As the child develops, this knowledge becomes more refined. By the time of school entrance the child has mastered a complex set of rules appropriate for interaction with family and peers. The chapter by Terrell describes this process and provides an understanding of the rules the child has developed in the first five years. She describes development in the basic discourse areas and demonstrates how the child learns to increase the size of discourse units. Once the child enters school another set of discourse rules must be learned. These rules are designed to facilitate learning and cooperation in groups. Bloome and Knott present an overview of ethnographic classroom research. They demonstrate that classroom rules have both social and academic ends and that the mastery level of these rules contributes to classroom success and failure.Their discussion highlights the complexity of discourse rules and the number of factors that influence their creation and usage. Tattershall and Creaghead's chapter focuses on the child's transition from home to school. They identify a number of differences between the two settings, but point out a common discourse framework as well. In discussing the differences between the two contexts, Tattershall and Creaghead suggest that knowledge of the differences between home and school rules contributes to classroom success.

As Bloome and Knott point out, there are similarities in typical classroom discourse that are maintained from classroom to classroom along with a number of individual rules. However, discourse rules do change with variation in context. Thus these rules change outside of "typical" academic interactions. Discourse characteristics of gym classes, playgrounds, and lunchrooms will differ in some ways from those of classrooms. Special learning situations present variations in discourse rules as well. The number of participants, the methods of learning, and the goals of learning all contribute to the creation of discourse rule variations for the nontypical or disabled child who receives assistance outside of the regular classroom. In addition, the nature of interactions as well as the specific abilities and disabilities of certain populations may produce some discourse behaviors that are uncharacteristic of typical school children.

A second set of questions focuses on the concerns of the nontypical child in the school setting. These can include children who exhibit learning problems or other problems that require assistance outside of the classroom or children who are in special classrooms primarily but are mainstreamed into regular classes for part of each day. It can also include children who are from cultures that differ from the primary culture and school setting. These children may possess discourse rules contrary to those used in typical academic settings. We can ask if the discourse rules of special learning contexts such as individualized and small group teaching differ from those found in typical classrooms. We can also ask if these rules differ in classrooms for children with specific disorders. If so, do they differ because of communication characteristics of the children or because of the learning requirements of those settings? We can also ask if these children who come to school with one set of discourse rules from home and perhaps learn another set for their special setting might be expected to experience difficulty mastering still another set of rules for the typical classroom.

The section of the book Discourse Variations in School considers discourse differences with which only some children in the school setting must deal. Iglesias discusses discourse differences experienced by normally developing children from different cultures. He focuses on the discourse skills of Hispanic children as a sample group. Iglesias notes that the similarities between home and school provide dominant-culture children with a basic framework to which classroom discourse rules can be added. In contrast, children from nondominant cultures need to learn both a system of interaction rules and a linguistic code in order to participate in academic learning. Iglesias argues that educators' understanding of the communication knowledge these children bring to school and programs based on this understanding are essential for meeting the academic needs of these children. Donahue's chapter highlights the discourse abilities of learning disabled children. She points out that these students possess discourse rules that differ from some of those typically used in classrooms and suggests explanations for their development. Griffith, Johnson, and Dastoli focus on discourse characteristics of classrooms for the hearing impaired and compare these with discourse patterns found in typical classrooms. They highlight some of the problems faced by hearing impaired children as conversational participants and suggest areas of solution. Calculator discusses discourse characteristics of mentally retarded individuals in residential and school contexts. He also provides insight for facilitating discourse with this population. In a comparison of classroom and therapy room discourse rules, Spinelli and Ripich identify similarities in these teaching and learning contexts as well as differences. They suggest that the differences can create difficulties for children participating in both contexts, whereas the similarities present opportunities to facilitate carryover from clinical to classroom contexts.

The third set of questions revolves around how information about school discourse can be of use to special educators. First, we can ask how the discourse rules of different settings can be determined. Second, we can ask how this information can be used in assessing and managing communication problems of nontypical children in an academic setting. Finally, we can ask if we are placing extra burdens on children who receive learning support in school settings. Are these children being required to learn a set of discourse rules that hardly overlap with those used in other contexts?

The section Intervention and Discourse addresses these questions by discussing how information about discourse can be used for remediation in a school setting. Although many of these ideas are oriented to communication impaired populations, they are also relevant for communicatively different ones. Ripich and Spinelli outline a model employing ethnographic research methods for assessment of children's discourse problems within the classroom environment. They discuss how this information can be utilized in intervention programs involving the classroom teacher and the speech-language pathologist. The chapter by Tomblin and Liljegreen considers the role of social penalties in defining a communication disorder. They propose a management model based on the child's communication successes and failures in social contexts. Bedrosian presents a framework for topic and conversational control and outlines an approach for assessing and facilitating discourse competence.

In the final chapter of this book, we integrate the discussions of the authors of these chapters and highlight recurring themes. In addition we evaluate the significance of the discussions for the practicing professional.

Together the chapters in this book present an expanded view of the role of communication at school. Communication is seen as more than an individual student's ability to understand and use linguistic forms and meaning; communication is seen as the key to entering the learning system. Without the knowledge of how to participate with teachers and peers in the learning process, that is, in the discourse rules of school, academic success is unlikely. This book describes school discourse and examines the ability of children with communication differences and deficits to successfully access the learning system. It highlights problems and offers suggestions for these problem communicators.

REFERENCES

Bates, E. (1976). *Language and context.* New York: Academic Press.

Brown, P., and Levinson, S. (1978). Universals in language usage: Politeness phenomena. In E. Goody (Ed.), *Questions and politeness.* Cambridge: Cambridge University Press.

Chapman, R. S. (1981). Exploring children's communicative intents. In J. F. Miller (Ed.), *Assessing language production in children.* Baltimore: University Park Press.

Crystal, D. (1980). *A first dictionary of linguistics and phonetics.* Boulder, CO: Westview Press.

Gallagher, T. M. (1981). Contingent query sequences within adult-child discourse. *Journal of Child Language, 8,* 51–62.

Gallagher, T. M. (1983). Pre-assessment: A procedure for accommodating language use variability. In T. M. Gallagher and C. A. Prutting (Eds.), *Pragmatic assessment and intervention issues in language.* San Diego: College-Hill Press.

Garvey, C. (1977). The contingent query. In M. Lewis and L. Rosenblum (Eds.), *Interaction, conversation, and the development of language.* New York: John Wiley and Sons.

Green, J. L., and Harker, J. O. (1982). Gaining access to learning: Conversational, social, and cognitive demands in group participation. In L. C. Wilkinson (Ed.), *Communicating in the classroom.* New York: Academic Press.

Halliday, M. A. K., and Hasan, R. (1976). *Cohesion in English.* London: Longman.

Mandler, J. M., and Johnson, N. S. (1977). Remembrance of things parsed: Story structure and recall. *Cognitive Psychology, 9,* 111–151.

Mehan, H. (1979). *Learning Lessons.* Cambridge, MA: Harvard University Press.

Sinclair, J., and Coulthard, R. M. (1975). *Towards an analysis of discourse: The English language used by teachers and pupils.* London: Oxford University Press.

Snow, C. E. (1977). The development of conversation between mothers and babies. *Journal of Child Language, 4,* 1–22.

Spinelli, F. M., and Terrell, B. Y. (1984). Remediation in context. *Topics in language disorders, 5,* 29–40.

Stein, N., and Glenn, C. (1979). An analysis of story comprehension in elementary school children. In R. Freedle (Ed.), *New directions in discourse processing.* Norwood, NJ: Ablex Publishing Corporation.

Wilkinson, L. C. (Ed.) (1982). *Communicating in the classroom.* New York: Academic Press.

PART II

NORMAL DISCOURSE DEVELOPMENT

Chapter 2

Learning the Rules of the Game: Discourse Skills in Early Childhood

Brenda Y. Terrell

Consider a conversation between three five year old boys as they play a game with colored toy soldiers:

Child 1: Whose turn is it?
Child 2: It's my turn.
Child 3: No, you're blue and I'm red. It's my turn now.
Child 1: Okay, you take a turn now. I'm yellow and I'll be next.
Child 2: Blue then yellow then red. Okay?
Child 1: Okay.
Child 3: Okay.

The children in this conversation are playing a game and trying to decide who takes the next turn. They work out the rules, agree on whose turn is next, and proceed with the game. Simultaneously with their game of soldiers, these children are also participating in another game. The rules of this second game are so well known to them that they never have to discuss them (and probably could not if asked). For this second game there is no discussion and few disagreements about whose turn is next or what to do with a turn. When there is a disagreement, these children know devices for solving the problem. Unlike when they play their game of soldiers, these children play this second game every time they interact. They play the game with their parents, their siblings, and their teachers. All of the other children in their kindergarten class play the same game with their parents and their siblings. Parents play the game among themselves and with colleagues in the office, friends on the tennis court, and the exercise instructor at the spa. The game that these children and most children and adults play every day of their lives is the game of communication. We all know the rules well and rarely make errors (except on those occasions when we speak first and think later) that we cannot immediately correct.

Brown (1958) suggested the "word game" as a hypothesis for the way that children learn the names for things in the environment and the meanings for words in the language. Austin (1962) suggested the "language game" as an explanation for how we follow rules to accomplish verbal acts. However, both Brown's word game and Austin's language game are subsumed by the communication game. We begin to learn and play by the rules of the communication game before uttering words or any other linguistic forms. It may be our knowledge of the communication game that makes possible our acquisition and use of language. But what are the rules and where do they come from?

THE FIRST PLAYERS AND THE FIRST RULES

This volume focuses on discourse competence in the educational setting. However, the basic structure of communication and the rules for participating in the game of communication are learned long before the process of formal education begins. Although there are modifications of these basic rules for the educational environment, and players such as teachers, cafeteria personnel, and school peers are introduced, the basic rules remain closely aligned with those learned the first times that the game was played.

The game of communication is first introduced during the period of infancy. The primary players during this period are the infant and the caretaker. The quality of the early interactions between these participants sets the stage for and determines the course of development of sociocommunicative and other skills (Brazelton and Tronick, 1980; Snow, 1981; Wilcox and Terrell, 1985). The first part of this chapter will describe the events and accomplishments that occur during the period of infancy and serve as the base for the development of discourse competence.

Three periods or stages of communicative development have been defined (Bates, 1976; Clark, 1978). Bates labels these the perlocutionary, illocutionary, and locutionary stages. The perlocutionary period corresponds to that stage in development when many of the infant's behaviors, both gestural and vocal, have a communicative effect on the caretaker without there being any communicative intent on the part of the infant. Context is a critical variable in defining this infant behavior-caretaker response set as communicative. For example, the infant cries (infant behavior) upon waking near a regularly scheduled feeding time (context). The mother interprets the cry as communicating hunger and responds by feeding the child. During this early period the child's behavior is not intended as communicative but is more likely a response to some physiological stimulus. However, the behavior, that is, the cry, has signal value for the adult. The continued pairing of the child's unintentional communicative signal with the adult's response sets in motion a system that forms the basis for the child's communicative development. Because of this pairing of infant behavior and adult response, the child develops an understanding of the signal value of behavior. This understanding of the communicative effect of behavior is critical for further communicative development (Snow, 1981).

Once the signal value of gestural and vocal behavior is established for the infant, these behaviors are used to achieve communicative goals, that is, the attainment of either attention, aid, or objects from the adult. When the child shows voluntary and intentional use of these behaviors, illocutionary stage communication has appeared. Observationally, perlocutionary and illocutionary stage behaviors can be distinguished based on (1) the infant's attention to the adult who can produce the desired result and (2) the infant's persistence in performance of the behaviors until the result is obtained (or the infant is completely frustrated). For example, the child who wants more juice may vocalize and look toward the caregiver and hold an empty cup up until the caregiver responses. Words are not a part of the communicative frames of the perlocutionary and illocutionary stages. Nonetheless these behaviors are communicative and often become conventionalized just as words do.

It is during these two periods, prior to the appearance of verbal or locutionary communication, that the underpinnings of discourse competence are established. All the necessary components of structured conversational interactions — topic initiation, turn-taking conventions, conversational repairs, and so on — can be found in the caregiver-infant interactions of the perlocutionary and illocutionary periods. Although rudimentary, the rules of discourse are used and "taught" by the caregiver during these early phases of development.

One of the necessary prerequisites for conversation is the capacity for joint attention (Keenan and Klein, 1975). The joint regulation of attention and activity is one of the initial achievements of early infant-caregiver interactions. Joint regulation first centers on affective behaviors with the adult cuing into and modifying his or her behavior so that it is consistent with the infant's level of arousal (Als, 1982; Brazelton, 1982; Stern, 1977). Dyadic play, and finally object play with the caregiver, later become the focus of joint regulation (Als, 1982; Brazelton, 1982). Bruner (1975, 1977) has suggested that joint attentional focus during games and routines such as peek-a-boo and give and take are necessary not only for nonlinguistic communicative development but also for the development of language.

Conversational Topic in Early Interactions

The joint regulation of attention, particularly when an object focus is present, appears to be the precursor for the notion of topic and topic initiation in conversational discourse. In verbal discourse, topic can be simply defined as what the conversation or speaker's message is about: the focus of the discourse. In order for there to be successful interactions during the prelinguistic period, caregiver and infant must also share attentional focus. This joint attentional focus is an agreement on the visual and often tactile center of the interaction.

Topics of preverbal interactions can be initiated by either the child or the adult. Infants as young as four months have been found to follow the adult's line of regard (Bruner, 1975, 1977) and there are numerous examples in the literature (e.g., Shaffer, Collis, and Parsons, 1977; Snow, 1977; Trevarthan, 1974) of adults using the object focus of the child as the focus of their comments and actions.

Once topic is established in conversational discourse, the speaker is obliged to comment on the topic. When the infant and the caregiver achieve joint attention, the caregiver generally acts on or verbally comments on the interactional focus. The child shows the comment aspect of this prelinguistic notion of topicalization (i.e., joint attentional focus) by giving some indication that the topic is indeed shared. The child does this primarily through gaze management. Once the object focus of the interaction is visually established, the child makes eye contact with the adult. This assures that both interactors are "on topic" and serves as the child's comment on the topic (Bruner, 1975, 1977). At later points in development this topic confirmation becomes vocal.

Infants show their understanding of the procedures of topic initiation through their use of protodeclaratives and protoimperatives (Bates, 1976; Bates, Camaioni, and Volterra, 1975) during the illocutionary period. With these nonverbal behaviors infants offer an object focus for interaction with the adult. That the topics of this nonverbal discourse are definite for the children in these interactions is illustrated in their persistence when the adult misinterprets the intention of the behaviors. For example, if the infant desires that the adult "do something" with the object (protoimperative) and the adult merely responds with attention (protodeclarative), the child will repeat or elaborate the vocal or gestural behavior as an attempt to gain compliance.

Turn-Taking in Early Interactions

Another consequence of the interactions between caregiver and infant is the emergence of a pattern of dialogue. A central component of dialogue in nonverbal as well as in verbal exchanges is turn-taking between the participants. Understanding the centrality of turn-taking then is another achievement of early caregiver-child interactions. Most of the gestural and vocal games played by caregiver and infant involve a pattern of turns and allow for the practice of many of those skills necessary for sociocommunicative competence. Snow (1981) outlines three such skills: (1) taking a turn as a necessary component of social interaction, (2) understanding how a particular turn can be used, and (3) understanding how the turn content can be varied given the constraints of the game or routine.

The appearance and disappearance games played by two mother-infant dyads described by Ratner and Bruner (1978) illustrate how early games provide a training ground for each of the outlined skills. These games generally provide a restricted and highly routinized format. This format allows the child to make clear predictions about what is to occur next and how his or her turns or the caregiver's turns should be used. Mothers often mark each juncture in the game with its own type of vocalization, further emphasizing structure and signaling the exchange of turns for the child. Over the course of the game any of its specific components may be elaborated, thus giving practice in how turn content can be varied. These early games also demonstrate an interchangeability of role structure that is analogous to the reversibility of hearer-speaker roles in discourse.

Turn-taking conventions in discourse allow for smooth interchanges between speaker and listener (Prutting and Kirchner, 1983) and for the coordination of speech so that all participants can achieve their respective goals (Clark and Clark, 1977). Although in adult-adult discourse the primary aim appears to be "getting a turn," the mother's primary aim in early interactions with her infant appears to be getting the baby to take a turn (Snow, 1977). Snow suggested that to achieve this aim mothers adopt a "conversational model" for their interactions. This mode of interaction directed the verbal input to infants during the period when the children were 3 to 18 months old and thus allowed mothers to teach and the infants to practice turn-taking behavior. The preponderance of interrogatives, post-completers, tag questions, and greetings seemed designed to serve as turn-allocation devices in the speech of mothers to infants. In the earliest interactions mothers accepted almost any behavior, either voluntary or involuntary, as the child's turn. However, with further development the mothers' requirements for what was adequate and appropriate turn content increased. The mothers' increasing constraints on what was appropriate turn content is of course related to the increasing motor and vocal skills of the child but appears also to be related to the child's increasing awareness of his or her role in the interchange. By the age of 14 months children have been observed to initiate vocal turn-taking sequences and to play a central role in maintaining the flow of conversation with their mothers (Dunn and Kendrick, 1982).

Ninio and Bruner (1978) observed interactive book reading in a mother-infant dyad when the child was between the ages of 8 and 18 months. They reported nearly perfect turn-taking cycles from the beginning of their observations, with no more than one per cent of the turns showing overlap. This clearly indicates that turn-taking skill was established in this infant quite early. Trevarthan (1974, 1977, 1980) found that mothers of two month old infants were using this conversational mode and allowing infants to take their turns. He proposed that this mode of interaction is as much a function of infant behavior as it is a function of the mother's spontaneous teaching strategy. He further proposed that the foundations of interpersonal communication and intersubjectivity are possibly innate and are useable by infants as early as eight weeks of age.

Infants are exposed not only to the procedure for turn-taking during their early interactions with caregivers but to the timing of turn-taking as well. As a part of their turn-taking instruction, mothers use a "mature time frame" for dialogue and allow just as much time between their own vocalizations or verbalizations for the infant's response as would be allowed for the listener to take a turn in adult-adult conversation (Stern, 1977).

After their first experiences with the communication game infants know much about the rules for true conversational dialogue. They are exposed to the duality and reversibility of their roles, some of the conventions for topic selection, elaboration, and maintenance and turn-taking. Although many of these behaviors are adult initiated and directed, it is clear that adult knowledge of discourse rules structures these early interactions. From these early experiences with playing the communication game children learn the requirements of and practice their roles in discourse competence.

COMPLICATING THE GAME:
THE PRESCHOOL YEARS

Once the child enters the locutionary period of communicative development, the options for how to initiate and play the communication game are significantly increased. There are now available both verbal and nonverbal means of conveying messages and expressing discourse competence. As the child's semantic and syntactic competence increases, so do the expectations of those with whom they play the game. Although adults who interact with language learning children appear to make some allowances for the less sophisticated skills of their young partners, they expect that children will make some active contribution to keeping the interaction going, will make their comments topically relevant, and will make conversational repairs. In this section of the chapter those advancements in discourse competence that occur during the preschool years will be discussed.

An Expanded Notion of Topic

During the preschool years the notion of conversational topic is greatly expanded beyond that of the early infant-caregiver interactions. During the early periods of development (i.e., perlocutionary and illocutionary periods) children learn the procedure for initiating topic. With the onset of verbal language during the locutionary period, children can use words to introduce and respond to conversational topics. Because words are more specific than gestures children can be more successful in making the focus of interaction with others definite.

A further skill necessary for discourse competence is the ability to maintain a topic across several exchanges of conversational turns. To sustain a topic across turns it is necessary to attend to the utterances of each speaker and to make a contribution relevant to the topic. Topic-relevant comments in conversation require that each participant's contribution be to some degree contingent on the speech of the previous speakers. Bloom, Rocissano, and Hood (1976) have described the discourse contributions of children at Brown's linguistic Stages I and II (mean length of utterance [MLU]) as largely noncontingent. Although these children made comments that were primarily adjacent to adult utterances, their comments did not add new information to the conversational topic. When an adult system definition of topic contingency, such as that used by Bloom and colleagues is used, it may be the case that topic-relevant and contingent responses are limited at Stages I and II. This, however, is a reflection of linguistic and not discourse competence. When a child-based definition is employed, the discourse competence of children at these stages is clear.

Children at early Stage I (MLU 1.0) make many of their contingent responses nonverbally (Prelock, Messick, Schwartz, and Terrell, 1981). When the two year old picks up and examines or throws a ball in response to the adult's "There's your big ball," this can be considered a topic-relevant and contingent response. Through his or her actions the child not oly acknowledges the topical focus but also provides a means for the adult to verbally extend the conversation (e.g., "You threw it."). The child's "comment" not only shares the topic but also adds to the topic. This behavior is consistent with the conversational interactions of the earlier periods of development. Additionally, it may also be a nonlinguistic example of the principle, "New functions are first expressed by old forms" (Slobin, 1973). The new function expressed is extended topic maintenance. Maintaining a topic across several turns is first done with the most well-established communicative device, nonverbal communication, and once established nonverbally can be later expressed through language.

Keenan and Klein (1975) described multiple strategies used by twins during the early preschool years to sustain interaction and topical focus in child-child interactions. Among the strategies were (1) simple repetition of the previous speaker's utterance, (2) affirmation or denial of the previous utterance, (3) repetition of the previous utterance with a change in a single linguistic or paralinguistic feature, and (4) extension of the previous utterance by predicating something new. The most complex of these, extension, is most consistent with the contingent response of Bloom and colleagues, but extension did not occur frequently in these child-child interactions during the period from age 2:9 to approximately 3:9.

In addition to these verbal strategies for extending discourse, Keenan and Klein found these children to sustain conversations for longer than 20 turns when these conversations involved exchanges of sound play. The children listened to the previous child's vocalization and then repeated or modified its phonological shape in their responses. By adhering to the rules of conversation, taking turns and making contingent responses, these children could extend interaction when referential content had been exhausted. This type of sound-play exchange provides the opportunity to practice conversational skills in much the same way described by Bruner for earlier periods. To participate in this interaction it is necessary to attend to and acknowledge the speaker's previous utterance and use elements of those antecedent utterances to formulate a response. Both skills are necessary for successful discourse. True topic maintenance by adult standards probably requires conceptual and linguistic development beyond that of the early preschool years. Children at this level however have available the procedure and form necessary for this skill.

Turn-Taking Made More Complex

Even though preschoolers may have the ability to take turns and maintain topic focus across turn exchanges, they often continue to appear conversationally incompetent. The rules of the game at this point have changed slightly. In the early infant-caregiver interactions the turn-taking rule was "give the baby a turn." During the preschool period the rule changes and is now more equivalent to rules in adult-adult conversations, in which each participant must manipulate conversation to gain a turn. This rule shift may generate or at least contribute to the apparent conversational incompetence demonstrated by children during this period.

Preschoolers have difficulty in managing interruptions and also do not have well-developed devices for acknowledging and terminating topics (Ervin-Tripp, 1979). Thus they may find it difficult to gain a turn in on-going discourse. In adult-adult interactions, if a speaker wishes to change the topic of conversation, the present topic must be acknowledged and a termination signal sent before the new topic is introduced (e.g., "Yeah, that's true. You know, the other day I was thinking . . .") (Wilcox and Terrell, 1985). Preschoolers do not have these devices available for acknowledgment and termination. Owing to processing constraints, children at this level find it difficult to monitor the conversation and determine the appropriate point to "jump in." They cannot monitor the speech of others and simultaneously remember their own contributions. Because of this latter deficiency preschoolers find it more difficult to participate in multi-party interactions with adults and older children than in dyadic interactions (Ervin-Tripp, 1979).

Interactions with age peers, however, reveal their knowledge of conversational rules. In these interactions, turn overlap generally occurs at points in the conversational flow that are transition relevant (Gallagher and Craig, 1982). Overlaps are observed to occur most often when the previous speaker self-selects to take the next conversational turn or when one speaker dominates the conversational floor, thereby limiting the number of speaker transition points.

Because during the early stages of linguistic development children lack the specific devices for verbally terminating and initiating topics, their contributions are often viewed as irrelevant. Consequently they are sometimes ignored by older listeners (Ervin-Tripp, 1979), and topic introductions may be unsuccessful. However, these children have the skill to readjust when their topic introductions fail and make relevant and contingent responses to the topics on the floor (Prelock et al., 1981).

Adjusting to the Listener: Conversational Repair and Speech Style Modifications

To successfully engage in conversational discourse each participant, when in the speaker role, must consider and attend to the needs of listeners. Listeners differ in what they require from speakers. If the amount of information shared between speaker and listener is limited, then speakers must make their messages explicit. Listeners who have limited linguistic abilities require messages that are reduced in complexity. Authority figures and listeners of otherwise high status require that speakers are polite and deferential. As competent discourse participants, speakers must evaluate their listeners' needs and determine if messages have been comprehended. Such determinations are made on the basis of listener feedback as well as on the speakers' knowledge of the quality of their own messages. Evaluation of message quality is important because the feedback from listeners is sometimes inaccurate (Beal and Flavell, 1983).

Preschoolers seem cognizant of the requirement to respond to listener cues regarding messages that are not clear. One device used by listeners to alert speakers to unclear messages is the contingent query. As defined by Garvey (1977), a contingent query is a question that is addressed to the immediately prior speaker. The question is embedded in a larger stretch of discourse. In using a question of this type the questioner indicates that the earlier speaker's message was in some way unclear or that additional information is desired or needed for full comprehension. The use of a contingent query obligates the earlier speaker to respond. If no response is forthcoming there may be an interruption in message comprehension. Children's use and comprehension of the requirements imposed by the contingent query have been studied extensively (e.g., Gallagher, 1977, 1981; Garvey, 1975, 1977). In addition, children's methods of conversational repair have also been given attention (e.g., Gallagher, 1981; Konefal and Fokes, 1984; Wilcox and Howse, 1983; Wilcox and Webster, 1980).

Children who are in early Stage I and who are as young as two years old seem to understand their obligation to respond to a contingent query (Gallagher, 1981), and in conversations with other children (Garvey, 1975) preschoolers responded to queries from their listeners a major portion of the time. In preschool interactions two year olds failed to respond only 40 per cent of the time. Although they generally respond to queries, there appears to be some developmental ordering in the types of queries to which children can appropriately respond (Gallagher, 1981). In adult-child interactions the query most frequently responded to appropriately in linguistic Stages I to III is the simple request for confirmation. This query generally takes the form of a yes-no question; either full repetition of the child's original utterance using question intonation or some modified (elaborated or reduced) repetition of the utterance. Children at all three stages showed specific response strategies to this query type as well as to a category of neutral query (e.g., "What?", "Huh?", "I don't understand"). Only a portion of the children at Stages II and III showed distinctive responses to queries that required repetition of a specific grammatical constituent (e.g., "You did what?").

Children in these stages of development also use contingent queries in their interactions with adults. Most frequently used were requests for confirmation and the neutral query. The query requiring repetition of a specific constituent was generally used only by Stage III children.

Although basically proficient in participating in contingent query sequences, it is not until first grade that children seem to accurately evaluate a listener's comprehension when listener feedback is inaccurate. Using an experimental design, Beal and Flavell (1983) showed that children in preschool and kindergarten found it difficult to reject listener's inaccurate statements regarding their comprehension of messages even when the children themselves were aware of the quality of messages (i.e., whether or not the messages provided complete information). First graders, like adults, were able to use their evaluations of message quality to make determinations about whether or not listeners actually understood.

When faced with listener feedback indicating the need for clarification, how do children make conversational repairs? During early and late Stage I, when faced with listener misinterpretation of messages, children seldom abandon their attempts to communicate. Alternatively, they repeat utterances when faced with a neutral query (e.g.,"What?") or recode their utterances when listener feedback or response is inappropriate to the intent of the utterance (e.g., responding to a request as though it were a declarative). Across Stages III through V of linguistic development children begin to show some individual preferences for certain repair strategies (Konefal and Fokes, 1984). Across this range of development there is a definite decrease in the use of repetition as a repair device and an increase in the use of revision. Among varying categories of utterance revision older children show more elaboration than reduction of constituents. For children at the upper end of Brown's developmental continuum (Stage V) there appears to be little preference for a particular type of repair strategy. As children become proficient in the use of various types of syntactic strategies, there is less need to rely primarily on one.

Competence in social discourse requires a repertoire of speech styles. As adults we use a different style of speech with the boss at the office, a housekeeper, our spouse, children, and close friends. For the preschool-aged child the move to school in the preschool, kindergarten, and primary grades requires the ability to use various speech styles. Teachers are different from peers and also different from parents. Although teachers are adults they do not share the same amount and kinds of information with children as do parents. In conversing with parents about school occurrences this is also true: There is less shared information. The school-aged child is continually required to shift back and forth between registers.

Piaget's proposal that preschool speech was basically egocentric and the results of investigations using referential communication tasks

(Glucksberg and Krauss, 1967) would appear to indicate that a repertoire of listener-adapted speech styles is beyond the ability of the preschool child. However, observation of children in natural interactions and variation of the age and status of the persons addressed indicates that this too is an early developing ability. Two year olds have been shown to discriminate among forms of address relative to politeness. Although they recognized some forms as more polite, they did not accurately report why one form was more polite (Bates, 1976).

In using directives, four and five year olds are more polite when making requests than when commanding, and they include more politeness markers when addressing adults and age peers than when addressing younger children (James, 1978). In addressing speech to younger children, preschoolers demonstrate many of the characteristics of mother's speech to children. They simplify their speech by using strategies such as shorter, less complex sentences, frequent repetition, more questions and attention-getting devices, and a simple phonology (Sachs and Devin, 1976; Shatz and Gelman, 1973).

In modifying the style of their speech children are sensitive not only to age differences in listeners but also to differences in developmental status. Guralnick and Paul-Brown (1984) found that in addressing children who are developmentally delayed (primary cognitive deficit with commensurate linguistic skills), five year olds reduced utterance complexity, used more repetitions, and more gestures. The ability to modify interactional style based on age assures success in interacting with teachers, classmates and the "big kids" in the upper grades. The ability to modify style on the basis of developmental status will aid in interactions in mainstreamed classrooms.

CONCLUSION

This chapter can be summarized as "Discourse competence in early childhood: What they know and when they know it." The game of communication begins during infancy. With continued interactions and a variety of new experiences the game is played in many different contexts and with numerous players. Children first learn the basic rules with some modifications, and they also learn how to modify the rules depending on the context and the players. When the process of formal education begins, their skills are in place. Once through the preschool years, evaluation of children's discourse abilities would deem them ready for the new frontier of school. They're ready to play the communication game with almost anyone!

REFERENCES

Als, H. (1982). The unfolding of behavioral organization in the face of a biological violation. In E. Z. Tronick (Ed.), *Social interchange in infancy: Affect, cognition and communication*. Baltimore: University Park Press.

Austin, J. L. (1962). *How to do things with words*. Cambridge, MA: Harvard University Press.

Bates, E. (1976). *Language in context*. New York: Academic Press.

Bates, E., Camaioni, L., and Volterra, V. (1975). The acquisition of performatives prior to speech. *Merrill-Palmer Quarterly, 21,* 205–206.

Beal, C. R., and Flavell, J. H. (1983). Young speakers' evaluation of their listeners' comprehension in a referential communication task. *Child Development, 54,* 148–153.

Bloom, L., Rocissano, L., and Hood, L. (1976). Adult-child discourse: Developmental interaction between information processing and linguistic knowledge. *Cognitive Psychology, 8,* 521–552.

Brazelton, T. B. (1982). Joint regulation of neonate-parent behavior. In E. Z. Tronick (Ed.), *Social interchange in infancy: Affect, cognition and communication*. Baltimore: University Park Press.

Brazelton, T. B., and Tronick, E. (1980). Preverbal communication between mothers and infants. In D. R. Olson (Ed.), *The social foundations of language and thought*. New York: W. W. Norton.

Brown, R. (1958). How shall a thing be called? *Psychological Review, 65,* 14–21.

Bruner, J. S. (1975). The ontogenesis of speech acts. *Journal of Child Language, 2,* 1–19.

Bruner, J. S. (1977). Early social interaction and language acquisition. In H. R. Schaffer (Ed.) *Studies in mother-infant interaction*. London: Academic Press.

Clark, H. H., and Clark, E. (1977). *Psychology and language*. New York: Harcourt Brace Jovanovich.

Clark, R. (1978). The transition from action to gesture. In A. Locke (Ed.), *Action, gesture and symbol: The emergence of language*. London: Academic Press.

Dunn, J., and Kendrick, C. (1982). The speech of two-and three-year-olds to infant siblings: "Baby talk" and the context of communication. *Journal of Child Language, 9,* 579–595.

Ervin-Tripp, S. (1979). Children's verbal turn-taking. In E. Ochs and B. Schieffelin (Eds.), *Developmental pragmatics*. New York: Academic Press.

Gallagher, T. (1977). Revision behaviors in the speech of normal children developing language. *Journal of Speech and Hearing Research, 20,* 303–318.

Gallagher, T. (1981). Contingent query sequences within adult-child discourse. *Journal of Child Language, 8,* 51–62.

Gallagher, T., and Craig, H. (1982). An investigation of overlap in children's speech. *Journal of Psycholinguistic Research, 11,* 63–75.

Garvey, C. (1975). Requests and responses in children's speech. *Journal of Child Language, 2,* 41–63.

Garvey, C. (1977). The contingent query: A dependent act in conversation. In M. Lewis and L. Rosenblum (Eds.), *Interaction, conversation and the development of language*. New York: John Wiley.

Glucksberg, S., and Krauss, R. M. (1967). What do people say after they have learned to talk? Studies in the development of referential communication.

Merrill-Palmer Quarterly, 13, 309–316.

Guralnick, M. J., and Paul-Brown, D. (1984). Communicative adjustments during behavior-request episodes among children at different developmental levels. *Child Development, 55,* 911–919.

James, S. L. (1978). Effect of listener age and situation on the politeness of children's directives. *Journal of Psycholinguistic Research, 7,* 307–317.

Keenan, E. O., and Klein, E. (1975). Coherency in children's discourse. *Journal of Psycholinguistic Research, 4,* 365–380.

Konefal, J., and Fokes, J. (1984). Linguistic analysis of children's conversational repairs. *Journal of Psycholinguistic Research, 13,* 1–11.

Ninio, A., and Brunio, J. (1978). The achievement and antecedents of labelling. *Journal of Child Language, 5,* 1–15.

Prelock, P., Messick, C., Schwartz, R. and Terrell, B. (1981). Mother-child discourse during the one-word stage. *Proceedings of the Second Wisconsin Symposium on Research in Child Language Disorders,* Madison, WI, Vol. 2, 67–74.

Prutting, C., and Kirchner, D. (1983). Applied pragmatics. In T. M. Gallagher and C. A. Prutting (Eds.), *Pragmatic assessment and intervention issues in language.* San Diego: College-Hill Press.

Ratner, N., and Bruner, J. (1978). Games, social exchange and the acquisition of language. *Journal of Child Language, 5,* 391–401.

Sachs, J., and Devin, J. (1976). Young children's use of age appropriate speech styles in social interaction and role playing. *Journal of Child Language, 3,* 81–98.

Schaffer, H. R., Collis, G. M., and Parsons, G. (1977). Vocal interchange and visual regard in verbal and pre-verbal children. In H. R. Schaffer (Ed.), *Studies in mother-infant interactions.* London: Academic Press.

Shatz, M., and Gelman, R. (1973). The development of communication skills: Modifications in the speech of young children as a function of listener. *Monographs of the Society for Research in Child Development, 38,* 152.

Slobin, D. I. (1973). Cognitive prerequisites for the development of grammar. In C. A. Ferguson and D. I. Slobin (Eds.), *Studies of child language development.* New York: Holt, Rinehart and Winston.

Snow, C. E. (1977). Mothers' speech research: From input to interaction. In C. Snow and C. Ferguson (Eds.), *Talking to children: Language input and acquisition.* Cambridge: Cambridge University Press.

Snow, C. E. (1981). Social interaction and language acquisition. In P. Dale and D. Ingram (Eds.), *Child language: An international perspective.* Baltimore: University Park Press.

Stern, D. (1977). *The first relationship.* Cambridge: Harvard University Press.

Trevarthan, C. (1974). Conversations with a 2-month old. *New Scientist, 62,* 230–235.

Trevarthan, C. (1977). Descriptive analysis of infant communicative behavior. In H. R. Schaffer (Ed.), *Studies in mother-infant interactions.* London: Academic Press.

Trevarthan, C. (1980). The foundations of intersubjectivity: Development of interpersonal and cooperative understanding in infants. In D. R. Olson (Ed.), *The social foundations of language and thought.* New York: W. W. Norton.

Wilcox, M. J., and Howse, P. (1983). Children's use of gestural and verbal behavior in communicative misunderstandings. *Applied Psycholinguistics, 3,* 15–27.

Wilcox, M. J., and Terrell, B. Y. (1985). Child language behavior: The acquisition of social communicative competence. In C. S. Mcloughlin and D. F. Gullo (Eds.), *Young children in context: Impact of self, family and society on development.* Springfield: Charles C Thomas.

Wilcox, M. J., and Webster, E. J. (1980). Early discourse behavior: An analysis of children's responses to listener feedback. *Child Development, 51,* 1120–1125.

Chapter 3

A Comparison of Communication at Home and School

Sandra Tattershall
Nancy Creaghead

Remember for a moment the feelings you had in anticipation of going to school for the first time. Relatives reminded you of the importance of this impending venture; parents purchased items for and planned around the event; and older children threatened you with frightening tales of electric paddles.

Children approach the "going-to-school" phase in their lives with wonder, curiosity, concern, and their own idea of what school is like. They have a "theory of the world in the head," according to Smith (1975, p. 11). This theory is based on past learning and influences children's current perceptions and interpretations. It determines their approach to new experiences and is their basis for imposing sense on their world. This theory of the world provides a foundation for learning.

Schema theory, as explained by Rumelhart (1984), corresponds closely to Smith's ideas. He describes a schema as "a kind of informal, private, unarticulated theory about the nature of the events, objects, or situations we face. The total set of schemata we have available for interpreting our world in a sense constitutes our private theory of reality" (p. 3). Rumelhart explains that a schema is an abstract unit of knowledge, representing the generic concepts in our memory. A schema can be thought of as a structured "whole with variable slots to be filled for specific instances of a concept" (Tattershall, 1984, p. 47).

These schemata guide comprehension of new experiences. For instance, young children have a doctor's office schema that includes receiving shots. Visits to other kinds of offices or introduction to an adult with the title "Doctor" apparently activates the Medical schema, as shown by the frequent question, "Am I going to get a shot?"

It is clear that preschool children have a theory of the world and schemata that they use in making sense of their experiences. Early-morning sounds and smells from the kitchen provoke the Breakfast schema, which can be further refined to the Sunday-Breakfast schema if Daddy is in his pajamas and offers the child the comics from the Sunday newspaper. The child has an organized set of associated bits of information that allows him to presuppose meanings. Further child schemata might include Getting-Dressed, Grocery-Shopping-with-Mother, Company-Coming, Going-to-Grandma's, Getting-a-New-Car, Bedtime, Discipline, and so on. One youngster known to the authors, upon noticing that his mother was angry, looked at her and said frantically, "Don't mean it." Based on past experience, his schema about discipline situations included Mother supporting her reprimands with "and I mean it." When he saw signs of anger, he presumed the predictable pattern or course of events and attempted to ward off the emphatic conclusion.

Preschool schemata often revolve around daily routines and are probably common to many children. There are, however, many differences in households, which causes children to differ in their specific world views. The Getting-Up-and-Getting-Ready schema for the child whose father stays home as a househusband differs from the schema of the child whose mother drops him at the daycare center on her way to work. The child from a poor, lower-class family views Doing-the-Laundry differently than does the child who watches a housekeeper wash the family clothes.

Tough (1973) suggested two patterns representing extremes in possible family types. There are homes in which adults give the instructions and children do not question them. Language is treated as a functional tool to get things done or to manage behavior. At the other extreme is the family that encourages children to question, look for cause and effect, and explore various interpretations; that is, to view the world as a series of interesting problems to be discussed. The children from these prototypical families will have different world views. Their adult-child talk schema will differ considerably. In his much debated work, Bernstein (1971) called these two styles of communication restricted and elaborated codes. He described the restricted code as a style of communication that is dependent on particular situational contexts and thus does not make meanings verbally explicit, in contrast to the elaborated code, which does make meanings verbally explicit. Bernstein equated the restricted code with the working-class family and the elaborated code with the middle-class family, and suggested that this difference was related to school success or failure. Wells (1981) contends that Bernstein's theory may be wrong on two points. First, the notion of only two codes is oversimplified, and second, the child's linguistic experience is not strictly tied to social class. However, he emphasizes an important and accurate part of his theory:

the way in which each individual child constructs his model of the world, and discovers his place and power of control within it, is most strongly influenced by the values and orientations that are encoded and transmitted in the everyday conversations he has with his parents and other adults in his immediate environment. (p. 259)

Each child's experience remains relatively unique and peculiar to his family until he goes to school. Because of the conformity required for large groups to function, school routines are perhaps more uniform than those in family situations.

In school, the child must learn that he has less leeway than in the typical one-on-one communication at home. He must revise his attention-getting strategies ("Hey" will not be allowed) and learn how to wait longer for his turn. He will develop schemata such as Reading-Time, Snack-Time, Following-Teacher-Directions, and Asking-Questions-in-Class. He will recognize that ". . . and don't talk to your neighbor!" is a comment unique to school and fits into an Independent-Quiet-Work-Period schema, with implications for not bothering the teacher either!

The child comes to school with rich, varied experiences—information and impressions organized into schemata. Many of these schemata will help in comprehending the new world of the school, but there will be unique school schemata to learn. The special discourse rules of written language and math will have to be learned. The constrictions of life in a large group with implications for turn-taking, topic introduction, and so on, will be new. The student role has its own definition, requiring variation from the at-home role. Those children who appreciate the similarities and differences in home and at school will have an advantage. This chapter will examine the unique and common characteristics of the two settings and will attempt to compare and contrast school versus home schemata.

COMMUNICATION REQUIREMENTS OF SCHOOL

Teachers' Expectations

Preschool and Primary. The authors interviewed teachers at various grade levels regarding their expectations of students. A preschool teacher of three and four year olds said she hoped they were potty trained, knew how to listen and to talk to another person while using appropriate eye contact, and had had some experience with crayons, scissors, pencils, and paper. This teacher remarked that she did not expect children to share or take turns because they would learn that in preschool. This same teacher outlined what a child must know in order to be promoted to kindergarten:

1. How to wait his turn, sit still, and listen in a group.
2. How to follow directions without repetition.
3. How to hold a pencil.
4. How to finish a reasonable task without undue frustration.
5. How to attend to a task for its purpose, not just to finish and go on to the next one.

Tough (1973) explained that educators expect children to learn certain skills before entering school: the ability to be independent of adults, to get along with other children and to care for toys and equipment.

Baron, Baron, and MacDonald (1983) queried kindergarten teachers about prerequisite skills for their classes. In regard to verbal and pragmatic skills, they expected that the child can:

1. Say his full name, his parents' full names, his address, and his phone number.
2. Talk loud enough.
3. Recognize his name in print.
4. Listen and sit quietly while others are talking.
5. Share, take turns, and play by the rules.

Preschool teachers, however, do not expect their young students to focus on reading and writing. Schickedanz and Sullivan (1984) found relatively few literacy events in an "excellent" preschool as compared with the number of literacy events these same children encountered at home. They found that their subjects observed their parents reading newspapers and books, writing thank-you notes, making lists, and so on. These children did not observe these literacy events at school, however, because their teachers tended to involve themselves in typical preschool activities. Preschool schemata must consequently be revised as children advance in school and encounter more written language than was found in early educational settings.

Baron and coworkers (1983) explained in their book for parents that first grade is a "big switch" from kindergarten, with more structure, less "mothering," and more stringent standards. Two first grade teachers interviewed by the authors of this chapter suggested the following abilities as desirable in beginning first graders:

1. The ability to attend to a task for at least ten minutes.
2. The ability to express themselves orally with teachers and peers.
3. The ability to retell the plot and describe the main character after listening to a story.
4. The ability to follow basic procedure for reading—left to right, top to bottom.

5. The ability to count objects and count aloud to ten.
6. The ability to say the alphabet in order.
7. The ability to see letter to sound relationships.
8. The ability to identify beginning sounds.
9. The ability to print their own name legibly.

In her interview comments, a second grade teacher showed concern about children's ability to work in a group ("Waiting your turn," "Time to talk," "Time to listen"). She wanted second graders to slow down, to know that ideas are important, and to know that reading is fun. She seemed less concerned with specific skills than the child's turn-taking habits, attention, and overall attitudes toward learning.

In summary, there appears to be primary emphasis among teachers of young students on the ability to work in a group and attend to task, on reading readiness and an appreciation for stories and books, and on eye-hand coordination.

Elementary and High School. Toward the middle of elementary school, teachers change in their expectations of students. Fourth grade teachers expect more independent work and see less need for repeated explanations. Children are often reminded that they "are no longer babies" and must be more responsible.

When a sixth grade teacher was asked what she expected of her students, she stressed organization (having materials ready for class) and responsibility for turning in assignments.

A seventh grade teacher expressed hope that her students knew basic classroom behavior—how to participate appropriately until routines specific to the new class are learned. This teacher felt that her seventh graders needed to acquire library and reference skills, study habits, an ability to think, and the maturity to cope with the next grade.

A ninth grade English teacher said that she hoped for students who were socially and emotionally mature, but she did not feel that maturity could be facilitated through instruction. She felt that ninth graders may need help from parents in budgeting time for long-range assignments. She stated that the most important new learning over the freshman year was in personalizing reading, that is, in not just reporting the main idea, supporting detail, and theme but in giving a personal reaction to what has been read. She explained that ninth graders must also learn to work in unity on group projects but do not seem ready for that until late in the year. They are apparently still learning to communicate effectively in groups.

Calfee and Sutter (1982) discussed these factors in planning or assessing students' group discussion skills in school:

1. Topic and questions: Can the student stay on topic and ask appropriate questions?

2. Rules of procedures: Can the student understand and follow the rules?
3. Leadership style: Can the student operate under various governing styles—autocratic, democratic, laissez faire?
4. Group composition: Can the student function in groups that vary in size and composition?
5. Time and place: Can the student ignore visual and auditory distractions or other influences?

The successful student must learn how to contribute to and learn in various settings in school. Organized group discussions with emphasis on content are perhaps unique to school and require unique communication skills.

Parents' Expectations

The authors also interviewed parents to discover their views on what was required at various grade levels. Parents of children entering first grade mentioned these requirements: The child must:

1. Be able to follow verbal directions: "Draw a line under...", "Put a circle around...", "Connect...", and so on.
2. Be able to demonstrate prereading and early reading skills: the knowledge that words tell something and that you can get information from pictures, where to start and end on a page, recognition of letters and initial sounds, and the ability to write all the letters. (Every parent mentioned this.)
3. Be able to describe an item, tell a simple story, and tell something in a paragraph.
4. Be able (1) to recognize numbers to 50 and (2) to count to 100.
5. Be able to listen, concentrate, and pay attention.
6. Be able to work or play in a group. (One mother said that this was accomplished in kindergarten.)
7. Be able to do what the teacher asks and know when to stop socializing and start working.
8. Be able to tie shoe laces, put on a coat, and use pencils, scissors, crayons, and so on.
9. Be responsible for personal belongings.
10. Be willing to leave Mom and deal with a full-day program.

These responses suggest that parents viewed preschool as the time for learning to operate in a group through play but saw first grade as more academic, a time to get down to the work of school. Both parents and teachers portrayed first grade as more "school-like."

A parent of a fourth grader commented that the emphasis this year would be on reading comprehension. Parents of junior high students stressed being responsible, self-directed, and developing good study skills. The parent of a ninth grader talked about his son's "need to manage time— more freedom, no one monitors." Also mentioned was a greater need to relate to peers, including those from differing socioeconomic backgrounds.

This particular group of parents seemed quite similar in their comments on school requirements to the teachers interviewed. Their children's schemata will probably be helpful in guiding the children's predictions and comprehension of what school is like.

Children's Expectations

In July, several pre-first graders were asked what they would do in first grade. One child emphasized how hard it would be compared to kindergarten. She said the teacher would be "meaner" and "make us answer more questions." All the children expected to learn how to read. These children obviously expected first grade to include more "grown-up" work than kindergarten.

A third grader said that in preschool he had learned to color; in kindergarten, to "read and spell and pronounce words"; in first grade, to "read bigger words in books and learn more numbers"; in second grade, to read more automatically ("Say the whole thing by just looking at 'em"). Third grade, according to our young reporter, was significant for multiplication tables and division, and he anticipated that next year he would "review third grade." The young child's school schema is somewhat incomplete, but our third grader has refined his observations to the specifics.

Two third grade classes were asked about the rules for behavior and participation in their classrooms. The written questionnaire included 20 questions like the following: What things are bad to do in your class? What makes your teacher angry? What makes your teacher happy? How do you know when it is time to be quiet, to take a test, to go home? This group of third graders were in general agreement about the requirements in their classrooms. The single most important requirement, according to these children, was to be quiet. This was acknowledged in answers to many different questions: "What makes your teacher angry?" "Talking." "What makes your teacher happy?" "Being quiet." "What things are bad to do in school?" "Talking." These children seemed to have clearly learned one school rule that does not apply at home. Children were not asked what things are bad to do at home, but the findings of Patterson and Cobb (1971) are pertinent. They coded family interactions in the homes of 24 aggressive boys aged 6 to 13. About 50 per cent of all the events that they observed were described as conversational talking. Based on these findings, it is not anticipated that children would say that they should not talk at home.

In spite of our potential first grader's dire view of how "hard" first grade will be, Frieze, Francis, and Hanusa (1983) reported that first and second grade children tended to be hopeful after both success and failure. They seemed to feel that they would do well if they tried again. In second grade, children assessed their success and failure more realistically, and attributed outcome to internal factors. They depended less on magic and luck and more on proven skills. The sophisticated third grade interviewee suggested that automatic word recognition occurs after two years of reading work. He has undoubtedly adopted the realistic view of how one achieves success. As the schema is filled in, children's predictions become more solid.

The expectations of teachers, parents, and children reported here suggest a school schema that outlines how to operate in a school group.

ARE THE RULES DIFFERENT?

The literature has suggested that children may need to learn a different set of communication rules when they enter school. MacLure and French (1981) discussed the similarities and differences between home and school in regard to question sequences, speaker selection, and topic choice.

Question Sequences

It has been suggested that questions at home have a two-part sequence that consists of simply the question and the answer.

Parent: Did you have a good time at Mary's?
Child: Yes.
Parent: What did you do?
Child: We played in the sprinkler.

At school, however, questions usually have a three-part sequence including the question, the answer, and the teacher's evaluation of the answer (Mehan, 1978; Sinclair and Coulthard, 1975; Stubbs, 1976).

Teacher: Who discovered America?
Child: Columbus.
Teacher: Right.

Questions outside school are usually "real" questions, in that the speaker really wants the information being requested. Many questions in school are pseudo, or test, questions; the teacher already knows the correct answer.

However, parents also ask test questions of their children. Examine the following example of a parent and child looking at a book.

Parent: What's that?
Child: Doggie.
Parent: Right, a doggie.

Another type of testing parents use is checking their children's preparation for appropriate behavior.

Parent: What will you say when you get ready to leave?
Child: I had a nice time.
Parent: Good for you.

Observations indicate that parents use a large number of interrogatives with their young children in order to encourage their participation in conversation (Garnica, 1977; Ervin-Tripp, 1977a). Corsaro (1979) found that 62.7 per cent of all adult utterances to children were interrogatives.

Teachers, however, spend relatively more time asking test questions, whereas parents spend relatively more time trying to get real information from their children. In observing adult-child interactions with two and four year old children, Camaioni (1979) noted only a few examples of the three-part question sequence, and these occurred only with four year olds. He suggested that this type of pedagogic interaction may become more common between children and adults as the child gets older.

Speaker Selection

In conversations between peers, a variety of possible strategies for selection of the next speaker exist. The current speaker may nominate the next speaker by asking him a question, or the listener may nominate himself as next speaker by talking at a pause or even by interrupting. In a casual group, everyone generally has equal opportunity to talk, although some may exercise that right more than others. In the classroom, the child rarely has the opportunity to nominate himself as the next speaker (Coulthard, 1977). This right is reserved solely for the teacher. Despite the fact that a group is present, communication usually follows the pattern teacher-child-teacher-child-teacher-child, in which the teacher is always the same person but the particular child may change. When self-nomination occurs, it is in the form of hand-raising, with the teacher reserving the right to have the final decision on who will talk.

MacLure and French (1981) suggest that the home environment offers a more equitable distribution of speaker rights than the school. Children can initiate conversations more freely at home and may have more opportunities to question or argue. Sacks (1974) notes that preschool children learn strategies that will insure permission to talk, such as the phrase, "You know what?" Children also learn outside school that when they talk to an adult, that adult can exercise his right to be in charge just as teachers do. The adult in both settings can decide when the child can talk or interrupt. The adult can also terminate the child's participation in the conversation (French and Woll, 1981; Speier, 1976).

It appears that both parents and teachers use certain devices to help the child participate effectively in communication interchanges. The adult first directs the child's attention to an object, an event, or a comment. He then provides opportunities that are consistent with the child's ability to respond. Research indicates that parents work to insure joint attention with their children (Corsaro, 1979; Schaffer, Hepburn, and Collis, 1983).

Topic Choice

Coulthard (1977) suggests that in school interaction, the teacher not only keeps the group on topic but also chooses the topic. He states that teachers often frame the lesson by beginning with, "Well, today we're going to talk about . . . ." Coulthard suggests that this does not happen in informal conversations because no one participant has that much control. A participant may make a concluding statement to end the conversation, but he would not presume to announce the topic for the day as teachers do.

Young preschool children have many opportunities to select the topic in communication with their caregivers (Corsaro, 1979; French and Woll, 1981). Mutual attention is often initiated by the young child to an object or event of interest. Subsequent comments by mother are generally elaborations on the child's topic. French and Woll (1981) note that parents may refuse the child's attempt to introduce a given topic, but children develop strategies for inducing adults at home to attend to their topic. The "You know what?" question noted previously is one device. Another is asking the parent a question that will require clarification. For example, if a child says, "Mom, how do you get grape juice stain out of something?", Mom is likely to ask where the grape juice was spilled. The adult, requesting clarification from the child, is drawn into the conversation. Although research regarding communication interactions between mothers and older children is sparse, parents would probably agree that children remain free to initiate topics at home and that they exercise this right frequently.

In spite of this freedom, there are also situations at home as in school in which adults initiate topics and give the child no options. These may be "teaching" situations, in which the parent wants to provide information or warning to the child about his future or past behavior. At home children learn to initiate topics and conform to those of adults. At school, they must adhere to the topic selected by the teacher.

Metalinguistics

Children use their language everywhere, but in school they must also become adept at reflecting on it. Metalinguistic and metapragmatic skills are seen outside of school in children's comments on or their repairs of communication breakdown, in their ritualized language games and vocal play, in their comments on conversational protocol, in their use of jokes and figurative language, and in their use of appropriate registers with different listeners (Van Kleeck, 1984). This development of language awareness outside of school is casual. In school, however, children must formalize these skills through conscious analysis of their knowledge, thus becoming more deliberate in their "instrumental" use of language (Van Kleeck, 1984, p. 136). Kindergarteners must identify sounds and letters; first graders talk about words and sentences; second graders encounter the quintessence of school metalinguistics: parts of speech!

We have suggested above that there are similarities and differences in home and school experiences regarding question sequences, speaker selection, and topic choice. MacLure and French (1981) suggest that the difference between the home and school environment lies in the relative balance between the types of communicative interactions found in each. They present evidence that the interactions between teachers and children are similar to the communication experiences that children have with adults outside of school.

Most children are adept at interpreting the rules for classroom interaction and operating within them. They are able to adjust to the imbalance between home and school rules just as they are able to learn different sets of rules for a variety of other adult and peer communication interactions. Shuy and Griffin (1981) note the expertise that primary school-aged children exhibit in dealing with fairly complex rules for group lessons. For example, they know that they must wait to raise their hands until the teacher has finished her preelicitation comments. They know that if they raise their hand, they must be prepared to answer. Finally they know when their answer has received a positive or negative evaluation despite the teacher's varied responses. In some instances, she may tell the child that he is right or wrong, but often that message is merely implied by her asking another child the same question. The first child then knows his answer was wrong. If she goes on to another question, he was right.

Knowing the rules of the classroom appears to be a prerequisite for learning content. The child must include in his school schema rules for who talks when, how, and about what. Abiding by these rules will elicit more positive attention and evaluation from the teacher. When children have difficulty in school—in following directions, in conforming to behavioral expectations, or in participating effectively in classroom lessons—it would be useful to determine the child's specific difficulty. Is the child's problem learning the new set of rules for school or switching to different rules in different settings?

It is clear that children must know the rules of the classroom. It is not clear, however, to what extent these rules are new to the child entering school.

THE VARYING ROLES OF PARENTS AND TEACHERS

The schemata regarding home and school communication are alike and different. For some children, one is simply an elaboration of the other, with more similarities than differences. Teachers use language (Vetter, 1982) to provide instruction, to focus attention, to direct or control behavior, to explain ideas, to structure discussion, to provide feedback, and to fulfill social functions. Children have heard parents talk in similar ways: "Here is how you turn it on," "Look here," "You'll sit there until you can behave," "You have to put this end through the loop," "Now tell Daddy where we went and what we saw," "That is not inside play," "How nice of you to call." The child with an elaborated code has heard it before, but there is a difference. Teachers who are also parents use similar language in both their roles but make certain changes. When they are in charge of a group, the teacher register comes out. They change their tone, vocabulary, body language, and content. And their own children know when Mom or Dad starts sounding like teacher! One of the authors once "tried out" a behavior management technique on her four year old son, who looked her in the eye and said, "Let's stop all this nonsense." He knew his mother was teaching and not mothering.

The magnitude of the difference between home and school for a given child may depend on the degree to which his parent plays the teacher role and the degree to which his teacher plays the parent role.

Parents

It appears that caregivers engage in teaching activities with their children. Camaioni (1979) stated that the social context of adult-child conversation is often a pedagogic situation, whereas with peers, the context is play. The parent may want to insure that the child learns from an ongoing or past experience or may want to prepare the child for a new experience. Parents differ in the relative amount of time devoted to teaching activities. Some parents use almost every experience as a teaching opportunity, whereas others may allow the child to learn more independently. Whatever the mode of the parent, there may be differences between the teaching strategies of parents and teachers.

The amount of perceptual and contextual support may differ in the two settings. For instance, mothers make use of routines and redundant sequences to enhance comprehension (Allen and Schatz, 1983); they determine the inferential ability of the child and modify the form of their directives accordingly. Schneiderman (1983) found that mothers of children between 18 and 42 months of age use three types of directives: (1) direct imperatives, (2) embedded imperatives, and (3) inferred imperatives. They found that embedded and inferred directives became more common as the children got older, but when children did not respond, mothers reverted to a more direct form. Schaffer, Hepburn, and Collis (1983) suggested that at home the young child's comprehension is closely tied to the context. The child is a part of the context in that his behavior affects the mother's verbal input. Although these observations have usually involved children under four years of age, it seems reasonable to conclude that contextual and perceptual support are readily available in home interactions even for the school-aged child, due to shared information and shared experiences. In addition, home interactions are often one-to-one and constant adjustment between speaker and listener can occur, unlike school interactions, whose ratio is more likely to be 1 to 25. It is not possible for the teacher to constantly monitor the comprehension of each child and adjust her communication according to the needs of each one.

Walkerdine and Sinha (1981) and Bridges, Sinha, and Walkerdine (1981) noted that parents take great care to understand their children's communication and to make sense to the child. In school the opportunity for the child to engage in this kind of sensitive dialogue with the teacher may be limited. When the child gives an answer in school, it is often evaluated as correct or incorrect without explanation as to why (Mehan, 1974). MacLure and French (1981) note that parents usually correct their children's incorrect responses, whereas teachers provide the correct answer only when the child cannot self-correct on request. The school situation may prohibit discussion that might reveal the child's reason for a mismatch between question and answer. This is especially true of the testing situation. The following example, given by a parent, illustrates the value of determining the child's reason for an incorrect response.

Billy, a fourth grader with pragmatic deficits, came home very upset because his teacher had accused him of being impudent. After talking to his "neighbor" in church, the teacher had told him to write 50 words on how to behave in church. Billy obediently struggled to think of 50 appropriate words. After a very long time, he had only a few words such as quiet, solemn, still, and prayerful. His teacher was angry because she thought that Billy was making a joke of her punishment. The mother was convinced that Billy did not understand the teacher's idiomatic use of "50 words" and truly thought that he was doing what he had been asked to do.

In one-to-one interactions at home the parent and child may be likely to agree on the purpose of their discussions. In contrast, high-school students who were interviewed about their school learning experiences noted that in some classes they were confused about the topic, the purpose of the discussion, or what benefit the subject might be to them (Gannaway, 1976). Stubbs (1976) concluded that pupils do not ask about the purpose of school communication because they expect not to understand. An additional interpretation might be that students are less likely to ask clarification questions in a group than in a one-to-one conversation.

Teachers

It was noted previously that parents vary in the degree to which they behave like teachers at home. It is also true that teachers differ in their motherlike qualities and behaviors. Naturally, this is somewhat dependent on the age of the children, but even first grade teachers demonstrate a range of behavior from motherly to academic. Leiter (1974) quoted the following principal's description of two first grade teachers from the same school.

> Now recognizing that. . .(First Grade Teacher A) is a different kind of person, what would be good for this child? Now does this child need somebody strongly oriented academically? Does she need that kind of strong hand? Here's a warm mother (tapping First Grade Teacher B's card). I came into the auditorium and she had Li on her lap. Li had gotten money at lunchtime but she didn't bring it quite by accident. . .and it just crushed her. And Teacher B instead of saying "It's all right now you just get in line and go," there she was sitting there with this child—you know it was beautiful. Now we're going to have some kids in here who are going to need a Momma-type. All right here's your Momma. (p. 35)

Although the aforementioned quotation illustrates a range of teacher types, there also tend to be certain similarities among teachers. Teacher talk was studied by Blumenfeld, Hamilton, Bossert, Wessel, and Muce (1983) and found to be quite consistent at various grade levels and with different social classes. Generally teacher talk focused on violations of classroom procedures. Teacher talk about performance ("You can do better!") seemed, in Blumenfeld and coworkers' study, to convince children to work harder. Teacher reprimands about bad work habits convinced children the habits were indeed bad. Teacher comments about talking, however, had little effect on children's attitudes. They viewed this as nagging. Apparently children in this study had a "good student" schema that agreed partially but not totally with that of teachers.

Nelson (1984) reported a study of teacher communication that described complexity, rate, and fluency in grades one, three, and six. First grade teachers were uniformly slower in rate (4.5 syllables per second) as compared with upper grade teachers, and their utterances were syntactically simpler. Third grade teachers' utterances retained the simpler syntax of their first grade colleagues, but the rate was faster (5.4 syllables per second). Sixth grade teachers spoke fast (5.3 syllables per second), and syntactic complexity was greater.

Cuda and Nelson (1976) found that first grade teachers used a high number of statements to direct attention and to control behavior. They focused on "how-to-do" in reading, writing, and math, and activities were highly context bound. There were many concrete materials, but there were also instances when abstract language was used (linguistic analogies, dual word meanings, and so on). First grade teachers used a variety of strategies to boost students' confidence for working in their math books.

By third grade, teachers were focusing on meaning as opposed to word decoding in reading. They asked more memory questions (specific recall) than any other type. In mathematics, teachers were still using primarily action requestives. Third grade teachers and students were focusing on content subjects (social studies, science) more than on the how-to aspects of early literacy. Verbal instruction was becoming more important.

At sixth grade, teachers in Cuda and Nelson's study talked about getting organized. (Gump [1975] reported that about half the time in the average elementary class is spent in this way!) Teachers talked more about content—relating information in reading to prior discussion and experience. Reading and writing had become tools for learning.

As children grow older their teachers assume more and explain less. They focus on content, the "what" of learning rather than the "how" emphasized in earlier grades. Sometimes there is a potential mismatch, however, between the everyday knowledge that a student brings to class and the expert knowledge required in the content-area classroom. Nicholson (1984) interviewed junior high students in the process of reading and writing assignments. He found that the teacher or text assumed background ("old") information that was often at odds with what students actually brought to the task. He suggested that junior-high teachers should question students to find out "how" they were arriving at the "what" that is so often the goal in content-focused later grades. This questioning to discover a child's confusion was noted earlier in the chapter to be more typical at home than at school.

Although there is a dependable "teacherishness" about teacher talk at different grades, there are also differences. As the students get older, the teachers' styles and content change in predictable ways. Students and teachers spend less and less time on how to learn and more time on content. They become more abstract or metalinguistic in their focus.

PEER INTERACTIONS

What has been suggested thus far is that teacher-child communication at school is a subset of adult-child communication outside school. It involves perhaps more stringent rules than the child has encountered in other situations with adults.

Peer interactions, however, may be very different from those of adults and children. Camaioni (1979) suggests that peer interactions take a variety of forms wherein each child may take responsibility for obtaining mutual involvement. In contrast, adult-child interactions tend to remain pedagogic in nature, no matter which participant initiates them. Camaioni found that children of different ages also engaged in pedagogic interactions. In communication between two and four year olds, the three-part question sequence tended to be more common than play sequences.

It has been shown that even preschool children have a variety of effective strategies for interacting with their peers (Slama-Cazacu, 1977). They are able to secure attention (Camaioni, 1979) and initiate and respond to simple topics (McTear, 1984). McTear says that younger preschool children exhibit two-part sequences that are fairly closed and not integrated into larger sequences. Before they enter the school years, however, they have learned to produce utterances that not only correspond to a preceding utterance but also set up expectations for further response.

It has been shown that preschoolers are able to use a variety of strategies for obtaining information (Brinton and Fujiki, 1982; Garvey, 1979) and directing others' behavior (Ervin-Tripp, 1977b; Kernan and Kernan, 1977). It has, however, been seen that both information and directive requests of young children are not always successful (Brinton and Fujiki, 1982). It has further been demonstrated that older preschool children are able to engage in task-directed interaction. Slama-Cazacu (1977) observed that the conversation of a small group of nursery school children focused on cooperating to accomplish a task even though some of their utterances diverged to related topics or a fantasy related to the task.

These same skills have been observed in peer-learning groups of school-aged children. Wilkinson (1984), Wilkinson and Dollaghan (1979), Wilkinson, Clevenger, and Dollaghan (1981), and others have observed primary and elementary school instructional groups. From their research, it is clear that school-aged children grow in their ability to make effective requests for information and to direct their peers' behavior, although it is equally clear that they also develop effective strategies to avoid compliance. Wilkinson (1984) defined the effective speaker in such groups as one who receives responses when he makes requests. She stated that in order to do this, he must (1) express himself clearly and directly, (2) stay on task, (3) be sincere, and (4) persist by revising his requests. Wilkinson found that in first grade reading groups, effective use of requests was positively related to reading scores. Interestingly, Shuy and Griffin (1981) found that teachers' evaluations of children's competence in asking questions did not coincide with evaluations obtained from video-taped observations, because the most effective children tended to direct their clarification requests to other children rather than to the teacher.

Evidence regarding the effect of peer-learning groups and peer tutoring on achievement is inconclusive. Webb and Kenderski (1984) examined achievement in peer groups as compared with whole-class settings. They did not find a significant difference between achievement in the two settings even though less interaction occurred in the whole class. They found that for average junior high school students, those children who provided information in mathematics groups produced higher achievement scores than did those who received information from their peers. These findings have been confirmed in other studies with junior high and upper elementary school children (Peterson and Janicki, 1979; Peterson, Janicki, and Swing, 1981). However, studies with above-average junior high and high school students showed a positive relationship between receiving explanations from peers and achievement (Webb, 1980a, 1980b, 1980c, 1982a, 1982b). Webb and Kenderski (1984) conclude that the high-achieving students may have been capable of adequately explaining the information, whereas the other groups were not. Studies of the effectiveness of peer tutors have confirmed these findings. Cooper and Cooper (1984) describe a study by Ellis and Rogoff (in press) in which eight and nine year olds were given a sorting task to figure out and then explain to six and seven year old children. The child tutors tended to either show what to do with little explanation or ask guessing game questions, both of which forced the learner to perform the task with little help. In essence, they did not help the learner develop strategies to prepare for the posttest. In contrast, adults tended to orient, explain, and in other ways prepare the children for the test. Unlike the peer teachers, they also changed their strategy from more to less control during the teaching process. In spite of the more effective strategies of the adult-teachers, it is important to note that the learners were more actively involved in the learning process during the peer-teacher situation.

One reason that peer tutors may be less effective is that they themselves are learning the task, the information, or strategies for dealing with the task. A second possibility is that they have less effective information-giving strategies. Research regarding referential communication suggests that the ability to take the listener's perspective and to determine the critical elements to be described continues to develop during the school-age years (Asher and Wigfield, 1981). Creaghead and Tattershall (1985) report that first and third graders had difficulty giving directions in a barrier game with no listener feedback, whereas fifth graders performed essentially like adults. Whitehurst and Sonnenschein (1981) found that five year old children did not improve their explanations simply by knowing that the listener was confused. They needed explicit feedback about the critical information to be communicated. This is an important point in regard to peer teaching. Neither participant may be sophisticated enough to know the critical element that needs to be communicated.

The aformentioned comments suggest that peer teaching may not be the most effective strategy for teaching. Cooper and Cooper (1984) point out, however, that "success cannot be assessed in all or none terms" (p. 91). They noted that the conversations of peer learning groups suggested that social as well as educational goals were being pursued and that the accomplishment of these two goals was not always equal. Children in peer groups may be learning more about the rules of group interaction than about the content subjects.

This discussion suggests three important issues. First, more information is needed about the skills required for peer group learning and how these skills are related to the communication strategies of children in and out of school.

Second, although there is little research regarding peer interactions of school-aged children outside the school, it seems likely that the strategies children use to negotiate with their peers during play and social and peer learning situations are similar. In comparison to home, however, school offers the opportunity for same-age and same-status peer negotiation and for the development of valuable task-related communication skills. It appears that the teacher-directed classroom is likely to provide more content learning but significantly less opportunity for the practice of these skills.

The third conclusion is that children will encounter peer-learning groups in at least some classrooms. Those children without adequate peer-group communication skills will be less able to learn from this format or to share their knowledge with other children. Learning may be enhanced when the teacher is aware of the strengths and weaknesses of her children and provides guidance in improving communication.

SUMMARY

We can summarize the comparison of home and school discourse by using the four basic components of a teaching-learning exchange

(Thompson, 1969). These are the sender, the receiver, the message, and the medium.

In school, the teacher is most often the sender or initiator of communication (Bellack, Kleibard, Hyman, and Smith, 1966), whereas parents may be less active as senders. At home children initiate many of the conversations. The familiar "uh-huh" nonattentive response of parents highlights the receiver role they often play in contrast to teachers' role as sender. This means that in school children are more often receivers of information, whereas at home they are both senders and receivers.

Messages both at school and at home may often focus on procedures: "Ms. Brown, do we have to put the date at the top?" "Mom, should I turn the oven on first or wait till the batter is mixed?" Because conformity is more necessary for efficient group management, however, procedure may be discussed more at school. Lindfors (1980) reported that procedural questions of children increase while social and curiosity questions decrease during the elementary school years. Academic content and procedures predominate as messages at school, whereas social or curiosity messages may have a greater place in the home.

The medium of communication can be spoken, written, or nonverbal. Much of what goes on in school is verbal. Griffin and Hannah (1960) reported that students spend from 50 to 90 per cent of their day listening, with high school students listening the most. It would be an unusual home in which teenagers listened 90 per cent of the time! A major difference between home and school, however, is in the use of written language as the medium for communication. Although families exchange notes, read newspapers, letters, and so on, the primary communication is oral, whereas school is more "literate."

The setting of school, with its larger numbers of children, its focus on academic information, and the pressures of accountability, dictates a different sender-receiver proportion, more restricted types of messages, and more written language than at home. Children learn to expect school to be like school in these ways. Those who do not appreciate the similarities and differences of home and school and therefore do not develop appropriate classroom schemata may fail in the student role.

REFERENCES

Allen, R., and Schatz, M. (1983). What says meow? The role of context and linguistic experience in very young children's responses to what-questions. *Journal of Child Language, 10*, 321–335.

Asher, S., and Wigfield, A. (1981). Training referential communication skills. In W. P. Dickson (Ed.), *Children's oral communication skills* (pp. 105–126). New York: Academic Press.

Baron, B., Baron, C., and MacDonald, B. (1983). *What did you learn in school today?* New York: Warner Books.

Bellack, A., Kleibard, H., Hyman, R., and Smith, F. (1966). *The language of the classroom.* New York: Teachers College Press.

Bernstein, B. (1971). *Class, codes and control* (Vol. I). London: Routledge and Kegan Paul.

Blumenfeld, P., Hamilton, V., Bossert, S., Wessel, K., and Muce, J. (1983). Teacher talk and student thought. In J. Levine and M. Waug (Eds.), *Teacher and student perceptions: Implications for learning.* Hillsdale, NJ: Lawrence Erlbaum Associates.

Bridges, A., Sinha, C., and Walkerdine, V. (1981). The development of comprehension. In G. Wells (Ed.), *Language through interaction: The study of language development.* Cambridge: Cambridge University Press.

Brinton, B., and Fujiki, M. (1982). A comparison of request-response sequences in the discourse of normal and language disordered children. *Journal of Speech and Hearing Disorders, 47,* 57–62.

Calfee, R., and Sutter, L. (1982). Oral language assessment through formal discussion. *Topics in Language Disorders, 2,* 45–51.

Camaioni, L. (1979). Child-adult and child-child conversations: An interactional approach. In E. Ochs and B. Schieffelin (Eds.), *Developmental pragmatics* (pp. 325–338). New York: Academic Press.

Cook-Gumperz, J. (1977). Situated instructions: Language socialization of school-age children. In S. Ervin-Tripp and C. Mitchell-Kernan (Eds.), *Child discourse* (pp. 103–121). New York: Academic Press.

Cooper, C., and Cooper, R. (1984). Skill in peer learning discourse: What develops? In S. Kuczaj (Ed.), *Discourse development progress in cognitive development research* (pp. 77–97). New York: Springer-Verlag.

Corsaro, W. (1979). Sociolinguistic patterns in adult-child interaction. In E. Ochs and B. Schieffelin (Eds.), *Developmental pragmatics* (pp. 373–390). New York: Academic Press.

Coulthard, R. (1977). *Introduction to discourse analysis.* London: Longman Group, Ltd.

Creaghead, N., and Tattershall, S. (1985). Observation and assessment of classroom pragmatic skills. In C. Simon (Ed.), *Communication skills and classroom success: Assessment of language-learning disabled students* (pp. 105–131). San Diego: College-Hill Press.

Cuda, R., and Nelson, N. (1976). *Analysis of teacher speaking rate, syntactic complexity, and hesitation phenomena as a function of grade level.* Presented at the American-Speech-Language-Hearing Association Annual Convention, Houston.

Ellis, S., and Rogoff, B. (in press). Problem solving and children's management of instruction. In E. Mueller and C. Cooper (Eds.), *Process and outcome in peer relations.* New York: Academic Press.

Ervin-Tripp, S. (1977a). Discourse agreement: How children answer questions. In J. Hayes (Ed.), *Cognition and development of language.* New York: Academic Press.

Ervin-Tripp, S. (1977b). Wait for me roller skate. In S. Ervin-Tripp and C. Mitchell-Kernan (Eds.), *Child discourse.* New York: Academic Press.

French, P., and Woll, B. (1981). Context, meaning and strategy. In G. Wells (Ed.), *Learning through interaction: The study of language development.* Cambridge:

Cambridge University Press.

Frieze, I., Francis, W., and Hanusa, B. (1983). Defining success in classroom settings. In J. Levine and M. Wang (Eds.), *Teacher and student perceptions: Implications for learning*. Hillsdale, NJ: Lawrence Erlbaum Associates.

Gannaway, H. (1976). Making sense of school. In M. Stubbs and S. Delamont (Eds.), *Explorations in classroom observation*. New York: John Wiley and Sons.

Garnica, O. (1977). Some prosodic and paralinguistic features of speech to young children. In C. Snow and C. Ferguson (Eds.), *Talking to children*. Cambridge: Cambridge University Press.

Garnica, O., and King, M. (1979). *Language, children and society*. New York: Pergamon Press.

Garvey, C. (1979). Contingent queries and their relations in discourse. In E. Ochs and B. Schiefflin (Eds.), *Developmental pragmatics*. New York: Academic Press.

Griffin, K., and Hannah, L. (1960). A study of the results of an extremely short instructional unit in listening. *Journal of Communication, 10*, 135–139.

Gump, P. (1975). Education as an environmental enterprise. In R. Weinberg and F. Wood (Eds.), *Observations of pupils and teachers in mainstream and special education*. Reston, VA: Council for Exceptional Children.

Kernan, C., and Kernan, K. (1977). Pragmatics of directive choice among children. In S. Ervin-Tripp and C. Mitchell-Kernan (Eds.), *Child discourse*. New York: Academic Press.

Leiter, K. (1974). Ad hocing in the schools: A study of placement practices in the kindergartens of two schools. In *Language use and school performance*. New York: Academic Press.

Lindfors, J. (1980). *Children's language and learning*. Englewood Cliffs, NJ: Prentice-Hall.

MacLure, M., and French, P. (1981). A comparison of talk at home and at school. In G. Wells (Ed.), *Learning through interaction: The study of language development*. Cambridge: Cambridge University Press.

McTear, M. (1984). Structure and process in children's conversational development. In S. Kuczaj (Ed.), *Discourse development: Progress in cognitive development research*. New York: Springer-Verlag.

Mehan, H. (1974). *Accomplishing classroom lessons: Language use and school performance*. New York: Academic Press.

Mehan, H. (1978). Structuring school structure. *Harvard Educational Review, 48*, 32–64.

Nelson, N. (1984). Beyond information processing: The language of teachers and textbooks. In G. Wallach and K. Butler (Eds.), *Language Learning Disabilities in School-Age Children*. Baltimore: Williams & Wilkins.

Nicholson, T. (1984). Experts and novices: A study of reading in the high school classroom. *Reading Research Quarterly, 19*, 436–451.

Patterson, G., and Cobb, J. (1971). A dyadic analysis of "aggressive" behaviors. In J. Hill (Ed.), *Minnesota Symposia on Child Psychology* (Vol. 5). Minneapolis: University of Minnesota Press.

Peterson, P., and Janicki, T. (1979). Individual characteristics and children's learning in large-group and small-group approaches. *Journal of Educational Psychology, 71*, 677–687.

Peterson, P., Janicki, T., and Swing, S. (1981). Ability x treatment interaction effects on children's learning in large-group and small-group approaches.

American Educational Research Journal, 18, 453-473.

Rumelhart, D. (1984). Understanding understanding. In J. Flood (Ed.), *Understanding reading comprehension: Cognition, language, and the structure of prose*. Newark, DE: International Reading Association.

Sacks, H. (1974). On the analysability of stories by children. In R. Turner (Ed.), *Ethnomethodology*. Harmondsworth, Middlesex: Penguin.

Schaffer, H., Hepburn, A., and Collis, G. (1983). Verbal and nonverbal aspects of mother's directives. *Journal of Child Language, 10*, 337-355.

Schickedanz, J., and Sullivan, M. (1984). Mom what does U-F-F spell? *Language Arts, 61*, 7-17.

Schneiderman, M. (1983). "Do what I mean, not what I say." Changes in mothers' action-directives to young children. *Journal of Child Language, 10*, 357-367.

Shuy, R., and Griffin, P. (1981). What do they do at school any day? In W. P. Dickson (Ed.), *Children's oral communication skills*. New York: Academic Press.

Sinclair, J., and Coulthard, R. (1975). *Towards an analysis of discourse: The English used by teachers and pupils*. Oxford: Oxford University Press.

Slama-Cazacu, T. (1977). *Dialogue in children*. The Hague, Netherlands: Mouton Publishers.

Smith, F. (1975). *Comprehension and learning: A conceptual framework for teachers*. New York: Holt, Rinehart and Winston.

Speier, M. (1976). The child as conversationalist: some culture-contact features of conversational interactions between adults and children. In M. Hammersley and P. Woods (Eds.), *The process of schooling: A sociological perspective*. London: Routledge and Kegan Paul.

Stubbs, M. (1976). *Language, schools, and classrooms: Contemporary sociology of the school*. London: Methuen.

Tattershall, S. (1984). Story grammar: Implications for reading instruction. *Kentucky Reading Journal, 5*, 47-50.

Thompson, J. (1969). *Instructional Communication*. New York: Van Nostrand Reinhold.

Tough, J. (1973). Focus on meaning: Talking to some purpose with young children. London: George Allen and Unwin.

Van Kleeck, A. (1984). Metalinguistic skills: Cutting across spoken and written language and problem solving abilities. In G. Wallach and K. Butler (Eds.), *Language learning disabilities in school age children*. Baltimore: Williams & Wilkins.

Vetter, D. (1982). Language disorders and schooling. *Topics in Language Disorders, 2*, 13-19.

Walkerdine, V., and Sinha, C. (1981). Developing linguistic strategies in young school children. In G. Wells (Ed.), *Learning through interaction: The study of language development*. Cambridge: Cambridge University Press.

Webb, N. (1980a). Group process: The key to learning in groups. *New directions for methodology of social and behavioral science: Issues in aggregation, 6*, 77-87.

Webb, N. (1980b). A process-outcome analysis of learning in group and individual settings. *Educational Psychologist, 15*, 69-80.

Webb, N. (1980c). An analysis of group interaction and mathematical errors in heterogeneous ability groups. *British Journal of Educational Psychology, 50*, 1-11.

Webb, N. (1982a). Predicting learning from student interaction: Defining the interaction variables. *Educational Psychologist, 18*, 33-41.

Webb, N. (1982b). Group composition, group interaction and achievement in cooperative small groups. *Journal of Educational Psychology, 74*, 475–484.

Webb, N., and Kenderski, C. (1984). Student interaction and learning in small-group and whole-class settings. In P. Peterson, L. Wilkinson, and M. Hallinan (Eds.), *The social context of instruction: Group organization and group processes*. New York: Academic Press.

Wells, G. (1981). Language, literacy and education. In G. Wells (Ed.), *Learning through interaction: The study of language development*. Cambridge: Cambridge University Press.

Whitehurst, G., and Sonnenschein, S. (1981). The development of informative messages in referential communication: Knowing when versus knowing how. In W. P. Dickson (Ed.), *Children's oral communication skills*. New York: Academic Press.

Wilkinson, L. (1984). Research currents: Peer group talk in elementary school. *Language Arts, 61*, 164–169.

Wilkinson, L., Clevenger, M., and Dollaghan, C. (1981). Communication in small instructional groups: A sociolinguistic approach. In W. P. Dickson (Ed.), *Children's oral communication skills*. New York: Academic Press.

Wilkinson, L., and Dollaghan, C. (1979). Peer communication in first grade reading groups. *Theory into Practice, 18*, 267–274.

Chapter 4

Teacher-Student Discourse

David Bloome
Gladys Knott

INTRODUCTION

The purpose of this chapter is to provide a framework for understanding classroom discourse as both a communicative context and a social accomplishment. Classroom discourse is viewed from the perspectives of teachers and students, and the discussion is based on researchers' recent work on classrooms. Much of the work is represented in disciplines such as sociolinguistics, ethnography, ethnomethodology, and anthropology.

The chapter is organized into five sections. In the first section, The Nature of Classroom Discourse, three broad constructs are discussed:

1. The communicative context of classroom lessons is neither given nor prescribed but is constructed through the face-to-face interaction of teachers and students. Simply stated, teachers and students build on each other's communicative behavior as they work together to meet curricular goals and carry out everyday classroom activities.
2. Meaning is situation-specific. Teachers and students interpret each other's communicative behavior based on the communicative context established. An utterance or other communicative behavior in one classroom situation may mean something different in another classroom situation.
3. Classroom discourse involves multiple layers of interaction. Teacher-class discourse, teacher-student discourse, and student-student discourse are among embedded layers of classroom discourse.

In the next three sections, three issues will be discussed that illustrate classroom discourse as both a communicative context and a social accomplishment. Representative findings from recent work on classroom discourse are presented. The first issue concerns the nature of classroom discourse across classroom settings and situations. Of special concern are the changing demands for appropriate participation across contexts both within and across classrooms. The second issue concerns written language in the classroom. Of special concern are (1) how the communicative context influences written language, (2) how written language influences the communicative context, and (3) how written language is defined as reading and writing. The third issue concerns classroom discourse and cultural continuity and discontinuity across home and school settings. Of special concern are the implications of discontinuity for evaluation, communication, and instruction. Also of concern are implications for the creation of classroom "successes" and "failures."

In the fifth and last section, we discuss communication disorders in the classroom. Of special concern is a framework from which communication disorders can be described. The framework suggests that a description of communication disorders needs to be based not only on knowledge of individual communicative behavior but also on knowledge of classroom discourse as both communicative context and social accomplishment.

ON THE NATURE OF CLASSROOM DISCOURSE

Researchers exploring classrooms from the perspectives of sociolinguistic ethnography (Cazden, John, and Hymes, 1972; Cochran-Smith, 1984; Cook-Gumperz, Gumperz, and Simons, 1981; Gumperz, 1981; Green and Wallat, 1981; Hymes, 1981; Shultz, Erickson, and Florio, 1982; Wilkinson, 1982), ethnomethodology (Mehan, 1979; Heap, 1983) and anthropology (McDermott, 1976; Philips, 1982) have provided a series of constructs for understanding classroom discourse from the perspective of students and teachers (see Cazden, in press, and Green, 1983, for reviews of recent work in this area). Underlying this recent work is a view of classroom discourse as a communicative context. Classroom discourse is viewed as a context for both the academic and the social and cultural work that occurs in classrooms. That is, academic tasks and social and cultural tasks, knowledge, procedures, and evaluations are embedded within classroom discourse.

As a communicative context, classroom discourse is a resource teachers and students use to interpret each other's communicative behavior; that is, through classroom discourse teachers and students construct interpretive frameworks for understanding what is occurring in classrooms. Classroom discourse also provides standards (or expectations) for appropriate interactional behavior. Such interactional standards include who gets to talk, what gets talked about, and when, where, and how interactions are facilitated or impeded. As such, classroom discourse can be viewed as both an interactional context and an interpretive context.

As stated earlier, classroom discourse is both a communicative context and a social accomplishment. For example, although part of the task of teachers and students is to create a shared context for communication, another part of the task is to create an event that can be counted as a classroom lesson. In other words, through their concerted efforts, teachers and students need to create a social and cultural event that both they and the members of broader social and cultural contexts (e.g., school officials, parents, taxpayers) recognize as being a classroom lesson. The construction of classroom discourse reflects its dual nature as communicative context and social accomplishment.

Constructive Nature of Classroom Discourse

Classroom discourse can be viewed as a communicative context. Contexts are not given, in the sense that four walls, a blackboard and desks make a context, but rather contexts are constructed by what people are doing, how they are doing it, and with whom they are doing it (Erickson and Shultz, 1977, 1981; Green, 1983; McDermott, 1976). Through their face-to-face interaction, teachers and students establish rules for how they are to interact with each other and how they are to interpret each other's message.

Interactional rules are established for gaining access to conversations (Green and Harker, 1982), for turn-taking (Shultz, Erickson, and Florio, 1982), for constructing narratives (Michaels, 1981; Cook-Gumperz, Gumperz, and Simons, 1981), and for demonstrating group membership (McDermott, 1976), among other interactional purposes. These "rules"— which are often implicit—can be viewed as culturally driven expectations that become frames for appropriate behavior (Green, 1983).

Teachers and students establish communicative contexts during face-to-face interaction through the use of contextualization cues (Gumperz, 1976). Contextualization cues are verbal, nonverbal, and prosodic cues used by participants to signal what is happening and what constitutes appropriate communicative behavior as well as appropriate interpretations of communicative behavior. It is through the use of contextualization cues that teachers and students make the communicative context "visible" to each other. For example, consider what happens during transitions between events: Postural configurations shift, intonation patterns shift, and topics of conversation shift, among other changes in patterns of contextualization cues. As a "new" event forms (or as an "old" event reformulates or shifts direction), patterns of contextualization cues stabilize and members begin to act in concert.

Within events, teachers and students hold each other accountable for contextually appropriate behavior. For example, if a student talks out of turn or talks about an unrelated topic, both the teacher and other students are likely to admonish the errant student. Admonishment may be subtle, taking the form of skewed glances, smirking, or silence, or admonishment may be overt, such as when students are punished for talking at the wrong time. Breaches in appropriate behavior often lead to explicit statements of interactional rules: "It's not your turn to talk" or "Raise your hand and wait for the teacher to call on you." Breaches in appropriate behavior are means by which interactional "rules" are made visible to the class; that is, students can observe the errant behavior and its consequences and infer what constitutes appropriate behavior. Classroom goals provide the impetus for establishing a shared communicative context for teachers and students; that is, classroom discourse is purposeful and goal directed (Green and Wallat, 1981). One of the goals of classroom discourse is academic learning.

The discourse work that teachers and students need to do in order to accomplish classroom tasks (that is, the construction of a shared communicative context) involves both the academic task structure and the social participation structure (cf. Erickson, 1982). Erickson identified four components of the academic task structure: (1) the logic of subject matter sequencing, (2) information content of various sequential steps, (3) the "meta-content" cues towards steps and strategies for completing tasks, and (4) the physical materials through which tasks are manifested and accomplished. The social participation structure consists of the sequencing, distributing, and articulating of roles, rights, and obligations for communication by teachers and students (e.g., turn-taking procedures and group maintenance procedures) (cf. Erickson, 1982).

From this perspective, then, the discourse work that teachers and students do within and across lessons helps to define the communicative context, which in turn is defined by the academic task structure and the social participation structure. In other words, from participating in lesson construction students learn about how to do (how to participate in) the lesson as well as about academic content. Lessons, therefore, as well as the discourse within lessons, are social accomplishments.

One aspect of this lesson construction process that has been uncovered using this perspective is that for some teachers and students the focus of lessons is the production of a series of discourse events that can be counted as classroom lessons. That is, both teachers and students must *display* to each other behaviors that indicate appropriate procedures for completing the classroom lesson. Bloome (1983a) calls this phenomenon procedural display and metaphorically compares it to actors performing their parts in a play without necessarily learning the meaning of their lines or the meaning of the play.

Procedural display builds on the routinization of classroom lessons. That is, although communicative contexts are not given (are static) but rather are constructed, over time, a particular classroom event (e.g., reading group) will develop consistency in the patterns of the academic task structure and the social participation structure. In turn, the patterns may lead to the establishment of highly ritualized classroom discourse. As communicative contexts become highly ritualized, teachers and students may work to complete the ritual (as opposed to working for academic learning). That is, some teachers and students may become primarily concerned with "getting through" the lesson. For these teachers and students, "getting through" is important because finishing lessons (1) is an indicator of how much was done (which may inaccurately be equated with curriculum coverage and learning), and (2) allows for discretionary time (e.g., recess, relaxing).

Meaning as Situation-Specific

As stated above, classroom discourse provides a communicative context for interpreting teachers' and students' behavior. As Gumperz and Tannen (1979) state, to understand intended meaning, look at the context of communicative behavior:

> Any utterance can be understood in numerous ways and...people make decisions about how to interpret any given utterance or gesture based on their definition of what is happening at the time of interaction. In other words, they define the interaction in terms of a "frame" which is identifiable and familiar.
> (Gumperz and Tannen, 1979, p. 307)

One of the implications of viewing meaning as situation-specific is that the interactional meaning of utterances may differ from the literal meaning of their words. The interactional meaning may depend more on the utterance's placement and function within the stream of communicative behavior than on the literal semantic content of the words. For example, depending on the communicative context, a teacher utterance to attend to an academic task may be interpreted as an admonishment for students to adhere to an appropriate classroom interactional norm.

A second implication of viewing meaning as situation-specific is that there may be interpretive differences, depending on how teachers and students view what is happening. That is, differences in teacher and students perspectives—whether the result of cultural differences, linguistic differences, or simply differences in classroom roles—may lead to different interpretations of classroom behavior.

Farrar (1983) and Heap (1983) suggest a third implication of viewing meaning as situation-specific. They note that classroom discourse often consists of initiation-reply-feedback sequences (cf. Mehan, 1979). Through teacher initiations and student responses, a series of propositions are produced that potentially can be counted as knowledge in the classroom. Teacher feedback confirms which propositions are to count as knowledge and indicates which students may be held accountable for which propositions. In sum, through initiation-reply-feedback sequences, classroom discourse makes clear what counts as knowledge in the classroom.

A fourth implication of viewing meaning as situation-specific is that the intended academic meaning of classroom discourse may be interpreted in terms of the social, interpersonal workings of the classroom. For example, a classroom discussion on geographical features may result in the distribution of status and roles within the classroom (via how positive feedback is distributed, which student is able to respond to which questions, and so on). Conversely, the interpersonal working of the classroom (e.g., who will talk about what) influences the academic meaning and outcome of classroom discourse (Cochran-Smith, 1984; Green, Harker, and Golden, in press). For example, Green, Harker, and Golden (in press) showed that the way in which two teachers talked about the same story with students was related to differences in what students recalled about the story.

Although meaning is viewed as situation-specific, situations are embedded in broader contexts. Classroom lessons are embedded in schools that are embedded in communities that are embedded within a societal or ideological context. Therefore, interactional patterns in specific situations reflect broader contexts. Neither teachers nor students enter classrooms empty-minded. They have expectations from previous experiences in similar or related situations both inside and outside the classroom. These expectations may be transformed or confirmed during face-to-face interaction. Therefore, although meaning is specific to a given situation, it may also be related to other situations both in the past and in the future.

Multiple Layers of Classroom Discourse

Part of what needs to be considered in understanding how students and teachers interpret classroom discourse is where students and teachers stand within the multiple layers of classroom discourse. For heuristic purposes, three layers of classroom discourse can be identified: (1) teacher-class discourse, (2) teacher-student discourse, and (3) student-student discourse. Teacher-class discourse occurs when the teacher addresses the whole class. Teacher-student discourse involves interaction with a single student, either in private or within a group situation. (Typically, the term teacher-student discourse has been used generically to refer to both teacher-class and teacher-individual student discourse.) Student-student discourse refers to discourse between individual students and to discourse between a student and the remainder of the class.

Consider the multiple layers of discourse involved in a simple directive from a teacher to a student, such as, "John, turn to page 45." Although the teacher is explicitly addressing John (teacher-student discourse), the teacher is also addressing the whole class (teacher-class discourse). The teacher is telling all students that they should be on page 45 and that their behavior is being monitored. From the teacher's perspective, teacher-student discourse is always teacher-class discourse.

From the student's perspective, teacher-student discourse is also teacher-class discourse, but it is biased towards the teacher. For example, reconsider the teacher's directive to John. Although John must respond to the teacher, what John does is being monitored by the remainder of the class. Therefore, what John needs to do is not only to respond to the teacher but also to respond to the teacher in a manner appropriate to the expectations of his peers. In most situations like John's, there may be no difference between teacher expectations and student expectations for an appropriate response. However, at times there may be differences between what is considered an appropriate response by the teacher and what is considered appropriate by the remainder of the class. For example, consider what may happen when a teacher asks an especially hard question. A student who answers the question correctly may violate student expectations or norms about the appropriateness of "showing off."

Whereas student-student discourse can be instructional discourse (for example, teachers may arrange for students to work in a group), student-student discourse often involves covert conversations, such as the interchange that occurs when students talk together during seatwork. Although such covert conversations may appear to be off-task, research has also shown that covert student-student conversations may be directly related to the task (Bloome and Theodorou, in press). Students may help each other accomplish the task, providing resources or information. Indeed, covert student-student discourse may be responsive to what the teacher is attempting to accomplish. For example, Bloom and Theodorou (in press) describe a covert conversation among three girls during a teacher-directed instructional conversation. The girls' covert conversation focused on aspects of the academic task as they were being discussed by the teacher.

Within each layer of discourse, "rules" are established for what constitutes appropriate participation. Although the rules of different layers of discourse may be complementary, they can often conflict. For example, a teacher may assign a seatwork task and explicitly state that students are to work independently and without talking. However, the "rules" of student-student discourse may require students to cooperate with each other and to respond to other students' initiatives (Bloome and Theodorou, in press). Thus, students may find themselves having to respond to conflicting sets of expectations for discourse behavior.

Even when rules across layers of discourse are not conflicting, students must continuously monitor several layers of discourse. For example, consider an individualized classroom in which a teacher moves from student to student. When the teacher is involved with a student, it is inappropriate to bid for the teacher's help. A student needs to wait until the teacher is done before bidding for the teacher's attention. However, the student must also keep busy while waiting for the teacher to be available (Merritt, 1982).

Merritt (1982) suggests that teachers orchestrate multiple layers of classroom discourse through the use of verbal and nonverbal channels. Although through the verbal channel the teacher may be addressing teacher-student interaction, through the nonverbal channel (e.g., where the teacher chooses to stand or the teacher's posturing, hand movement, and eye contact) teacher-class discourse may be addressed.

CLASSROOM DISCOURSE ACROSS CLASSROOM SETTINGS AND SITUATIONS

Classroom Discourse Across Classrooms

On the surface level, two classrooms engaging in a similar activity (e.g., sharing time) would seem to provide students with similar experiences. However, detailed description of the communicative contexts may suggest important differences in the two classroom lessons that result in different sets of experiences for students. To illustrate how communicative contexts may differ across supposedly similar events in two classrooms, two related studies will be described in detail. The first study (Green and Wallat, 1981) involved the microanalysis of two 13 minute videotaped segments from two different classrooms. Each videotaped segment involved "circle time." The videotape segments were part of a larger data base gathered through a sociolinguistic ethnography of the two classrooms over a three year period. The second study (Green and Harker, 1982) involved a reanalysis of the thirteen minute videotape segments.

In the first study, Green and Wallat (1981) were concerned with the identification of generic classroom social rules through the comparison of detailed descriptions of two classrooms. However, the intent was also to capture the diversity of ways in which generic classroom rules might be manifested within teacher-student discourse. We discuss their findings in order to highlight one way to look at teacher-student discourse across classrooms.

Three of the social rules identified across the classrooms by Green and Wallat (1981, p. 186) were

1. Being a member of a group requires attending to cues that flag differentiated expectations for physical orientation and proximity (e.g., attending to communicative cues about where to sit or stand).
2. Being a member of a group includes responsibility for enacting different patterns of responses (e.g., students in a reading group are held responsible for appropriate behavior during all phases of a lesson, including responding to teacher questions, listening to teacher directions, concluding a lesson, and so on).
3. Becoming a member of a group involves attending to differentiated social meanings of cooperative effort. (Students are expected to act in accordance with the interactional goals of the group; for example, getting a task completed.)

Through microanalysis of videotapes of circle time in the two classrooms, Green and Wallat were able to describe similarities and differences in how the social rules listed before were manifested. Similarities between the two lessons included the amount of teacher talk (computed in terms of message units, not in duration of time), grouping practices, and same number of phases within lessons. Also similar were the teacher's goals towards helping children develop a sense of group and permitting children to receive individual recognition within the group. Beyond these similarities, comparisons of the lessons showed differences in the communicative contexts of classroom interaction.

For example, during circle time in both classrooms, teachers desired individual space for children. However, they differed in how they realized this goal. One teacher focused the children's attention on defining individual space by changing the configuration of students across phases of the circle time lesson. Students who had been sitting on the perimeter of a square rug were directed to form rows. The teacher formed the rows by calling on children according to the color of their clothing. This enabled the teacher to help children establish individual space for a new context as well as to create a new group structure (rows). Although the second teacher was also concerned about individual space, she directed students to find their own space around the edge of a rug in a circle. Students who did not find their own space were directed by the teacher to an open space in the circle. In each classroom, the teacher coordinated her verbal and nonverbal actions (e.g., singing and gestures) to form a group. The first teacher used both verbal and nonverbal cues to signal specific expectations for where individual children were to sit. The second teacher also coordinated verbal and nonverbal actions to form the group and to indicate that children in different places in the circle were welcome and were to join in the group activity.

In both classrooms, once the group was formed, the circle time lesson shifted. In one class, the lesson shifted to a structured lesson on the calendar. In the other class, the lesson shifted to news and views (sharing time). As phases of the lesson shifted, students had to recognize the shifts (which are made overt by the teacher's verbal and nonverbal actions) and reorient themselves to new demands for appropriate participation.

In brief, although both teachers established and signaled expectations for appropriate participation in circle time through verbal and nonverbal messages, the specific expectations for participation differed across classrooms. In other words, classroom communicative contexts have social rules or expectations for participation, but within a given classroom event, such rules are manifested in situation-specific ways.

In a related study, Green and Harker (1982) explored further comparisons across the two circle time lessons through a reanalysis of the same videotape data. Of special concern were the contextual, social, and thematic demands of the instructional conversations; that is, teachers and students need to know what the nature of the activity is, what the social nature of the group is at any given moment, and what thematic information is being exchanged. Green and Harker (1982) argued that failure to read all of these demands may lead to inappropriate behavior by the children.

Across the two classrooms, there were differences in how teachers cue students about the context and focus shifts. In the first classroom, cues were primarily verbal, whereas in the second classroom cues were prosodic and nonverbal (e.g., cues involved, voice intonation, gestures, and eye contact). In other words, how students knew what the context was (what activity is beginning or is taking place) in the two classrooms differed. The communicative demands placed on children in the two classrooms were different.

Strategies for establishing and maintaining social rules also differed across the two classrooms. In the first classroom, social rules were established through a large number of external, overt control strategies. In the second classroom, social rules were established and maintained through question-asking, continuance strategies (e.g., backchanneling), and requests for clarification and confirmation. In both classrooms, the kinds of strategies used were appropriate to the teachers' goals. The point is that across the two classrooms the social demands differed.

In terms of the thematic demands made in both classrooms, when students talk, their talk must be thematically related to the instructional topic. Breakdowns in the coherence of a lesson may involve the failure to tie discussion to the content or structure or the lesson's instructional theme. When breakdowns occur, repairs need to be made. Even when the instructional theme is similar across classrooms, the communicative demands made of students for how to link their talk to the instructional theme can differ.

Green and Harker (1982) suggested that "...although two teachers may have similar goals or stated expectations, they may not have similar social and communicative environments for children. Perhaps children in these classrooms are being socialized into different schooling processes" (p. 207).

Classroom Discourse Across Reading Groups

One implication of the previous discussion is that surface-level descriptions of classroom events (e.g., circle time, reading group) may gloss over important differences in communicative contexts. In order to understand the social, academic, and communicative demands made of students, detailed events are needed.

Detailed descriptions of teacher-student discourse in reading groups within the same classroom have shown that communicative contexts for high and low reading groups may differ. Differences in the structure and organization of teacher-student discourse within reading groups has been related to the time spent reading (Collins, 1981; McDermott, 1976), the evaluation of student reading behavior (Collins, 1981), and the tasks provided students (Collins, 1981). In addition recent research has suggested that different reading groups socialize students into different communicative norms (Eder, 1982). Each of these findings will be briefly reviewed.

Time Spent on Reading Instruction. In a study of a first grade classroom, McDermott (1976) showed how students in the top reading group spent more time on reading instruction than did students in the low reading group, although both groups met for the same amount of time (see Collins, 1981, for similar findings). In the top group, turn-taking was organized in a round-robin fashion. Each student knew when his turn was. There was no bidding for turns. Transitions between speakers occurred smoothly. In the low reading group, students bid for turns to read. However, because reading was a difficult and frustrating experience for most students in the group, students would often attempt to avoid their turns. The effect was that the group spent considerable time on turn-taking procedures and considerable time formulating and reformulating the group after each student read. The result was that the students spent less time engaged in reading instruction than the top group.

The difference between the top and low groups was not only in the structure of turn-taking but also in the interactional goals established in the group. In the top group, the goal was the practicing of reading. Both teacher and students worked towards the goal of giving students opportunities to practice the oral rendition of a text. In the bottom group, the goal was the avoidance of frustration and the accomplishment of "getting through" the lesson. For both teacher and students, the reading group proved a frustrating and otherwise undesirable task. Spending time on turn-taking and classroom interruption provided a way to alleviate the frustration. Thus, implementing round-robin turn-taking procedures in the low group would not necessarily have changed the time spent on reading or changed the essential nature of teacher-student discourse.

Evaluation of Student Reading. Collins (1981) found differences in how top and low reading group students orally read narrative text. Top reading group students orally read narrative text in a prosodic manner similar to that of the teacher. Bottom reading group students orally read narrative text in a prosodic manner that was different from the teacher's manner but was similar to how narrative text was prosodically rendered in their home culture. In effect, the teacher had an implicit model of how narrative text was to be prosodically rendered. Students who matched the model were viewed as better readers, whereas students who did not match the implicit prosodic model were viewed as poorer readers. Often, the degree to which students did or did not match the implicit prosodic model of narrative text-rendering masked skills and abilities for decoding and comprehending text.

Reading Group Tasks. Collins (1981) found that the ways in which students' oral reading of narrative texts were evaluated was tied to the kinds of tasks given to students. Students who rendered narrative text in a manner consistent with the teacher's implicit model (often top reading group students) were given comprehension tasks. Students who did not render text in the expected prosodic manner were given word-attack tasks.

Allington (1980) also found implicit differences between tasks given students in top and bottom reading groups. In bottom reading groups, teachers were more likely to interrupt when oral reading errors were made. Such interruptions focus student attention on oral rendering as opposed to comprehension. In addition, teacher interruptions provide opportunities for other students to interrupt.

Communicative Norms. Eder (1982) examined student initiations and teacher responses within reading groups of various levels. Student initiations can occur as a result of a teacher's invitation to students to initiate comments or without an explicit invitation. Eder (1982) found that at the beginning of the year there were differences in the communicative competence of students in the top and bottom reading groups. The result was that students in the top reading group gained access to the "floor" more often than other students. Further, the comments of the students in the top reading group were more often topically relevant than the comments of the other students. In both the top and bottom reading groups, the teacher discouraged nontopical comments. However, the teacher responded to interruptions differently in the two groups. In the top group the teacher discouraged interruptions, whereas in the bottom group the teacher responded to interruptions. Across the year, students in the top reading group made fewer interruptions. Eder (1982) argues that differences in the norms for interruptions between the top and bottom reading groups result in bottom group students not developing an understanding that reading turns should not be interrupted.

In effect, students in the bottom reading group were socialized into a different set of communicative norms than top group students. While the communicative norms acquired may be appropriate within the respective reading groups, the communicative norms of the bottom reading group are not appropriate outside the reading group. That is, if students in the bottom reading group apply the communicative norms learned in the reading group to other classroom situations, their communicative behavior may be viewed as inappropriate.

WRITTEN LANGUAGE IN THE CLASSROOM

Teachers and students talk considerably about written language, such as about a story that was read, a worksheet completed, a composition written, about blackboard assignments, and so on. Both the written language tasks students are asked to do and how teachers and students talk about those tasks influence the communicative context of classroom events.

Written language tasks include not only the tasks students are given in reading group but also any task that requires a student to use reading or writing. As Florio and Clark (1982), Bloome (1981), and others have noted, when a broad view of writing or reading is present, a great deal of writing and reading is seen occurring in classrooms.

Written language tasks can be viewed as having a prescribed dimension and a realized dimension. The prescribed dimension involves what the task designers hope to accomplish. They may intend for students to learn new vocabulary or to write summaries. When teachers and students begin to work on the task, the nature of the prescribed task may change. A prescribed task for learning new vocabulary words may be realized as a copying task; that is, instead of learning new vocabulary words, students may end up copying words and definitions out of a book without learning what the words mean or how to use them.

How written language tasks are realized depends, in large part, on the accountability system inherent in classrooms (cf. Doyle, 1984) and on teacher-student discourse within written language tasks. The accountability system involves the continuous need for teachers to evaluate student work formally or informally. Formally, student evaluation occurs through grades and written evaluations. Informally, evaluation occurs as part of ongoing teacher-student discourse. For example, researchers have found that conversational sequences of teacher initiation, student response, and teacher feedback occur frequently in classrooms (Mehan, 1979). Evaluation is an inherent part of such sequences (in the feedback component).

As Doyle (1984) stated, students orient the work they do in terms of the accountability system; that is, students will do that for which they are held accountable. Although students may be held accountable for accomplishing the goal prescribed for a written language task, often this is not the case (especially with more complex and higher-level tasks whose evaluation is more difficult and the criteria for evaluation more ambiguous). For example, students may be held accountable for completing a worksheet as opposed to knowing definitions of the new words on the sheet. Students may be held accountable for completing a basal reader instead of being able to comprehend stories at a specified difficulty level. In writing, students may be held accountable for neat papers, correct spelling, and grammar as opposed to clear, interesting, and purposeful composition.

The result may be what Bloome (in press) has described as text reproduction. Text reproduction includes the oral reproduction of written texts (e.g., oral rendition), the written reproduction of written texts (e.g., copying), the written reproduction of oral texts (e.g., dictation), and the oral reproduction of oral texts (e.g., imitation). Bloome (in press) suggests that in some classrooms the ways in which written tasks are realized produces text reproduction as the dominant mode of student-text interaction; that is, text reproduction becomes the social and communicative norm for student-teacher-text interaction. For example, Bloome (1983b) describes a first grade reading group in which teacher-student discourse fostered text reproduction. In that reading group, students were first asked to orally render a written text. The students were asked questions about the text rendered. Although on the surface the questions called for text information, the teacher-student discourse was structured so that appropriate answers had to be phrased in the exact words given in the text and had to be prosodically rendered in the same manner in which the text was originally rendered (e.g., word by word). Bloome (in press) also describes middle school classrooms in which text reproduction dominated teacher-student-text interaction. One question raised by Bloome's work is the kinds of student-text relationships into which students are being socialized.

DeStefano, Pepinsky, and Sanders (1982) also raise questions about teacher-student discourse during written language instruction. Their study of an inner-city first grade classroom suggested that what students learn during reading instruction is how to talk and how to act during reading instruction. That is, students learned little about comprehending extended written discourse (e.g., stories, essays) but did learn how to behave appropriately during reading instruction.

Although the work of Doyle (1984), Bloome (1983a, 1983b, in press), and DeStefano and co-workers (1982) may not describe all classrooms, their studies suggest that at least three principles affect teacher-student discourse: (1) Student-text relationships (how students approach reading and writing tasks) are influenced by the communicative context of the classroom (see also Mosenthal and Na, 1980) and by the accountability system inherent in the classroom. (2) The prescribed task may not necessarily be the task realized in the classroom. (3) During written language tasks, students must attend to norms for student-text interaction.

CLASSROOM DISCOURSE
AND CULTURAL CONTINUITY

The ways people organize language events are an extension of their culture (Heath, 1983). In other words, part of the cultural expectations for social events includes who speaks when, where, and about what (Erickson and Shultz, 1977, 1981; Shultz, Erickson, and Florio, 1982; Florio and Shultz, 1979); how narratives are structured and constructed (Scollon and Scollon, 1982); and what obligations speakers have to their audiences and audiences have to their speakers (Tannen, 1982). (Detailed discussions of language events as cultural events can be found in Gumperz and Hymes, 1972; Gumperz, 1982; Hymes, 1974; and Scollon and Scollon, 1982.)

When language events in classrooms are viewed as cultural events, questions can be raised about the participation of students from a broad range of cultural backgrounds. Of primary concern are (1) the cultural expectations and meanings inherent in classroom language events, (2) miscommunication among teachers and students from diverse cultural backgrounds, and (3) the adequacy with which students of diverse cultural backgrounds are accommodated within classroom language events.

The cultural expectations inherent in classroom language events can be revealed by comparison of classroom events to nonclassroom events. For example, Scollon and Scollon (1982) compared how narrative events in classrooms are organized with how narrative events are organized within Native American Athabaskan communities. In school, students are expected to render as given the text they are presented. There is no opportunity for the student to add to the text or to change the text. Individual interpretations and transformations of the text are not allowed. Within Athabaskan culture, opportunity is provided for individual interpretation and transformation of narratives. A narrative text is not viewed as a "given." Although a narrative text may follow a broad outline, individual interpretation and production of the narrative is allowed and expected. The ways of organizing narrative events within Athabaskan reflect the value placed on respect for the individual. The ways of organizing narrative events in the classroom reflect the value placed on the integrity of the text.

When students approach classroom language events in ways consistent with their home culture but not with the classroom, miscommunication and faulty evaluation may result. For example, Philips (1982) described how Native American children on the Warm Springs Reservation were viewed as appropriately behaving in some situations and inappropriately behaving in other situations (in a classroom taught by an Anglo-American teacher). In some situations, there was little difference between how the Native American children participated and how the Anglo-American children participated, but in other situations the Native American children did not seem to participate. The Native American children were viewed as misbehaving, disrespectful, or unable to participate in the classroom task. However, Philips (1982) reported that their behavior was consistent with appropriate behavior in analogous language events within the children's home culture. Simply put, the children were acting in ways consistent with expectations they thought were appropriate for the situation.

Researchers have described a broad range of ways in which

discontinuity between the culturally derived ways of organizing language events in classrooms and homes can manifest itself and result in miscommunication and misevaluation (Gumperz and Tannen, 1979). There can be discontinuity in the basic assumptions participants have about the communicative goals and activity inherent in classroom situations. For example, one of the communicative goals of classroom activities is to learn to read. Engaging in reading, with the primary purpose to learn to read, is a culturally based communicative goal not shared by all communities (Heath, 1983). Discontinuity can also exist in the interpersonal organization of certain spoken and written language events (Heath, 1983). For example, in classrooms reading is primarily an individual activity: An individual reads a text. However, outside of classrooms, reading is often a group activity in which several people may simultaneously read and discuss a text. There can also be discontinuity in the ways in which turns at talk are organized (Au, 1980; Shultz, Erickson, and Florio, 1982; Florio and Shultz, 1979). For example, in classroom situations, one person talks at a time and the teacher distributes turns at talk. However, within some communities, in analogous situations at home, several people may speak simultaneously, and turns at talk are not distributed by a single individual. Culturally based differences in the use of prosody can also result in miscommunication and faulty evaluation (Michaels, 1981; Collins, 1981; Gumperz and Tannen, 1979). For example, within some communities, the structure of narratives may be signaled through prosody as opposed to lexical cohesion. When children produce narratives whose structure is signaled prosodically, teachers may view the narratives as unorganized and rambling (e.g., Michaels, 1981).

One way to describe the culturally based ways of organizing language events is that for some students a cultural continuity between some classroom and home language events is present, whereas for other students there is discontinuity. Simply put, participation in classroom language events is a cross-cultural experience.

Bloome (1981, in press) has suggested that participation in classroom language events is, in part, a cross-cultural experience for all students. He found that successful participation in classroom events often required students to repress or deny their own background knowledge and respond to questions and tasks in terms of a "school" framework. For example, Bloome (1982) described how a ninth grade student failed a fourth grade reading task because the student answered questions based on the student's background knowledge. That is, although the student's answers made sense in terms of the student's experiences, they were not the answers required by the curriculum guide. "Successful" students could assume the framework of the curriculum guide and "correctly" answer the questions.

Interestingly, "successful" students could also recognize the legitimacy of answers based on their background knowledge but knew that such answers were not appropriate for successful completion of the task.

COMMUNICATION DISORDERS IN THE CLASSROOM

Communication disorders are typically viewed as a disorder in an individual's communicative abilities; that is, communication disorders are typically viewed as an *intra*personal phenomenon. Teacher-student discourse is, obviously, an *inter*personal phenomenon. In this section, we are concerned with looking at communication disorders within the context of teacher-student discourse; we are concerned with looking at an intrapersonal factor within interpersonal contexts. In this chapter, we have discussed at length issues involved in teacher-student discourse in an attempt to establish an interpersonal frame for looking at instruction, classroom lessons and learning, student behavior, and, in particular, at communication disorders as they may be manifested in classrooms. In this section, we first briefly consider the nature of communication disorders and then discuss issues involved in exploring communication disorders within the interpersonal context of teacher-student discourse.

Communications in humans includes the reception, expression, and use of verbal and nonverbal symbolic behavior (Knapp, 1978; Bryan, 1978; Knott, 1980; Green and Wallat, 1981). Traditionally, the verbal channel is defined to include listening, speaking, reading, and writing. Although the elements of the verbal channel are often segmented in classroom instruction, they are interrelated. The acquisition and development of one element facilitates progress in another. Conversely, a problem in the acquisition and development of one element of verbal behavior may impede progress in another (Wiig and Semel, 1976; Wallach and Butler, 1984; Smith, 1984).

Nonverbal communication consists of several channels; for example, paralanguage, kinesics, and proxemics. Although other modes (for example, the use of artifacts or tactility) are recognized, the elements just mentioned have received major attention. Briefly defined, paralanguage includes pitch, stress, intonation qualities, backchanneling, and other oral but nonverbal behaviors that assist a listener in perceiving how a message is to be understood (Duncan, 1969; Knapp, 1978; Gumperz and Herasimchuk, 1975). (Paralanguage is similar to prosody but includes related communication behaviors not typically associated with prosody, e.g., backchanneling.) Through intonation, for example, a listener may determine that a statement is a question and requires a response. Kinesics consists of gestures and body movements, including facial expression, posture, and eye movement. Information is communicated through each element or a combination of elements. Proxemics is defined as the perception and use of social and personal space as well as the observation of space boundaries in communication. For example, the distance between two or more persons in social interaction may indicate familiarity, sharing of mutual concern and interest, and so on, or in contrast, distance may serve to demonstrate that communication between two persons is not desired.

A significant role is played by kinesic, proxemic, and prosodic behaviors in human communication. In a definition of human communication, the elements of communication should be viewed within the context of a total communicative act. In human communication, verbal and nonverbal behaviors are shared simultaneously.

From this brief description of verbal and nonverbal components of human communication, a variety of problems in communication can be identified, as some children and youth participate in academic and social interactions in and out of classrooms. A common tradition, however, is to foster development of communication ability primarily on verbal behavior, particularly reading and writing in recent years. A major premise of the discussion here is that improvement of communication ability requires consideration of verbal and nonverbal communication. Interrelated with verbal communication are abilities in understanding, expressing, and appropriately using nonverbal communication.

Although an in-depth discussion of communication disorders in the classroom is beyond the scope and intent of this chapter, we suggest a general framework for identifying and describing problems in communication as they are presented in the classroom. Although we discuss techniques for identification and description, it is important to note that the techniques are only a means for applying a framework for interpreting student communicative behavior within a classroom situation. The constructs we have discussed earlier in this chapter constitute the interpersonal framework.

For descriptive purposes, students' verbal and nonverbal communication in regular classrooms can be observed systematically and recorded. This description of communication behaviors suggests educational programming needs. The description needs to take into consideration the nature of teacher-student discourse within which student communicative behavior is embedded and also needs to consider the classroom context within which educational programming will occur. For description of intrapersonal factors related to student communication, an appropriate measure on which evaluation of students' needs can be facilitated includes recent descriptions of children's acquisition and development of communication behavior (cf. Bloom and Lahey, 1978; Wallach and Butler, 1984). In other words, developmental norms may suggest whether a student has a communication disorder. However, as stated earlier, such measures need to be used in a way that considers and accounts for the interpersonal contexts in which students participate.

To make systematic observations and effectively describe students' communicative behavior, a structure to record and analyze data is needed. One type of structure includes a checklist of behaviors that delineate specific components of verbal and nonverbal communication. For example, to observe oral communication, it is necessary to consider the child's reception, expression, and use of different syntactic structures. Each parameter (for example, reception of messages) may further be delineated to include vocabulary, direct-indirect discourse, sequential events, comparative relations, and so on. The checklist suggests variables that may affect students' communication development and that are in need of educational programming consideration. The objective is to develop a structure that enables recording of sufficient data to generate a description of a student's communication behavior. However, a checklist by itself, that does not consider the interpersonal contexts within which communication takes place, such as the context of teacher-student discourse, may inaccurately describe and interpret communicative behavior. In brief, descriptions of students' communicative behavior, whether collected via a checklist or more sophisticated means, needs to be contextualized in terms of the communicative context in which students are involved. In classrooms, that communicative context, to a large extent, consists of teacher-student discourse. Knowledge about the nature of teacher-student discourse, how it constrains and facilitates communicative behavior and how it evolves and changes, and the demands it places on teachers and students, is needed in order to appropriately contextualize (or frame) students' communicative behavior.

Further, it is necessary to consider the conditions under which observations are made, the importance of particular aspects of communication behavior, the effects of the observer on the student and the nature of the communication interaction, including who is doing the interacting and when, where, and why the interaction is occurring. In addition, different observation settings are necessary to obtain reliable data. The process involves ongoing or continual settings rather than a single session to determine the educational program needs of students. The data can then be used to generate a comprehensive description of communication behavior. The description, based on functional communication in different academic and social contexts, suggests what the student's strengths and needs for improvement are.

In sum, the authors of this chapter suggest that the identification and description of students' communicative behavior, including the identification and description of communication disorders, require the application of a frame that considers both intrapersonal factors and interpersonal factors. In this chapter, we have emphasized the interpersonal factors, especially those involved in teacher-student discourse, that constitute part of a frame for exploring students' participation in classroom events.

ACKNOWLEDGMENT

The authors gratefully acknowledge Dr. Judith Green of The Ohio State University for providing critical and editorial comments on early drafts of this chapter.

REFERENCES

Allington, R. (1980). *Poor readers don't get to read much* (Occasional Paper No. 31). East Lansing, MI: Institute for Research on Teaching.

Au, K. (1980). Participation structures in a reading lesson with Hawaiian children. *Anthropology and Education Quarterly, 11*(2), 91–115.

Bloom, L., and Lahey, M. (1978). *Language development and language disorders*. New York: Wiley.

Bloome, D. (1981). *An ethnographic approach to the study of reading among black junior high school students*. Unpublished doctoral dissertation, Kent State University, Kent, Ohio.

Bloome, D. (1982). *School culture and the future of literacy*. Paper presented at the Future of Literacy Conference, University of Maryland, Baltimore.

Bloome, D. (1983a). Classroom reading instruction: A socio-communicative analysis of time on task. *32nd Yearbook of the National Reading Conference*. Rochester, NY: National Reading Conference.

Bloome, D. (1983b). *On asking literal comprehension questions: A socio-communicative perspective*. Paper presented at the American Educational Research Association meeting, Montreal.

Bloome, D. (in press). Reading as a social process in a middle school classroom. In D. Bloome (Ed.), *Literacy and schooling*. Norwood, NJ: Ablex.

Bloome, D., and Theodorou, E. (in press). Analyzing teacher-student and student-student discourse. In J. Green, J. Harker, and C. Wallat (Eds.), *Multiple analysis of classroom discourse processes*. Norwood, NJ: Ablex.

Bryan, T. (1978). Verbal interactions and social relationships of learning disabled children. *Journal of Learning Disabilities, 11*(2), 107–115.

Cazden, C. (in press). Classroom discourse. In M. Wittrock (Ed.), *Handbook of research on teaching*. New York: Macmillan.

Cazden, C., John, V., and Hymes, D. (Eds.) (1972). *Functions of language in the classroom*. New York: Teachers College Press.

Cochran-Smith, M. (1984). *The making of a reader*. Norwood, NJ: Ablex.

Collins, J. (1981). Differential treatment in reading instruction. In J. Cook-Gumperz, J. Gumperz, and H. Simons (Eds.), *School-home ethnography project*. Final report to the National Institute of Education. Washington, DC: U.S. Department of Education.

Cook-Gumperz, J., Gumperz, J., and Simons, H. (1981). *School-home ethnography project*. Final report to the National Institute of Education. Washington, DC: U.S. Department of Education.

DeStefano, J., Pepinsky, H., and Sanders, T. (1982). Discourse rules for literacy learning in a first grade classroom. In L. C. Wilkinson (Ed.), *Communicating in the classroom*. New York: Academic Press.

Doyle, W. (1984). Academic work. *Review of Educational Research, 53*(2), 159–200.

Duncan, S. (1969). Nonverbal communication. *Psychological Bulletin, 72,* 118–137.

Eder, D. (1982). Differences in communicative styles across ability groups. In L. Wilkinson (Ed.), *Communicating in the classroom*. New York: Academic Press.

Erickson, F. (1982). Classroom discourse as improvisation: Relationships between academic task structure and social participation structure in lessons. In L. Wilkinson (Ed.), *Communicating in the classroom*. New York: Academic Press.

Erickson, F., and Shultz, J. (1977). When is a context? Some issues and methods in the study of social competence. *Quarterly Newsletter of the Institute for Comparative Human Development, 1*(2), 5–12.

Erickson, F., and Shultz, J. (1981). When is a context? Some issues and methods in the analysis of social competence. In J. Green and C. Wallat (Eds.), *Ethnography and language in educational settings*. Norwood, NJ: Ablex.

Farrar, M. (1983). *Tacit knowledge of questioning strategies: An aspect of teacher's practical knowledge*. Paper presented at the American Educational Research Association meeting, Montreal.

Florio, S., and Clark, C. (1982). What is writing for?: Writing in the first weeks of school in a second/third grade classroom. In L. Wilkinson (Ed.), *Communicating in the classroom*. New York: Academic Press.

Florio, S., and Shultz, J. (1979). Social competence at home and school. *Theory into Practice, 18*(4), 234–243.

Green, J. (1983). Exploring classroom discourse: Linguistic perspectives on teaching-learning processes. *Educational Psychologist, 18*(3), 180–199.

Green, J., and Harker, J. (1982). Gaining access to learning: Conversational, social and cognitive demands of group participation. In L. C. Wilkinson (Ed.), *Communicating in the classroom*. New York: Academic Press.

Green, J., Harker, J., and Golden, J. (in press). Lesson construction: Differing views. In G. Noblit and W. Pink (Eds.), *Understanding education: Qualitative studies of the occupation and organization*. Norwood, NJ: Ablex.

Green, J., and Wallat, C. (1981). Mapping instructional conversations. In J. Green and C. Wallat (Eds.), *Ethnography and language in educational settings*. Norwood, NJ: Ablex.

Gumperz, J. (1976). Language, communication and public negotiation. In P. Sanday (Ed.), *Anthropology and the public interest: Fieldwork and theory.* New York: Academic Press.

Gumperz, J. (1981). Conversational inference and classroom learning. In J. Green and C. Wallat (Eds.), *Ethnography and language in educational settings.* Norwood, NJ: Ablex.

Gumperz, J. (1982). *Discourse strategies.* London: Cambridge University Press.

Gumperz, J., and Herasimchuk, E. (1975). The conversational analysis of social meaning. In M. Sanchez and B. Blount (Eds.), *Sociocultural dimensions of language use.* New York: Academic Press.

Gumperz, J., and Hymes, D. (Eds.) (1972). *Directions in sociolinguistics.* New York: Holt, Rinehart, and Winston.

Gumperz, J., and Tannen, D. (1979). Individual and social differences in language use. In C. Filmore, D. Kemper, and W. Wang (Eds.), *Individual differences in language ability and language behavior.* New York: Academic Press.

Heap, J. (1983). *On task in discourse: Getting the right pronunciation.* Paper presented at American Educational Research Association meeting, Montreal.

Heath, S. (1983). *Ways with words: Language, life and work in communities and classrooms.* New York: Cambridge University Press.

Hymes, D. (1974). *Foundations in sociolinguistics: An ethnographic approach.* Philadelphia: University of Pennsylvania Press.

Hymes, D. (project director). (1981). *Ethnographic monitoring of children's acquisition of reading/language arts skills in and out of the classroom.* Final report to the National Institute of Education. Washington, DC: U.S. Department of Education.

Knapp, M. (1978). *Nonverbal communication in human interaction.* New York: Holt, Rinehart and Winston.

Knott, G. (1980). Communication competence and secondary learning disabled students. *The Directive Teacher, 2*(3), 22–24.

McDermott, R. (1976). *Kids make sense: An ethnographic account of the interactional management of success and failure in one first-grade classroom.* Unpublished doctoral dissertation, Stanford University, CA.

Mehan, H. (1979). *Learning lessons: Social organization in the classroom.* Cambridge, MA: Harvard University Press.

Merritt, M. (1982). Distributing and directing attention in primary classrooms. In L. Wilkinson (Ed.), *Communicating in classrooms.* New York: Academic Press.

Michaels, S. (1981). "Sharing time": Children's narrative styles and differential access to literacy. *Language in Society, 10*(3), 423–442.

Mosenthal, P., and Na, T. (1980). Quality of text recall as a function of children's classroom competence. *Journal of Experimental Child Psychology, 30,* 1–21.

Philips, S. (1982). *The invisible culture: Communication in classroom and community on the Warm Springs Indian reservations.* New York: Longman.

Scollon, R., and Scollon, S. (1982). Cooking it up and boiling it down. In D. Tannen (Ed.), *Spoken and written language.* Norwood, NJ: Ablex.

Shultz, J., Erickson, F., and Florio, S. (1982). Where is the floor? Aspects of cultural organization of social relationships in communication at home and at school. In P. Gilmore and A. Glatthorn (Eds.), *Children in and out of school.* Washington, DC: Center for Applied Linguistics.

Smith, C. (1984). *Learning disabilities: The interaction of learner, task, and setting.* Boston: Little, Brown and Company.

Tannen, D. (1982). The oral/literate continuum in discourse. In D. Tannen (Ed.), *Spoken and written language: Exploring orality and literacy.* Norwood, NJ: Ablex.

Wallach, G., and Butler, K. (Eds.). (1984). *Language learning disabilities in school-age children.* Baltimore: Williams & Wilkins.

Wiig, E., and Semel, E. (1976). *Language disabilities in children and adolescents.* Columbus, OH: Merrill.

Wilkinson, L. (Ed.). (1982). *Communicating in the classroom.* New York: Academic Press.

PART III

DISCOURSE VARIATIONS
IN SCHOOL

Chapter 5

Cultural Conflict in the Classroom: The Communicatively Different Child

Aquiles Iglesias

If we wanted a mechanism for sorting each new generation of citizens into the advantaged and the disadvantaged, into the achieving and the underachieving, we could have done no better than to have invented the school system we have. (McDermott and Gospodinoff, 1981, p. 229)

In most societies, educational policies are congruent with child-rearing practices of the majority or dominant group within that society. As a result of this congruency between home and school practices, the transition from home to school is relatively smooth for children who are members of the dominant subgroup. However, in a pluralistic society such as exists in the United States the same degree of congruency between home and school does not exist for individuals who are members of some cultural or linguistic subgroup. As a result of the discontinuity that exists between home and school practices, these children often encounter difficulties that extend beyond the normal difficulties encountered by mainstream children.

It is often assumed that the communication difficulties encountered by cultural or linguistic minority children are due solely to communication code differences: the children speak a language that is different than that of their teachers. Although researchers (Au and Jordan, 1981; Heath, 1983; Philips, 1972) have consistently stressed that the lack of congruency between discourse rules the children bring from home and those required for successful participation in the classroom is the major cause of the academic difficulties encountered by these children, educational programs continue to function as if linguistic differences are the only cause of the problem.

The purpose of this chapter is to describe the discourse characteristics of classrooms in which cultural and linguistic minority children are enrolled. Although the major emphasis will be on the Hispanic population, specifically the children of Main City School District, the discourse characteristics of this population and the problems encountered by them are very similar to those of other cultural and linguistic minority children throughout the country.

FROM HOME TO SCHOOL

All societies have procedures whereby children are socialized to become adults. This socialization process begins in the home via the interaction of the child and his significant others. During this socialization period, the child learns the cultural norms of his community; that is, the child learns all the rules of appropriate behavior as well as the values and beliefs that underlie overt behavior. In addition, through their daily interactions with their significant others, children acquire the significant others' linguistic system and the rules for participating in linguistic dialogues within that culture. The children's acquisition of these communication skills is gradual and their communication systems undergo transformations as a function of the communicative demands they encounter in various social situations. The linguistic, academic, and interactional demands placed on children will vary across and among cultural subgroups (Blount, 1982; Super and Harkness, 1982).

It can be assumed that certain features of our own socialization process are part, or should be part, of the socialization process of other people as well. This ethnocentric view leads to the postulation of certain hypotheses on what should be considered "adequate" socialization practices. For example, we assume that mother-child interactions should be child-centered ("Get into the child's world and talk about what he is doing"), mothers should provide syntactically and lexically simplified input ("Talk just above your child's level"), and children should be active participants in an interaction ("Encourage your child to initiate topics and ask questions"). Although these aspects of child socialization might be consistent with our culture, they are inconsistent with the socialization process in other cultures (Goody, 1980; Heath, 1983; Ochs, 1983).

It is difficult, if not impossible, owing to the paucity of research and the heterogeneity that exists between and among cultural and linguistic minority groups, to predict with any degree of certainty the socialization practices that will be used by any one family. However, this author's own experience working with parents suggests that parents make certain assumptions about the skills that will be demanded of their children in situations outside the home. Through some of their daily routines, parents will train their children to have these skills. It must be pointed out that the interactional and academic skills the parents are teaching, either consciously or unconsciously, may or may not be compatible with the expectations of the school district. For example, if the parents feel that their children are expected to label items and events, then the parents will engage in question-answer routines in which the questioner knows the answer; if the parents feel that prereading skills are not required of children entering school, then the parents will not teach that particular skill. The validity of the parents' assumptions is tested when the children enter school.

The moment children enter any kind of formal educational situation (preschool, kindergarten, and so on), the specific goals of the socialization process change. Rather than learn the cultural norms of their community, children are expected to learn and abide by the cultural norms of the school, cultural norms that are consistent with the values, traditions, and expectations of the dominant group in the society. As pointed out by Saville-Troike (1979, p. 141), in reference to the American educational system, "It is one which serves primarily to prepare middle class children to participate in their own culture."

At least for the first years, the curriculum in our educational institutions is organized so that the academic skills the middle-class mainstream children have learned at home are reinforced and practiced. In addition, the instructional approaches used by middle-class mainstream parents to train their children in these skills during the preschool socialization period are almost identical to the ones that the children will experience in the classroom. For example, the question-answer routine the parents used to teach colors, shapes, names of objects, and so on is the same kind of routine used by teachers in our educational system to teach that particular content. Thus, prior to entering school, middle-class mainstream children have considerable experience in the content to be trained as well as the rules for interacting in the classroom. As a result of this early training, which is congruent with educational expectations, success is virtually guaranteed for middle-class mainstream children.

It is not surprising that, as a group, cultural or linguistic minority children tend to do poorly in our educational system. Middle-class mainstream children would also do poorly if they were enrolled in a program in which instruction was in a language other than their own, in which the content of the curriculum was different from that taught by their parents and the rules of interaction were incongruent with the rules of home discourse.

REAL SCHOOLS, REAL CHILDREN, REAL PROBLEMS

Any comprehensive explanation of the discourse skills of cultural and linguistic minority children must be addressed within the full context in which these skills are exhibited, a context that extends beyond the classroom. Thus, the political, social, linguistic, and cognitive factors that impinge on the interactions must be fully described. The community, school, teachers, and children to be described are real. However, in order to protect the privacy of all, names of people and places are fictitious. The discourse characteristics of the children and the teacher will follow the description of the context in which these interactions occur.

The Community

Main City typifies, in many ways, the classic stereotype of the aged, blighted urban center of the northeastern United States. Once a healthy, vibrant center of business, commerce, and industry, the city began deteriorating about 30 years ago and has followed a well-documented downward spiral. Today nearly all of the significant business and commerce has moved out, leaving for the most part only heavy industry and impoverished residents. The city's median income is the fifth lowest in the state, with 70 per cent of the families living below poverty level and more than 50 per cent receiving financial assistance. Although the area has two major employers, a large number of its residents work only seasonally in nearby farms.

In addition to experiencing a decline in population, the population of Main City has also changed dramatically in composition. During the last decade the racial and ethnic composition changed from a minority population of 26 per cent to a minority population of over 50 per cent, with a high concentration of Hispanic and black families with young children. The present racial and ethnic composition is reflected in the school population: blacks (63.4 per cent), Hispanics (30.0 per cent), white non-Hispanic (6.3 per cent), and Asian (0.3 per cent).

Main City, like any other speech community, consists of a group of people who share a set norm of rules for the use of language and share at least one common linguistic code. Members of this community employ a variety of codes depending on the situation and the participants in the situation. They use different languages (Spanish, English) and different dialects (black English, Spanish-influenced English, standard English). This speech community is not a static one, owing to the contact of its members with members of other speech communities in the area and the constant migration of Spanish speakers into the community.

Members of the speech community are a linguistically heterogeneous group. Some are monolingual speakers of English, some are monolingual speakers of Spanish, and the large majority, commonly referred to as bilinguals, fall between the ends of the continuum. Only in rare cases are cultural and linguistic minority children exposed solely to individuals at one end of the continuum. The most probable scenario would be that of a child exposed to some monolingual Spanish speakers and a large number of bilingual speakers.

In order to be effective communicators within their community, the children must acquire the forms appropriate to the speaker and the situation. In some cases the children might be expected to speak only one language, and in other cases it is appropriate to code switch ("Come here y ponlo allí" ["Come here and put it there"]) or to use borrowed words ("La teacher estaba washeando las mesas" ["The teacher was washing the tables"]). The particular forms the children are exposed to and expected to use, and thus their competence in any one particular language, varies among children as a function of the linguistic skills of the participants with whom the children interact.

The Schools

The district has an enrollment of 19,500 students. At the beginning of the school year there were 1,400 students identified as Limited English Proficient (LEP). These are children whose difficulty in understanding and speaking English limit their opportunity to learn successfully in classrooms in which the language of instruction is English. Eighteen per cent of the LEP children are enrolled in kindergarten classes, with the majority of these children concentrated at Broad Elementary School.

Broad Elementary is a highly structured school, where teachers, students, and parents are required to follow the rules established by the principal. This is an extremely quiet school. If one was not aware that school was in session, one would assume that the school was deserted.

The Programs

The United States Supreme Court in its landmark decision *Lau v. Nichols* (1974) held that school districts must devise programs to ensure equality of educational opportunity for students of non-English background. In 1975, the Office of Civil Rights proposed a set of guidelines, referred to as the Lau Remedies, to aid school districts in complying with the Supreme Court decision. The Lau Remedies specified that when a school district had 20 or more LEP students from one language group, the child's native language was to be used for instruction until the child had sufficient English skills to function in an English-only classroom.

Compliance with the Lau Remedies has varied considerably throughout the country. O'Malley (1982) estimates that approximately one third of the LEP students were enrolled in classes where the medium of instruction was the child's dominant language. School districts that offer instruction in the child's native language, as the Main City School District does for grades kindergarten through 12, follow the following procedure: (1) Children are identified as speakers of a language other than English, (2) children's language dominance is assessed, and (3) children are placed in different classrooms based on their "dominant" language.

The identification procedure consists of parents completing a home-language survey, in which they are asked whether a language other than English is spoken in the home. Only those children whose parents state that a language other than English is spoken at home are further assessed. Parents of cultural and linguistic minority children who do not want their children enrolled in bilingual programs usually report that "only English is spoken in the home." These children are automatically assigned to English-only classes.

If a language other than English is the primary home language, then a language-dominance test is administered in order to evaluate the student's proficiency in listening to, speaking, and writing English. Students who score below the 20th percentile on this test are identified as LEP and placed in a "bilingual classroom." Although a discussion of the assessment of language dominance is beyond the scope of this chapter, it should be noted that a cursory assessment of the child's use of English is used to determine placement.

DISCOURSE IN BILINGUAL KINDERGARTEN CLASSROOMS

Each classroom is in itself a minicommunity controlled by the teacher. The teacher's goal is to train children in particular skills, in a short period of time, to a large group of children. In order to accomplish this goal the teacher determines the activities or tasks to be accomplished and the rules for participating in these activities. These teacher-controlled situations will place different communicative demands on the children.

What follows is a description of the discourse in two bilingual kindergarten classes. Bilingual kindergarten classes were selected for two reasons. First, if a discontinuity exists between home and school communication, then these differences are best observed when the children enter school. Although entry into our educational system can and does occur at any grade level, the majority of cultural and linguistic minority children enter our educational system at the kindergarten level. Second, because teachers in bilingual classes speak English and Spanish, the discourse that occurs in these classrooms should not be constrained by the children's inability to speak English.

Classroom 1

Classroom 1 is a kindergarten class at Broad Elementary School. The teacher is Hispanic and speaks English with a heavy accent. She has been teaching in this school for the last three years. The teacher's aide (TA) is also Hispanic, and her English skills are marginal. Most of the TA's time is spent preparing materials. During group activities (rug time) the TA's function is to keep the children quiet and on task.

Although the class is supposed to be composed of only LEP children, 5 out of the 19 children are neither Spanish-speaking nor Hispanic. All of the LEP children attend English as a Second Language (ESL) class for 20 minutes a day. Because the LEP children leave for ESL in groups of three, the class is composed of 11 LEP students and 5 non-LEP students for at least 50 per cent of the instructional period.

The children spend most of their day in their assigned seats doing table activities. Every day the teacher has at least two, sometimes three, 20 minute group activities that are conducted in the rug area. Interactions during "rug activities" and "table activities" differ considerably. The majority of teacher-student interactions are either teacher-initiated directives or teacher-initiated product elicitations, with directives being the most frequent. Product elicitations occur almost exclusively during "rug time" activities. During these activities allocation is always by individual nomination. Acknowledgment of correct response is almost nonexistent.

Children rarely initiate interactions. The majority of such initiations are done by the non-LEP students. Peer-peer interactions are strongly discouraged and occur only during free periods: before the pledge of allegiance, during snack time, and during recess. The majority of the children's utterances occur during "rug time" activities. In this kind of activity the teacher usually addresses the children in English, and the children respond in English. (Whenever Spanish is used, the translation will be provided in brackets. T stands for teacher, and children are designated individually by C1, C2, C3, and so on.) The following is an example of a typical rug activity.

Example 1. The teacher is conducting the activity. All the children are required to stand in a straight line and to take their turn at knocking down plastic bowling pins. The children are then required to count the number of pins they knocked down. The TA walks up and down the line nonverbally telling the children to stop talking and to be quiet.

T	John, roll the ball.
C1	(C1 rolls the ball and knocks down three pins.)
T	How many pins did you knock down?
C1	One, two, three.
T	(Moves C1 towards the end of the line.)
	Okay, next.
C2	(Maria rolls the ball and knocks down five pins.)
T	How many?
C2	(No response.)
T	Let's count.
	One, two, three, four, five.
	You knocked down five.
	¿Cuantos tumbastes? [How many did you knock down?]
	Five.
C2	Five. (Maria goes to the end of the line.)
T	(Looks at the next child and then looks at the bowling pins.)
C3	(C3 rolls the ball and knocks down all of the pins.)

All rug activities are highly structured. Turns are allocated automatically, and the first child in the line is required to do the task after the teacher instructs him or her to do so either verbally or nonverbally. After the child completes the task the child moves to the end of the line and the next child has a turn. In this example, the use of Spanish is limited to the teacher's brief interaction with Maria (C2). Maria's silence is interpreted by the teacher as Maria's inability to perform the task. After providing the answer, the teacher asks a more specific question using Spanish and answers her own question, and Maria imitates the teacher's utterance.

Interactions during "table activities" are very different from rug activities; children are expected to work at their tables and to be quiet. Teacher utterances are either in English or in Spanish. The teacher usually goes around the room providing comments and directives. The following is an example of a typical table activity.

Example 2. The teacher is conducting the activity. The TA is sitting at her desk preparing materials for the next lesson. Children are to color a picture of a rabbit. The rabbit is to be colored exactly as specified by the teacher.

C1	(Uses another child's crayons.)
T to C1	Take your own. (Crayon boxes have student's name printed on front.)
	Don't you know your name?
to C2	Sientate mi amor. [Sit down, dear.]
	Sit down.
to C3	Nadie se tiene que copiar del tuyo. [No one has to copy from yours.]
to C4	Pick up the crayons from the floor.
to C5	You know why she is covering hers? Because she didn't do the face right.
to C2	Hector, sit down please and be quiet.
C3	(Inaudible.)
T to C3	Pues usalo. [Then use it.]
to C6	Pero atiende Carolina. [Pay attention, Caroline.]
to C7	Bien clarito. [Very lightly.]
to All	¿De quien son estas crayolas? [Who do these crayons belong to?]
to C3	¿Tuyas? [Yours?]
	¿De ellas? [Hers?] (Gives crayons to C4.)
to C5	You do it lightly. (Begins to color the child's paper.)
	Like this.

Sometimes the teacher engages in question-answer routines. These routines often occur when the teacher is trying to impress someone; they occur every time the principal, supervisor, or guests enter the classroom. These activities are never part of her lesson plan. She always prefaces these routines by telling the children that they are going to review work that they had previously done.

Example 3. The teacher is carrying out a group activity in the rug area. The principal enters the room, and the teacher immediately goes over to the TA's desk and begins talking to the TA about the materials to be used for the next table activity. She then returns to the children, who have been sitting quietly.

T	Let's have a review of the letters we practiced.
	We will have a short review.
	What number is this, Alicia?
C3	(Child other than Alicia responds.)
T	Wait a minute. Wait a minute. I didn't call you.
	Is your name Alicia?
C3	No.
T	Alicia.
C2	Six.
T	What number is this, Ivan?
C4	Three.
T	What number is this, Juan?
C5	Two.

During these question-answer routines children are individually nominated, and the teacher's acknowledgments of correct responses are rarely observed. If a child incorrectly answers a particular question, the teacher either repeats the question or provides the answer.

Example 4

T to C5	How many oranges?
C5	Nine. (The correct answer is five.)
T	How many?
C5	Nine.
T to C6	How many oranges?

Example 5

T to C1	How about this one?
C1	A triangle. (The correct answer is an oval.)
T to C1	This is an oval.
C1	This is an oval.
T to C7	What color is this?

A unique characteristic of this teacher is her use of negative statements about the children. Statements such as the following are common in many of her daily interactions with the children. Even some of her compliments do not sound positive.

Example 6

T   ¿Tú no has coloreado esto todavia? [You haven't colored these yet?] ¡Que lento! [How slow!]

Example 7

T   ¡Que ocho mas feo! [What an ugly eight!]

Example 8

C	It's nice. (Referring to the child's completed work.)
T	It's nice. A little ripped but it's nice.

Classroom 2

Classroom 2 is also a kindergarten class at Broad Elementary School. The teacher is Hispanic and speaks English and Spanish fluently. Although she has several years of teaching experience, this is her first year at Broad Elementary. The TA in this class speaks only Spanish and she spends all her time preparing materials.

Activities are carried out in either small groups or large groups. The rules of participation vary considerably during these two situations. Small group activities occur while LEP children go to ESL classes. During this time the teacher has two small groups, a group of six LEP children and a group of five non-LEP, non-Hispanic children. Each of the two groups do different activities.

During small group activities children who are not with the teacher are allowed to speak among themselves. Thus, a considerable amount of peer-peer interaction occurs during this time. They also interrupt the lesson that the teacher is carrying out with the other group. These interruptions are usually requests for assistance. The following is an example of a small group activity.

Example 9. Non-LEP children are working at their table. One of the LEP groups is at ESL and the other is working on the concept of big and small (grande y pequeño). The LEP children are seated on the floor in a semicircle.

T   Ahora. [Now.]
     Vamos a ver estos juguetes que tengo aquí. [Let's look at the toys I have here.]
     Tenemos dos camiónes. [We have two trucks.]
     Tenemos a big truck and a (Pause) small truck. [We have a big truck and a (Pause) small truck.]
     ¿Cómo es esté? [What is this one like?]
C1   Big.
T   Big.
     ¿Es grande, verdad? [It's big, isn't it?]
     Esté es un camión (Pause) grande. [This is a big truck.]
     A big truck.
     ¿Maria, cuál de estos dos es el mas pequeño? [Maria, which one of these two is the smallest?]
C2   Esté. [This one.]
T   That's the smallest.
     El mas pequeño. [The smallest one.]
     Ahora. [Now.]
     Vamos a hacerlo ahora con los tigres. [Let's do it now with the tigers.]
     Este tigre no es como los tigres de verdad. [This tiger is not like a real tiger.]
     ¿Cómo son los tigres de verdad? [What are real tigers like?]
C3   Grande. [Big.]
T   ¿Grande, verdad? [Big, right?]
     ¿Cuál de esos dos tigres, Juan, is the smallest one? [Which of those tigers, Juan, is the smallest one?]
C4   (Child points.)
T   Muy bien. [Very good.]
     Este es el mas pequeño, the smallest one. [This one is the smallest one, the smallest one.]

Before asking any questions, the teacher makes sure that the children are paying attention by saying, "Ahora" ["Now"]. She then provides the children with a small description of the pictures. This is followed by a question in either English or Spanish. Correct responses are acknowledged, and the teacher usually repeats the child's answer in the language that the child did not use. If the child answers nonverbally the teacher provides the answer in English and Spanish.

Whenever the child answers incorrectly, the teacher engages in an extended sequence similar to that illustrated in the next example. In these sequences the teacher first provides the question in another language. If this fails, she attempts to teach the concept.

Example 10

T   Which one of these two is the smallest?
C5   (Points to the wrong one.)
T   ¿Ése es el mas pequeño de los dos? [That one is the smallest of the two?]
      ¿Cuál de los dos elefantes es el mas pequeño? [Which of the two elephants is the smallest?]
C5   Esté. (Points to the wrong one.) [This one.]
T   Si los ponemos uno al ladito del otro. . .[If we put one next to the other. . .]

Prior to a discussion of the interactions during large group activities, it is important to understand the function that these activities serve in this classroom. Large group activities are used by this teacher to teach content areas that are not formally assessed by the district. The curriculum for kindergarten specifies the skills to be taught each month. For example, during the month of October the colors to be taught are orange and black and the shapes are triangle and square. Children's mastery of these specific contents are assessed at the beginning and at the end of the year. Teachers' performances are somewhat measured by their ability to teach these skills. In addition, each month has a theme: October has Halloween, November has Thanksgiving, and so on. This content is never assessed by the district. As will be seen in the next example, the teacher's teaching style changes drastically during these large group activities. This could be due to the content being taught or to the number and composition of the participants (12 LEPs and 5 non-LEPs).

Example 11. The children are sitting in a semicircle. The teacher is showing the children the bulletin board for the month of November. The bulletin board contains a picture of the *Mayflower* and the Pilgrims among other Thanksgiving pictures. The previous month the students had studied about Christopher Columbus.

T   Bobby, can you tell me something about the month of November?
C1   (No response.)
C2   (Raises her hand.)
T   Iris.
C2   November.
T   Can you tell me something else besides November? The date is November but I want to hear something we celebrate. Something special during the month of November. They came to America on a ship called the. . .

C3   *Santa Maria.*
T   This is not Christopher Columbus. This is a new month and a different holiday. Who came? Who remembers the name of the boat? Do you remember the name?
C2   (Raises her hand.)
T   Iris.
C2   *La Niña.*
T   No, this is not *La Niña.*
C2   *La Santa.*
T   Tampoco. [Neither.]
       May...May...May...
C3   May.
T   *Mayflower.*
C3   *Mayflower.*
T   This is the *Mayflower.* Who came on the *Mayflower?* Who are they?
C2   They are people.
T   What are they called?
C3   November.
C4   Turkeys.
T   Pilgrims.

Comparison of Classroom Rules

Let us look at the communication skills taught in Classroom 1 and Classroom 2 to see the skills the children will have after leaving these classes. In Classroom 1 the demand for participation only occurs during "rug time" activities. During these activities each child is allocated a turn and is expected to comply with the teacher's request for information. Children's utterances are limited to brief answers. During "table time" the students are required to work on their activities and be quiet. Verbal interactions are strongly discouraged. In Classroom 2 the demand for participation also varies as a function of the situation. During small group activities the children's utterances are primarily short answers to questions. Turn-allocation is by individual nomination. Peer-peer interaction is tolerated and topics initiated by students, even if they interrupt a lesson, are accepted. During group activities the demand for participation is almost nonexistent. Turn-allocation is by invitation to bid, and with the exception of the few students who always raise their hands, turns are rarely allocated to any other students.

What have these children learned? In both classes they have learned that their communication in the classroom should be limited to short answers; one-word responses appear to serve the purpose. They have learned that when they are being taught academic skills they should wait until they are called upon to answer. In Classroom 2 they have been further trained to talk to their peers and to interrupt at any time, as long as they are not the ones being taught. Through their classroom interactions these children have learned to be "shy," "noninquisitive," and in some cases, "disruptive"—characteristics often used to describe Hispanic children.

Moving Beyond Kindergarten Classrooms

Perhaps the most striking thing about both bilingual classrooms is their similarity to regular kindergarten classrooms. This similarity is understandable if one considers that these are American classes taught by American teachers. It appears that except for the use of the child's native language during some of the instruction, no accommodations of the type advocated by sociolinguists have been made for these children. For example, no attempt has been made to ensure that the participation structure in the classroom is congruent with the participation structure of the community (Au and Jordan, 1981; Heath, 1983). It can be argued that unless accommodations are made these children are destined to encounter difficulties throughout their schooling. The children may not fail completely, but their performance in a system that strives for mediocrity will be marginal at best.

During the first few years of schooling teachers often attribute any difficulties that these children might encounter to their linguistic background. If the children fail to answer correctly, the teacher repeats the question in a simplified form in the children's native language. The teachers are also conscious of the children's cultural background. These children's lack of proficiency in English constantly reminds the teacher that the children are "different."

However, by the time the children reach third grade, if not sooner, they will be enrolled in English-only classes. Their earlier lack of English skills, which served their teacher as a reminder of their differences, are no longer present. These children are now expected to function as any other child; in reality, as any other middle-class child. At this stage, difficulties will no longer be attributed to the children's cultural or linguistic background but to "low intellectual capacity." What teachers at this level fail to realize is that the communicative demands of their classroom are different from those of earlier grades and that many of these children have not been trained, either at home or in their previous classes, in the particular skills required for success in higher grades.

A particular skill required for success in higher grades is the use of decontextualized, temporally organized, cohesive narratives. Successful participation in some assignments, such as writing essays or discussing a reading assignment, requires that the children rely primarily on linguistic cues, rather than paralinguistic or situational cues, to carry the intended message. The narrative must also be organized so that the events flow in a plausible way. One way to achieve flow in a narrative is by stating events in a temporal sequence. The use of temporal sequence and referential cohesion, referring back to persons and objects that occurred earlier in the narrative, result in cohesive narratives.

Although considerable variation exists, the interactions in which many of the cultural or linguistic minority children have engaged prior to entering school have been context-embedded situations in which the children have been able to negotiate meaning. In other words, the children have been able to use nonlinguistic cues such as props, gestures, and vocal inflection to support their narrative. In addition, the children are provided with immediate feedback when the message has not been understood. If the children are enrolled in classrooms in which the majority of the day is spent in interactions similar to those of Classrooms 1 and 2, then the children will not have the opportunity to expand or modify their narrative skills. As a result of this lack of experience, the children will not have a skill required in higher grades.

REAL SOLUTIONS

Some of the cultural or linguistic minority children will have the interactive and academic skills necessary to function in the classroom, but their only difficulty will be their lack of English skills. For these children the solution is a simple one: Teach them a new code to add to their previously learned knowledge. For other children the solution is not as simple. Their problems are not due just to the lack of linguistic skills in English. These children come to school with discourse rules and academic skills that are not compatible with those expected by our educational system.

Although currently available programs are identical for both types of children, the outcomes are not. The children who need to learn only the linguistic skills do so and succeed. The system is prepared to accommodate their needs. The outcome for the other children is not as positive. The programs in which they are enrolled further enlarge the differences with which they enter the system.

No one program can be advocated for such a diverse population. However, for any program to be successful with this population it must incorporate a systematic training of the children's parents and teachers. Parents are often unaware of the communication demands being placed on their children in the school situation. As stated previously, this author's experience working with parents indicates that once these parents are aware of these demands they will incorporate the training of these skills in their everyday routine. Teachers must become more aware of the communicative demands they are placing on the children and how these demands match the demands that will be placed on these children in later years.

One program that has incorporated the systematic training of teachers and parents of LEP children is the one currently in effect for prekindergarten and kindergarten LEP children in the Main City School District. The two major components of the program, teacher training and parent training, are discussed in the following paragraphs.

The objectives of the teacher training program were to provide teachers with a way to monitor and to modify classroom communicative interactions in order to promote the linguistic, social, and cognitive development of the students. Two hours per week for 12 weeks, teachers received theoretical information on classroom interactions, practical approaches to modifying instructional approaches, and the opportunity to modify their instructional approach. For example, one of the lectures dealt with turn-allocation rules. Teachers were informed of the different ways in which they could allocate turns, the verbal and nonverbal cues used for turn-allocation, and the communicative demands placed on the children as a function of the turn allocation-rules used. After a discussion of the advantages and disadvantages of the different turn-allocation rules, the teachers were encouraged to use the different turn-allocation rules in their classrooms. The teachers' lessons were then monitored by an outside observer, and the teachers were provided with a summary evaluation of each of their student's communication in the classroom as well as a summary of their own communication with these children. Thus, teachers were able to monitor the effect of their modified instructional approach. As a follow-up to the formal training sessions, the teachers received further help on a consultation basis.

The objectives of the parent training program were to familiarize the parents with the academic and communicative skills required in the classroom and to provide the parents with the skills necessary to help their children meet the teacher's expectations of successful students. During monthly meetings, parents were provided with information on the specific academic skills being discussed that particular month, the instructional approach the teacher was going to use, and the procedure by which the teacher was going to assess the mastery of the skills trained. Parents were also provided with techniques that they could use at home to help the children acquire the academic and discourse skills required in the classroom. In addition, parents were encouraged to attend the children's classroom on a regular basis.

Although it is too early to determine the effect of the program on the children's ability to succeed in the educational system, preliminary results are highly encouraging. Teachers have modified their instructional approach and in doing so they have been able to improve the children's communication skills. One area in which significant progress has been made is in the number of children who are participating in classroom interactions. Furthermore, parents involved in the training sessions have taken an active role in the teaching of the academic and discourse skills required in the classroom.

The major premise in designing this program was that without changes in the educational system many LEP children would not succeed. Providing the children with the same educational programs available to middle-class children was not sufficient. Although this was the same conclusion reached by the United States Supreme Court in the *Lau v. Nichols* (1974) decision, the programs in which LEP children are currently enrolled continue to function as if these children are middle-class, mainstream children who speak another language. Success within our educational system cannot be guaranteed for these children unless (1) we begin to realize that the communication skills these children bring to school are not always congruent with those required for successful participation in our educational system, and (2) we begin to implement programs that specifically meet these children's needs.

REFERENCES

Au, K. H-P., and Jordan, C. (1981). Teaching reading to Hawaiian children: Finding culturally appropriate solutions. In H. T. Trueba, G. P. Guthrie, and K. H-P. Au (Eds.), *Culture and the bilingual classroom. Studies in classroom ethnography*. Rowley, MA: Newbury House.

Blount, B. G. (1982). Culture and language of socialization. Parental speech. In D. Wagner and H. W. Stevenson (Eds.), *Cultural perspective on child language*. San Francisco: W. H. Freeman and Co.

Goody, E. (1980). *Questions and politeness: Strategies in social interaction*. Cambridge: Cambridge University Press.

Heath, S. (1983). *Ways with words*. Cambridge: Cambridge University Press.

Lau v. Nichols, 414 U.S. 563 (1974).

McDermott, R. P., and Gospodinoff, K. (1981). Social context for ethnic borders and school failure. In H. T. Trueba, G. P. Guthrie, and K. H-P. Au (Eds.), *Culture and the bilingual classroom. Studies in classroom ethnography*. Rowley, MA: Newbury House.

Ochs, E. (1983). Talking to children in Western Samoa. *Language in Society, 11*(1), 77–104.

O'Malley, M. (1982). *Children's English and service study. Educational needs assessment of language minority children with limited English proficiency.* Rosslyn, VA: National Clearinghouse for Bilingual Education.

Philips, S. U. (1972). Participant structures and communicative competence: Warm Spring children in community and classroom. In C. B. Cazden, V. P. John, and D. Hymes (Eds.), *Function of language in the classroom.* New York: Teachers College Press.

Saville-Troike, M. (1979). Culture, language, and education. In H. T. Trueba and C. Barnett-Mizrahi (Eds.), *Bilingual multicultural education and the professional: From theory to practice.* Rowley, MA: Newbury House Publishers.

Super, C. M., and Harkness, S. (1982). The development of affect in infancy and early childhood. In D. Wagner and H. W. Stevenson (Eds.), *Cultural perspective on child language.* San Francisco: W. H. Freeman and Co.

Chapter 6

Communicative Style in Learning Disabled Children: Some Implications for Classroom Discourse

Mavis Donahue

Engaging in talk may be among the most complex of human activities. Even mundane verbal exchanges require that two partners share an elaborate set of expectations for how the interaction should proceed. First, they must share a linguistic code—that is, phonologic, syntactic, and semantic knowledge—for conveying and interpreting ideas. Second, they must share an equally complex set of interactional rules for governing not only how the flow of meaning is sustained from one speaking turn to the next but also how the sequence and form of conversational turns are organized. These rules for how to initiate and maintain a dialogue form the structure within which the exchange of ideas can be accomplished.

In spite of the enormous complexity of the linguistic and social knowledge underlying successful discourse (e.g., Duncan and Fiske, 1977; Keenan and Schieffelin, 1976), subtle violations of these rules are easily detected by conversational partners. We seem to form rapid and often negative impressions about speakers and listeners who follow conversational conventions that differ from ours (Gumperz and Tannen, 1978). Those who interrupt, who fail to give feedback, or whose remarks are ambiguous or non sequiturs are not likely to be sought-after conversational partners. In fact, participants may be more willing to accept a speaker whose language is grammatically incorrect than one whose remarks are inappropriate.

One context that may be particularly intolerant of individual differences in discourse styles is the classroom. As other chapters in this volume indicate, classroom discourse rules not only are complex but also vary enormously from one context to another. Such diverse activities as lining up for lunch, completing math worksheets, working in small groups on science projects, and participating in whole-class instruction for social studies may each require variations in discourse-rule use. Children who fail to conform to these often bewildering norms for participating in the work of teaching and learning are at risk for being devalued by both teachers and classmates. Ethnographic studies suggest that teachers make rapid judgments about a child's learning potential and that these judgments appear to be based at least as much on the appropriateness of the child's speech as on the linguistic form or content of his or her message (Cicourel et al., 1974; Mehan, 1979; Schultz, 1979).

One group of children that may illustrate this link between school achievement and the acquisition of classroom discourse rules is learning disabled (LD) children, who, by definition, are not able to meet the expectations set forth in the classroom's curriculum. A concern for these students' understanding and use of classroom discourse rules seems motivated on several grounds. First, the classroom is typically the arena in which these children's learning difficulties first surface; many learning disabilities are not identified until the children fail to cope with the social, verbal, and cognitive demands of formal schooling. In fact, there is some evidence that interactional difficulties rather than academic failure alone trigger the referral and identification process for LD children (Ysseldyke, Algozzine, Shinn, and McGue, 1982).

Further, failure to adapt to classroom discourse rules for appropriate participation in talk may not only reflect but also *contribute* to LD children's difficulty in learning academic skills. As children age, the gap between high achievers and low achievers continues to widen; this is due in part to the fact that children who are skilled at mastering rules of classroom discourse are thereby afforded greater access to rich learning experiences through peer and teacher dialogues (Dickson, 1982; Eder, 1982; Merritt, 1982).

One reason that LD children are particularly vulnerable to this "the rich get richer" cycle (Wilkinson and Spinelli, 1982) relates to the well-established finding that these children have difficulty achieving social acceptance from normally achieving (NA) classmates (Bryan, 1974a, 1976; Bruininks, 1978; Scranton and Ryckman, 1979; Siperstein, Bopp, and Bak, 1978). Typically, studies of classroom discourse have focused on the teacher as socializing agent, in that children's task of learning to make sense of classroom life depends on their understanding of teachers' verbal and nonverbal cues to appropriate responses (e.g., Bremme and Erickson, 1977; Mehan, 1979). However, the role of classmates in facilitating not only academic achievement but also acquisition of classroom interaction rules is becoming increasingly apparent to researchers (e.g., Peterson, Wilkinson, and Hallinan, 1984a). Therefore, the quality of a child's relationships with peers may be a critical factor in predicting the degree to which he will adapt to the norms of classroom interaction. Further, the research literature on behavioral correlates of peer acceptance among normally developing children may be a useful site for identifying what communicative skills may be related to classroom discourse knowledge (e.g., Asher and Renshaw, 1981).

Finally, it is reasonable to hypothesize that the acquisition of classroom discourse rules will pose particular challenges for LD students, in light of the accumulating evidence that these children are deficient in both the linguistic and the social prerequisites to situationally appropriate speech. Many LD children have been found to exhibit problems in the knowledge of linguistic structure, ranging from subtle difficulties in word finding or the use of inflectional endings to pervasive delays in the comprehension and production of vocabulary and syntactic-semantic structures (e.g., Denckla and Rudel, 1976; Donahue, Pearl, and Bryan, 1982; Fletcher, Satz, and Scholes, 1981; Idol-Maestas, 1980; Vogel, 1975; Wiig and Semel, 1980). Further, the interpretation of social and situational cues to others' attitudes and feelings has also been found to be problematic for LD children (e.g., Bryan, 1977; Dickstein and Warren, 1980; Pearl and Cosden, 1982).

Surprisingly, there are virtually no studies that examine the implications of LD children's linguistic and social deficits for their acquisition of discourse rules in the classroom (cf. Hood, McDermott, and Cole, 1980). However, a number of recent studies have assessed various aspects of LD children's communicative competence in other settings. Although these studies typically used contrived experimental tasks rather than naturalistic observation of classroom settings, some possible patterns of how LD children communicate can be interpolated from these data.

The purpose of this chapter, then, will be (1) to review studies of LD children's classroom behavior and communicative development; and (2) to draw implications of these findings for understanding LD children's acquisition of classroom discourse rules. This discussion will point out the critical role that effective classroom communication plays in LD children's prognosis for academic and social growth as well as generate hypotheses for research in this neglected area.

LEARNING DISABLED CHILDREN'S
CLASSROOM BEHAVIOR

One body of data that may be useful for gaining insight into the nature of LD children's classroom discourse skills is the research comparing the behavior of LD children when mainstreamed into regular classrooms with that of normally achieving (NA) peers. Although the purpose of these observational studies was not to examine classroom discourse per se, their findings are relevant to a general description of LD students' knowledge of rules governing communication in a classroom context. In coding verbal and task-oriented behaviors similar to those important to classroom ethnographers, several studies demonstrated clear differences between the classroom behavior of LD children and their NA classmates.

The most consistently reported finding of these classroom observation studies has been that LD students spend less time than NA classmates engaged in task-oriented activities (Bryan, 1974b; Bryan and Wheeler, 1972; Dorval, McKinney and Feagans, 1982; Feagans and McKinney, 1981; Forness and Esveldt, 1975; Gettinger and Fayne, 1982; McKinney, McClure, and Feagans, 1982; Richey and McKinney, 1978). Although reported in studies using a variety of observational methods, subject characteristics, and instructional settings, this pattern of more frequent off-task behavior in LD students is still difficult to interpret. The most obvious conclusion is that it corroborates the well-documented evidence that LD children have attentional deficits on structured tasks (Hallahan and Reeve, 1979). However, another plausible interpretation suggests that LD children may be faced with academic tasks in the regular classroom that are too difficult for them, and they therefore are less motivated than NA classmates to maintain attention.

Whatever the source, it is likely that this increase in off-task behavior influences the social ecology of LD children's classrooms. Of course, off-task activity does not necessarily lead to behaviors that are disruptive or annoying to classmates or teachers; many LD children seem to develop strategies for "getting by" in the classroom by engaging in non-task-oriented behaviors that often escape notice (e.g., doodling, flipping through pages) (Bryan, 1974b). However, research on teacher perceptions indicates that teachers not only are well aware of LD students' difficulty in attending to classroom tasks (e.g., Bryan and McGrady, 1972) but also are attuned to these children's problems in social interaction. For example, Feagans and McKinney (1981) found that teachers rated LD students lower than NA students on the dimensions of task orientation, verbal intelligence, independence, extroversion, creativity and curiosity.

Teachers considered LD children to be less socially skilled and less verbally facile (Bryan and McGrady, 1972).

Further, teachers' interactions with their LD students seem to reflect their perceptions that these children are not active or independent learners. Several studies have found that teachers interact more frequently with LD students than with their NA classmates (Chapman, Larsen, and Parker, 1979; Dorval et al., 1982; Feagans and McKinney, 1981; Forness and Esveldt, 1975). The quality of these interactions also seems to differ from the way in which the teachers talk with NA children. Depending on the instructional context and whether the student or the teacher initiated the interaction, LD children have been found to elicit both more praise and more criticism from their teachers (Bryan, 1974b; Chapman et al., 1979). Typically, however, teachers' dialogues seemed to focus on encouraging the LD child to attend to the task at hand, whether the participants engaged in instruction or classroom procedures.

Generally, then, LD children seem to be "out of sync" with the daily rhythms of classroom life. One consequence is that, although LD children talk with their teachers as frequently as do NA classmates (Bryan, 1974b; Dorval et al., 1982), teachers are much more likely to ignore the verbal initiations of LD youngsters (Bryan, 1974b). A possible explanation for this is provided by Dorval and colleagues (1982), who found that LD children's bids for teacher attention were more likely than those of NA classmates to be considered contextually inappropriate, in that they interrupted or distracted other participants. LD students may fail to read the nonverbal and situational cues that indicate when a prospective conversational partner is "available" for particular kinds of interaction; therefore, timing as well as linguistic features may contribute to the ineptness of their bids.

For the teacher, then, maintaining the LD child's appropriate participation in classroom-setting activities demands a great deal more interactional "work" than does managing the NA child. Some evidence suggests that LD children's classmates may not be as willing to put forth the additional effort that may be needed to have a cooperative exchange of talk. Although LD students have been found to interact with classmates as frequently as NA controls (Schumaker, Wildgen, and Sherman, 1982), their verbal initiations were more likely to be ignored, and they were more often the targets of insulting remarks from their classmates (Bryan and Bryan, 1978; Bryan, 1974b). The affective quality of LD children's speech to other children has also been found to be more hostile and less considerate (Bryan, Wheeler, Felcan, and Henek, 1976; Bryan and Bryan, 1978). These findings are not surprising, in light of the sociometric data that LD children are not generally well accepted by their classmates (e.g., Bryan, 1974, 1976; Bruininks, 1978; Scranton and Ryckman, 1979; Siperstein, Bopp, and Bak, 1978).

In summary, LD children's experiences in the classroom are not typical of those of NA classmates. The causal relations among these differences in teacher and classmate behavior and LD children's academic, attentional, and interactional difficulties are, obviously, impossible to delineate. At the least, however, these differences in classroom experiences may help to explain why LD children may construct models for appropriate communicative behavior in the classroom that deviate from those of their classmates. Possible differences in discourse style in the classroom can be inferred from the following studies of LD children's performance on experimental communicative tasks.

LD STUDENTS' COMMUNICATIVE SKILLS

Consistent with the recent shift in language development research from a primary focus on linguistic structure and content to an interest in language use (i.e., communicative or pragmatic competence), a number of recent studies have examined the communicative development of LD children. This research can generally be categorized in terms of three interrelated dimensions: (1) a repertoire of communicative intentions or speech acts whose linguistic forms are adjusted to the characteristics of different listeners or situations; (2) the ability to produce and understand propositions by taking into account what information in the linguistic and nonlinguistic context is—and is not—shared between two communicative partners, and by using this knowledge to provide and elicit adequate descriptions (these aspects are called "coherence" and "repair" in the Spinelli and Ripich model); and (3) the understanding of the rules for participating in cooperative conversational turn-taking (e.g., how to initiate and maintain a conversation, how to manage the orderly exchange of conversational turns, and how to introduce and monitor topics (termed "attention" and "turn-allocation" by Spinelli and Ripich).

Adjusting Communicative Style to Listener Characteristics

Formulating messages whose form and content reflect an awareness of the needs and feelings of listeners obviously underlies all three dimensions of communicative competence. However, one skill that particularly taps a speaker's ability to adjust the content of a message to take into account a listener's feelings is tactfulness. Pearl, Donahue, and Bryan (in press) used a role-playing paradigm to investigate first through fourth grade children's strategies for delivering bad news, for example, telling a classmate that he or she had been rejected for the starring role in the class play. Developmental and group differences indicated that LD and younger children were less likely than their comparison groups to couch their messages in terms that would allow their listeners to save face or to feel better. These findings seem to reflect LD children's deficits in predicting or knowing how to protect the feelings of others (e.g., Dickstein and Warren, 1980; Pearl and Cosden, 1982).

Another measure of communicative competence is the degree to which syntactic and communicative aspects of children's speech vary when addressed to different listeners (e.g., Ervin-Tripp, 1977; James, 1978; Shatz and Gelman, 1973). Some recent studies have involved similar paradigms to examine LD children's ability to modify their communicative style as a function of listener characteristics. In a study by Bryan and Pflaum (1978), children were asked to teach a bowling game to a same-aged classmate and to a kindergarten-aged child. LD boys were found to produce less complex utterances than the control children; however, interactions of sex and group status emerged when the two listener conditions were compared. The prediction that LD children would not vary the syntactic complexity of their speech as a function of listener age was supported only for LD boys, perhaps because of their limited range of syntactic-semantic resources. LD girls and nondisabled boys responded in the expected pattern by using less complex speech when interacting with the younger child. Surprisingly, the nondisabled girls used more complex speech in this condition, apparently perceiving the "teacher" role with the younger child to call for more formal register.

A role-playing paradigm was used to separately assess children's ability to appropriately vary the politeness and persuasive characteristics of their requests as a function of listener social status (Donahue, 1981). Children were instructed to pretend that they needed newspapers for a school project and to convince each of four imaginary listeners to give up his newspapers. The listeners varied on the dimensions of power and intimacy.

Results showed within-group sex differences that were similar to those reported by Bryan and Pflaum (1978). LD girls differed from nondisabled girls only in the finding that the former produced more polite requests to all listeners. LD and nondisabled boys were found to have an equivalent repertoire of linguistic forms to express politeness, and both groups were able to vary their requests as a function of listener features. However, nondisabled boys' requests attended to intimacy, whereas those of the LD boys attended to power. Nondisabled boys were more polite to low-intimate than to high-intimate listeners. Surprisingly, LD boys produced more polite requests to low-power targets (i.e., peers) than to high-power targets.

Analyses of persuasive appeals confirmed these social-cognitive deficits. Compared with nondisabled boys, LD boys produced fewer and a smaller variety of persuasive appeals as well as fewer appeals requiring sophisticated levels of listener perspective-taking. Again, variations in appeals levels of the LD and nondisabled boys did not reflect the same dimensions, in that the intimacy dimension was salient for LD boys, whereas normal boys were influenced by the power factor. Thus, LD boys were able to vary the politeness of their requests and the elaboration of persuasive appeals as a function of listener features, although less appropriately than nondisabled boys.

IMPLICATIONS FOR CLASSROOM DISCOURSE

The findings that LD children are less able to frame messages and persuasive appeals in terms that accommodate their listeners' attitudes suggest that they are deficient in a set of skills with important implications for classroom adjustment and peer acceptance, that is, the ability to effectively resolve social conflict. Knowing how to defuse the inevitable dispute over access to toys, materials, or rights among children has been shown to be related to appropriate classroom behavior (Spivack and Shure, 1974), friendship formation (Gottman, 1983), peer popularity (Asher and Renshaw, 1981), and to interpersonal understanding (Stone and Selman, 1982). The need for conflict resolution strategies is obviously not limited to children; two communicative skills that were judged by adolescents, parents, and professional judges to be critical to social adjustment in teenagers were negotiating conflict situations and resisting peer presssure. During role-playing tasks, LD adolescents were found to be deficient to NA classmates in both skills (Schumaker, Hazel, Sherman, and Sheldon, 1982).

It seems likely, then, that LD youngsters will fare poorly in loosely structured small group activities where squabbles are likely to occur. Consider a scenario in which an LD child's rights to a ruler are challenged during a group map-making session; lacking the social-cognitive resources to tactfully refuse or to suggest a compromise, the child might relinquish the ruler passively and stop working or resort to aggressive or hostile behavior. In either case, purposeful activity is disrupted for the whole group. As this pattern becomes apparent to the teacher, she may restrict the LD child to seatwork assignments or to teacher-supervised activities, thereby limiting the child's opportunity to observe and model more skillful social exchanges among classmates. Since the frequency of talking and working together during learning tasks has been shown to have a beneficial effect on achievement (Cohen, 1984), difficulty in dealing with conflicts will also inhibit academic learning.

Interestingly, in the Donahue (1981) study, the requests made by LD girls to all listeners and by LD boys to classmates were excessively polite, suggesting that these children were adopting a deferential posture to avoid conflict. However, more polite requests, which are typically less direct and less explicit, may not be optimal for discourse during small group tasks. One examination of students' requests during math seatwork in small groups found that direct requests were more likely to elicit appropriate responses from partners. Further, the use of effective requests (i.e., direct, on-task, sincere requests addressed to a specific listener) was related to achievement on the task at hand, sociometric status, and receptive vocabulary scores (Peterson, Wilkinson, Spinelli, and Swing, 1984b). Polite requests may not only be more difficult to interpret as a request (e.g., "Maybe you know how to do this"), but also may be easier to ignore than direct questions (e.g., "Will you show me how you did Number 8?"). Thus, LD children's efforts to gain help and participate in the group may be ineffectual.

A final point relates to the finding that LD boys were capable of modifying the politeness and persuasive characteristics of their appeals yet appeared to do so in ways not typical of other children. For example, LD boys directed their most sophisticated persuasive appeals to strangers rather than to familiar listeners. It is possible that LD children are aware of the general social norms for effective requests yet believe that their status as marginal members of the group calls for a different set of communicative behaviors. Renshaw and Asher (1982) made a similar distinction between children's knowledge of social interaction strategies and children's goals for social interaction. In other words, LD children as low-status participants may have evolved a model for appropriate communicative behavior that accommodates goals for social interaction that differ from those of popular children. This social-cognitive explanation for LD children's discourse styles seems to account for the findings of the following studies.

Conveying and Comprehending Information

Children's ability to convey and comprehend information effectively is clearly another component of communicative competence that depends on underlying social and linguistic skills. Referential communication tasks have been used to examine LD children's performance in the communicative roles of both speaker and listener. Noel (1980) measured both the descriptive characteristics and the communicative effectiveness of messages by asking LD and NA boys to describe ambiguous figures to an adult experimenter. Although the LD boys were not found to differ from the nondisabled children in the number of words or attributes used in their descriptions, they were more likely to refer to the shapes of the figures (e.g., "It's pointed"), whereas their nondisabled peers were more likely to provide general labels (e.g., "It looks like a tree") for the stimuli. In the second phase of the study, the latter strategy was found to be more useful to listeners. The tape-recorded messages of the nondisabled students were found to elicit more correct picture selections from both LD and NA listeners than did the clues of the LD boys.

During a less-controlled communicative task involving peer dyads, Spekman (1981) also found LD boys to be less proficient than nondisabled boys on measures of the ability to produce informative descriptions of block designs. Although no differences were found in the amount of time or the number of conversational turns exchanged between normally achieving dyads and dyads including an LD partner, the block arrangements of the normally achieving dyads were more accurate than those of the LD dyads. Thus, dyads including an LD child were less efficient in their exchange of information. The LD children in the speaker role were found to produce less informative descriptions, suggesting that they had difficulty identifying the essential or new information and presenting it in an effective way.

The results of both studies suggest that LD boys are less skilled than nondisabled boys in formulating descriptions that are useful to their partners. In contrast to these message-production findings, LD boys in the listener role were found to be as proficient as nondisabled boys at using the information conveyed to select or construct the correct referent.

NARRATIVE SKILLS

Other studies suggest that LD children's difficulty in formulating and conveying information is not limited to the description of unrelated referents but extends to the production and comprehension of discourse units beyond the sentence or single-description level. The ability to comprehend and reproduce a sequence of instructions was examined in a group of newly identified first grade LD children (Feagans and McKinney, 1982). Subjects were taught to retrieve candy from a "trick" box by manipulating a series of knobs and buttons. Instructions were repeated until the children successfully opened the box; then they were asked to teach the trick to a puppet. Relative to nondisabled children, LD subjects not only needed more instructions in order to master the trick but also conveyed less complete directions, even after the puppet requested clarification.

Using both cross-sectional and longitudinal designs, Feagans and Short (1984) assessed the development of narrative comprehension and production in reading-disabled and NA children. As in Feagans and McKinney (1982), comprehension was tested first by having children use props to nonverbally enact story narratives that had been read to them. When full comprehension was demonstrated, children were asked to retell the stories in their own words. In general, there were no consistent group differences in narrative comprehension; however, there were reliable cross-sectional and longitudinal differences between reading-disabled and nondisabled controls on several measures of narrative production. Compared with those of nondisabled peers, LD children's narratives included fewer words and idea units, a smaller proportion of syntactically complex sentences, and a greater proportion of pronouns whose referents had not been previously specified. The longitudinal study indicated that although the performance of both groups improved from first through third grades, the disparity between reading disabled and NA children remained the same.

The findings of two other studies (Caro and Schneider, 1983; Schneider, 1982) also may help to explain how linguistic features of LD students' descriptions may cause them to be difficult for listeners to process. LD adolescents with expressive language problems were compared with NA adolescents during noninteractive tasks that required them to describe a formal operations problem-solving task and a brief filmed episode to a listener who had no contextual information. The investigators assessed the ability to produce cohesive texts, which were defined as narratives or explanations whose sentences are tied together in logical ways. This ability entailed such skills as creating referents by appropriately using a linguistic device that signals whether a topic is new information to one's listener or has already been mentioned in the dialogue (e.g., "a lady, some friends" versus "the lady, she, they"). This measure is similar to the category of nonreferential pronouns used by Feagans and Short (1984). Another aspect of text cohesion is the ability to use connective devices that link a sentence to a previous sentence or episode (e.g., "also, another thing, so this shows that...."). Compared with normal students, the LD adolescents used fewer appropriate referent-creating features and connective devices during both tasks. That is, their narratives and explanations were less likely to be adapted to their listener's need for explicit and cohesive information.

Donahue (1984a) also examined an aspect of communicative competence that provides a more direct link between syntactic knowledge and communicative effectiveness, that is, the ability to understand and use grammatical devices for distinguishing given or already mentioned ideas in discourse from propositions that are new and therefore informative. This depends not only on the social-cognitive ability of speakers and listeners to differentiate what knowledge they share and what information needs to be made explicit but also on a repertoire of syntactic strategies for producing and interpreting this distinction (Clark and Clark, 1977).

Using Hornby's (1971) paradigm, Donahue (1984a) examined children's comprehension and production of five sentence types for marking new propositions, that is, active, passive, cleft, and pseudocleft sentences, and sentences with contrastive stress. Generally, LD children were the equals of nondisabled subjects in the comprehension of these syntactic structures. On a production task, LD children were found to rely on strategies for marking new information that required less complex syntactic structures; they were less likely than nondisabled children to employ passive, cleft, and pseudocleft sentences. However, unexpectedly, LD children made effective use of their syntactic repertoire in that their utterances still were as likely as those of nondisabled subjects to correctly distinguish given from new propositions. In contrast to the studies described previously, these findings provide an example of a communicative task for which LD children *were* able to provide informative descriptions, in spite of their limited syntactic resources for doing so.

Implications for Classroom Discourse. Although performance during contrived narrative and referential communication tasks may not be identical to spontaneous exchanges of information in classrooms, occasions for giving instructions and describing events occur frequently in everyday interaction as well as during teacher-directed discussions. Skill in conveying information is likely to be salient to both teachers and classmates. Even young children have been found to be less accepting of peers who offer ambiguous messages (e.g., Deutsch, 1974; Gottman, Gonso, and Rasmussen, 1975; Rubin, 1972). The findings, then, that the descriptions and narratives produced by LD children are not particularly easy for their listeners to process may relate to their difficulties in interacting with peers.

A consistent finding in the classroom interaction literature has been that the frequency of offers of explanations to classmates is correlated with academic achievement (e.g., Webb and Kenderski, 1984). However, the findings of the referential communication studies suggest that even if LD students had mastered the relevant academic skills, they would not be particularly effective at peer tutoring. For example, Cooper, Marquis, and Ayers-Lopez (1982) found that the degree to which child-teachers could identify referents for their listeners was highly related to the success of the teaching episodes. Further, children seem to learn quickly which classmates are desirable "teachers," and often resist taking the learner role with a child whose skills are not valued.

It seems likely, then, that LD children's attempts to assume a teacher or narrator role in classroom discussions will often be met with failure. Problems in language structure undoubtedly contribute to their difficulty in organizing and formulating coherent descriptions and narratives. For example, Silliman (1984) found that classmates' willingness to attend to language-disabled children's narratives was more influenced by production factors, that is, disfluencies and false starts, than by level of narrative complexity. Obviously, longer speech events place a greater demand on a conversational partner's patience and interest; therefore, LD children's problems in language structure are probably more apparent to listeners during narratives than during single-utterance conversational turns.

REPAIRING COMMUNICATIVE BREAKDOWN

Grice (1975) proposed that conversational partners are able to accomplish a cooperative exchange of information through the mutual adherence to four simple principles. Speakers make an effort to be informative, truthful, relevant, and clear; in turn, listeners interpret their utterances by assuming that speakers have indeed followed these maxims. However, a successful exchange will not occur unless both partners are also skilled at establishing what background knowledge they share and what new information needs to be made explicit. One aspect of this skill is the ability to maintain the exchange of information when speakers overestimate what their listeners know and a communicative breakdown occurs. Cooperative listeners are expected to indicate that their partners' messages are unclear and specify what further information is needed; cooperative speakers are expected to revise or expand their remarks.

For children who have difficulty in the production or comprehension of language structure, understanding of the rules for repairing communicative breakdown is particularly important. The success of these children's social interactions may depend on their ability to recognize when a listener is confused and to revise the message, as well as on their skills at requesting clarification of others' unclear utterances. Several studies have examined these two aspects of LD children's skills in repairing communicative breakdowns.

The role of effective message encoder entails on-line monitoring of the listener's comprehension by recognizing explicit or subtle signals of the listener's not understanding. Pearl, Donahue, and Bryan (1981) found that LD children are generally not deficient in their responsiveness to their listeners' need for more information. LD children in grades 3 through 8 had no difficulty interpreting and complying with indirect and even nonverbal feedback. Spekman (1981) also found that LD boys (aged 9 to 11 years) did not differ from nondisabled boys in their ability to provide appropriate replies to their listener's requests for more information.

At least on these highly structured referential communication tasks, then, LD children seem to be proficient at responding to even subtle signals of communicative breakdown. However, a different picture emerges when the responsibility for initiating the communicative breakdown falls to the LD child. Providing useful feedback to a speaker on the adequacy of his messages requires two fairly independent subskills: the linguistic ability to appraise the adequacy of a message by monitoring its information value and to formulate a request for more information; and the understanding of the social rules underlying conversational interaction that cooperative listeners take responsibility for indicating to their partners when a message is unclear.

Two studies (Donahue, Pearl, and Bryan, 1980; Donahue, 1984b) examined both aspects of this model for responsive listening using a referential task in which children played the role of listener (Cosgrove and Patterson, 1977; Ironsmith and Whitehurst, 1978). In both studies, the child's task was to listen to a clue provided by an experimenter and then select one of four pictures of the same object, which differed in terms of binary features. Some messages were fully informative, providing enough details to identify just one picture. On the other trials, the experimenter *created* a communicative breakdown by giving clues that applied to two pictures or to all four pictures.

Donahue and colleagues (1980) found that children in grades 1 through 8 had no difficulty identifying the correct picture after hearing the informative clues. However, both younger children and LD children were less likely than their comparison groups to request clarification of the inadequate messages. Consequently, they made significantly fewer correct picture choices.

Although some possible explanations were explored in this study, none seemed to adequately account for LD children's failure to initiate the repair of the communicative breakdowns. Their performance did not seem to be due to language problems that would interfere with their ability to recognize inadequate messages or to formulate appropriate requests for more information. A message-appraisal task showed that LD children in grades 3 through 8 did not differ from their normal age-mates in the ability to identify inadequate clues (cf. Kotsonis and Patterson, 1980).

These findings, then, seem to indicate difficulty in the second component underlying message-clarification skills, that is, the understanding of the conversational rule that the obligation for initiating the repair of communicative breakdown falls to the listener. Even though most LD children had the linguistic ability to recognize ambiguous messages and formulate questions about them, they failed to perceive the situation as one in which these skills were relevant. The failure to acquire this rule led the LD children to assume a less active and therefore less cooperative role in the conversation.

A similar pattern of findings in studies of younger normal children's communicative skills has been characterized as a performance or "strategy deficit," termed by Whitehurst and Sonnenschein (1981) as "knowing how versus knowing when" to use existing skills. Donahue (1984b) assessed this strategy-deficit explanation for LD children's inactive listening by testing the effects of an intervention designed to emphasize and provide practice in question-asking, that is, by having children play the game Twenty Questions with an experimenter. Although grade and group differences replicated the findings of Donahue and co-workers (1980), the intervention did not increase the inactive listeners' use of requests for clarification.

The finding that LD children's performance proved resistant to brief training seems to rule out a strategy-deficit hypothesis. However, a second hypothesis may clarify their failure to be active listeners by pointing out a more basic difference in the understanding of conversational rules. These children's history of communicative and social difficulties may have led them to doubt their own comprehension skill and overestimate their partner's ability to provide adequate messages. If these children found it unlikely that an adult would violate the Gricean principles of informativeness, honesty, relevance, and clarity, they could only conclude that their inability to select just one referent must be due to their *own* misunderstanding of the task.

An analysis of children's picture-selection strategies provided support for the latter hypothesis: children who failed to request clarification of inadequate messages almost invariably selected the picture with the fewest features, apparently under the assumption that the adult would have specified the additional details if she had intended the other referents. This response reflects an overreliance on the Gricean principle that cooperative speakers provide informative messages but do not include more details than are necessary. The consequence is that LD listeners appear to be shirking their responsibility to indicate when they have not understood, thereby shifting the burden of responsibility for a successful exchange of information to the adult.

Implications for Classroom Discourse. LD children's overreliance on Gricean principles may indicate potential problems in dialogues with teachers. Unfortunately, no adults, not even teachers, are "ideal cooperative conversational partners" (Garvey, 1977); teachers in the regular classroom may have particular difficulty adjusting the complexity of their questions and instructions to the comprehension levels of LD children, and these students' lack of feedback will exacerbate the mismatch. Furthermore, many aspects of "teacher talk" violate the normal expectations for how to interpret an utterance. For example, "test" questions fail to comply with the conversational rule that sincere speakers do not ask for information already available to them. Teacher requests are notoriously indirect; for example, the statement "I'll give you to the count of three," in tandem with a stern look functions to stop a prohibited activity. Yet a great deal of shared knowledge is required to correctly derive the illocutionary force of that utterance. In addition, a teacher's attempts to help a child to expand or clarify a partially correct answer are sometimes bewildering; the child is placed in the uncomfortable position of trying to second-guess the teacher. Unsuccessful attempts to construct a plausible interpretation of what response is expected may cause the child to be perceived as slow, inattentive, or even rebellious (e.g., Mehan, 1979; Schultz, 1979).

Skills in repairing communicative breakdowns also seem to be prerequisite to successful peer learning exchanges. Cooper and associates (1982) report that requests for clarification were frequent and typically effective. However, children often had to reformulate their requests several times to solicit help from a classmate. LD children's communicative skills during clarification episodes in the classroom are difficult to predict from the findings of the referential communication research described above. Although these students seem to be able to revise their utterances in response to a listener's request, the quality of their reformulated messages has not been investigated. Further, LD children's behavior as "inactive listeners" during the referential communication tasks may have little relevance to conversations with peers; their failure to initiate clarification seems to be due to their expectations for informative messages from adults. Whether LD children's estimates of peers' communicative skills are also unrealistic is not known.

Initiating and Maintaining Conversation

An interesting pattern emerges from the studies of LD children's skills in exchanging information and repairing communicative breakdowns during structured tasks. In situations in which other partners assume major responsibility for maintaining the dialogue, thereby providing clear cues for what responses are expected, LD children seem to be as competent as nondisabled children. However, if the context calls for the child to take the initiative, LD partners seem to evade their conversational obligations. Several studies have attempted to determine whether a similar pattern of behavior emerges when LD children participate in more spontaneous conversations.

GROUP DECISION-MAKING

Three studies used a group decision-making task to examine LD children's conversational skills with peers and with their mothers. In the first study (Bryan, Donahue, and Pearl, 1981), triads were formed by matching LD and nondisabled children in grades 3 through 8 with two same-sex classmates. Each child independently ranked 15 possible gifts for their classroom (e.g., a gerbil, perfume for the teacher, a calculator, a Star Wars game). Then the triad was asked to rank the items again by discussing their choices and reaching a consensus.

Based on the correspondence between their first two choices and the first two choices subsequently made by their group, LD children in all grades were found to be less persuasive than were nondisabled controls. An examination of LD children's strategies for participating in these discussions explains why they had less effect on their triad's decisions. Although LD subjects produced as many conversational turns, they clearly assumed a less assertive role in the task. These findings appear to confirm the hypotheses generated by the findings of the referential communication studies.

When a response that was predictable from the context was required, the LD children appeared eager to participate. Compared with NA subjects, the LD children were more likely to agree with their classmates' opinions and to respond to their requests for opinions. They were as likely as nondisabled subjects to nominate a particular gift as a topic for discussion. Given the nature of the task, all three strategies provided an easy opening into the conversation. However, communicative intentions that may demand more sophisticated syntactic-semantic skills or social risk-taking were avoided, in that LD children were less likely than nondisabled children to disagree or to attempt to negate their partners' arguments. They also seemed unwilling to assume the group leader's role, providing fewer "conversational housekeeping" utterances, that is, utterances whose purposes were to keep the group on task. Finally, LD children rarely made bids to claim the conversational floor.

Although this style of interaction seemed to provide an easy and even adaptive means for LD children to participate in the task, the consequence was that they had little impact on their group's decisions.

Donahue and Prescott (1983) replicated these findings with a group decision-making task adapted for use with younger children. Triads of LD and NA children in first and second grades were asked to work together to sort pictures of possible gifts for their class into three boxes representing how much they liked each item.

When disputes occurred, LD children were as likely as non–learning-disabled (NLD) children to contribute conversational turns, initiate topics, and agree or disagree with their classmates' opinions. Nevertheless, the LD youngsters were *still* less able to win the final move in the disputes. Thus, young LD children's opinions were less likely to be accepted by their classmates, even though they seemed to be playing an active role in the dispute episodes. These findings suggest that the passive conversational style of older LD children may have evolved from their social history of being ignored in earlier years; by middle childhood these children may have given up on attempting to influence their classmates' ideas.

Thus, one obvious explanation for LD children's deferential conversational style may be their past experiences of peer rejection. However, this hypothesis does not account for the recent finding that this unassertive style is not limited to talk with familiar peers but extends even to interactions with their mothers (Bryan, Donahue, Pearl and Herzog, 1984). In a variation of the group decision-making task, LD and NLD children and their mothers were asked to rank 15 items in the order of their usefulness to an expedition to the moon. As in the peer interaction study, LD children were more likely to agree and less likely to disagree with their mothers than were NA controls. Furthermore, LD girls engaged in less conversational housekeeping than nondisabled girls.

TALK SHOWS

Like the tennis player who can return the ball but cannot serve, the LD children seem to carry their own conversational weight only when they receive clear turn-yielding signals from partners. While this approach may allow the children to "get by" in most spontaneous interactions, how do they fare when assigned the responsibility for initiating and maintaining control over a dialogue? In two studies, LD and NLD children were placed in a socially dominant position by asking them to play the role of a television talk show host.

In the first study (Bryan, Donahue, Pearl, and Sturm, 1981), children in grades 2 and 4 were each asked to interview a classmate about favorite movies and television programs. Even though LD hosts contributed the same amount of talk to the dialogue as did NLD hosts, they were still less skilled at initiating and sustaining the exchange of ideas. Relative to control children, they were less likely to use the most task-efficient strategy for getting guests to talk, that is, questioning. In addition, of the questions that LD hosts did direct to their guests, a smaller proportion were open-ended questions that elicited narratives or extended descriptions. When responding to their host's questions, guests of LD children were less willing than guests of NLD children to go beyond the literal meaning of the questions to elaborate on the topics. Even more striking evidence of LD children's difficulty in maintaining control over the dialogue was provided by a comparison of the number of partners who reversed roles. In 9 of 40 dyads, the guests took over the interviewer's role: 8 of those 9 dyads included LD hosts.

Why are LD children unable to play the assertive role even in a setting in which conversational dominance is not only appropriate but expected? These findings may be due to deficits in linguistic or conversational knowledge or may merely reflect difficulties in knowing how and when to use their skills. The purpose of the final study (Donahue and Bryan, 1983) was to explore these issues by examining the effect of modeling on conversational skills. LD boys in grades 2 through 8 and NA controls played the role of talk show hosts by interviewing a classmate.

Before each interview, each host listened to one of two brief audiotaped models: the intervention model consisted of a dialogue in which a child interviewer produced frequent open-ended questions, conversational devices, and contingent comments and questions; the control condition presented a monologue in which the subject heard only the responses of the guests, in order to control topic availability.

As hypothesized, LD hosts who heard the monologue condition were less talkative and produced fewer contingent comments than NLD children; however, exposure to the dialogue model significantly increased LD children's use of these behaviors as well as their production of open-ended questions. The effectiveness of such a brief model in activating these responses provides support for the hypothesis that these children may have already acquired these conversational skills but were unable to discern which social contexts call for their use.

Unexpectedly, the dialogue model did not lead to equally positive changes in the guest children's performance; in fact, this condition actually decreased the use of elaborated responses by guests of older LD children. Further, guests were more likely to request clarification of the utterances of LD hosts, especially those in the dialogue condition. These findings suggest that linguistic deficits may have made the LD hosts' open-ended questions and comments more difficult to understand or to expand on.

The performance of the talk show *guests* suggests a different source of LD children's conversational style. Perhaps they are unwilling to use the full range of their conversational skills because they are aware, at some level, that some strategies will tax their language abilities. Their experiences of communicative interactions may have convinced them that the dialogue flows more smoothly if they restrict themselves to asking questions that are easy to answer and avoid spontaneous comments. Some support for this explanation emerged from an examination of LD children's perceptions of conversational skills. Interviews with each subject after the videotaping indicated that the LD children were well aware of their difficulties in conversational interaction. The explanation that LD children's conversational style reflects their awareness of their social and language deficiencies seems consistent with the findings of studies discussed in previous sections.

IMPLICATIONS FOR CLASSROOM DISCOURSE

In general, these findings portray the LD conversational partner as eager to fulfill conversational responsibilities while compensating for linguistic inadequacies. Like the doubles tennis player with a limited set of strokes, the LD child seems to hover on the edge of the interaction, watching for an easy opening into the conversation. By seeking out opportunities for participating that provide rich linguistic and contextual support, the LD child gives the appearance of keeping the conversational ball in play. Meanwhile, he or she is equally adept at avoiding those contexts that demand linguistic fluency and conversational initiative.

What parallels can be drawn between this portrait of the LD child as a conversational partner, and what is known about the communicative skills needed for successful small-group interaction in the classroom? Other studies have demonstrated that students perceived as good readers were more active and influential participants than less skilled readers during a board game that necessitated group decision-making (Stulac, 1975; Rosenholtz, in press; Cohen, 1982; all reported in Cohen, 1984). The findings that LD children adopted a similarly unassertive conversational style during the group tasks just described are particularly compelling in light of the fact that not only were the tasks nonacademic in nature but students in all three studies were also explicitly told that there were no right or wrong answers to the decisions. It seems likely that LD students would be even less willing to disagree or debate with their classmates during a group task more typical of school work, for example, math worksheets and science projects.

Interestingly, these less-controlled communicative tasks provide further evidence that LD children may be at a disadvantage in communicative contexts where conflict-resolution skills and persuasiveness are valuable. Their relative lack of social influence and assertiveness is likely to result in fewer opportunities to participate in dispute episodes. This may in turn have negative consequences for these students' further cognitive and social development, in that the conflicts that arise between peers have been shown to enhance the development of reasoning. For example, in dyads of normally developing children working together on Piagetian conservation tasks, conserving children were found to win a greater number of the arguments about the task; however, the nonconserving children's performance was facilitated merely by participating in the conflicts (Silverman and Stone, 1972; Silverman and Geiringer, 1973). Furthermore, the implicit or explicit messages conveyed during children's arguments seem to serve an important socializing function in that they reflect norms for interaction, for instance, sharing, fairness, and compromise (Genishi and DiPaolo, 1982; Stone and Selman, 1982).

Attempting to adopt a dominant role in conversation seems to be another particularly difficult task for LD children as well as for those who interact with them. For example, LD group members in the Bryan, Donahue, and Pearl (1981) study seemed to avoid the use of communicative functions typical of a group leader, in that they were less likely to try to direct the task to completion or to make a bid for the conversational floor. Interestingly, Peterson and colleagues (1984b) also found that higher-ability students in small group tasks produced more "procedural requests," defined as those remarks concerned with pacing, time management, and monitoring the group's work. Further, the frequency of these requests seemed to be related to other group members' achievement. The presence of a "task master" seemed to serve a meta-cognitive function by modeling for other group members some effective strategies for completing the task. Further, the frequency with which procedural requests were directed to low-ability students was negatively correlated with both their on-task behavior and their achievement. Thus, the typically inattentive LD child would be most likely to elicit procedural requests from these self-appointed task masters, yet he or she would rarely choose to take on this role.

CONCLUSIONS: THE NEWCOMER HYPOTHESIS

One model that may be useful in conceptualizing LD children's classroom discourse skills is the "newcomer" hypothesis; namely, that LD children, like unpopular children (Putallaz and Gottman, 1981), communicate with teachers and classmates in a style similar to that of a naive participant or newcomer to the classroom. Of course, an obvious factor providing support for this hypothesis is that LD children who receive special instruction in resource rooms are actually absent from the mainstream classroom on a regular basis. Thus, they often miss events or activities that are later used for instruction, for example, a guest speaker in the morning whose topic becomes the theme for storywriting in the afternoon. Even missing small events that later form the basis for a joke or an example made by the teacher or a classmate may contribute both to the LD child's miscomprehension and to feelings of being an outsider. Unfortunately, since LD children are *not* newcomers, their "naive" behavior is probably not afforded the same patience and tolerance by teachers and classmates that the incompetence of a newly arrived child would elicit.

A further complicating factor in the LD child's efforts to overcome his newcomer status is the degree of mismatch between discourse rules in the regular classroom versus the resource room. For example, it is likely that rules for soliciting teacher help are less formal in the resource room than in the much larger regular classroom. Thus, acquiring effective strategies for getting the classroom teacher's attention may be hampered by "interference" from resource room norms, possibly resulting in behavior that appears bumbling or rude to the classroom teacher. Clearly, both regular education and special education teachers need to become aware of and make adjustments for the discrepancies between communicative norms in the mainstream classroom versus the special education setting.

The newcomer hypothesis seems to account for two recurring themes that emerged from the review of LD children's communicative style. First, the findings of many studies suggest that LD children are not necessarily deficient in communicative knowledge but have simply constructed a different set of norms for appropriate participation in particular speech events. This can not be attributed solely to the evidence that LD children may have less access to feedback from teachers and classmates; instead, based on the *nature* of their interactions, LD children may be deriving rules for expected communicative behavior from qualitatively different data.

As Eder (1982) and Merritt (1982) suggest, differences in teacher agenda for low-achieving children may have the inadvertent effect of creating a "subculture" whose participants are socialized to communicate in a way that is not considered acceptable by the larger classroom culture. Eder (1982) provides an example of a first grade classroom where, at the beginning of the school year, interruptions during reading turns were fairly frequent in all reading groups. However, the teacher typically reprimanded interruptions occurring during high-ability groups, yet tolerated and even acknowledged interruptions of reading turns of poor readers. By the end of the year, "low-group members did not develop an understanding of reading turns as a speech event in which other members do not speak or engage the reader in discussion (Eder, p. 261)." Aside from the obvious negative implications of this pattern for learning to read, it exemplifies how low-achieving children may be socialized to communicative norms that probably do not apply to other classroom contexts.

Finally, a second recurring issue relates to the social-cognitve interpretation of LD children's communicative style, that is, that it reflects their awareness of their newcomer or outsider status. This position also suggests that LD children's repertoire of communicative skills is not deficient; rather, they may select communicative strategies that meet social goals different from those of NA classmates. Like the newcomer, polite requests and a tentative conversational style may allow the LD child to hover on the edge of communicative interactions without offending. Meanwhile, this "low-profile" participation enables the child to gather data and test hypotheses about what communicative behavior is expected and valued by the "majority" classroom culture.

Ironically, as discussed previously, this communicative style may inadvertently work against the LD child's efforts to make sense of classroom discourse rules, by limiting opportunites to clarify messages, offer opinions, negotiate, and engage in sustained dialogue with others. On the other hand, the actual effects of particular communicative styles on academic and social success are not known. Efforts to change children's communicative behaviors should await an understanding of the degree to which their style enables them to function adaptively within the classroom. Teaching a child communicative behavior that does not accommodate his or her current working model of classroom discourse rules may upset an intricate and delicately balanced network of social relationships.

REFERENCES

Asher, S. R., and Renshaw, P. D. (1981). Children without friends: Social knowledge and social skills training. In S. R. Asher and J. M. Gottman (Eds.), *The development of children's friendships.* Cambridge: Cambridge University Press.

Bremme, D., and Erickson, F. (1977). Relationships among verbal and nonverbal classroom behaviors. *Theory into Practice, 16*(3), 153–161.

Bruininks, V. L. (1978). Peer status and personality of learning disabled and nondisabled students. *Journal of Learning Disabilities, 11,* 484–489.

Bryan, T. H. (1974a). Peer popularity of learning disabled children. *Journal of Learning Disabilities, 7,* 621–625.

Bryan, T. H. (1974b). An observational analysis of classroom behaviors of children with learning disabilities. *Journal of Learning Disabilities, 7,* 26–34.

Bryan, T. H. (1976). Peer popularity of learning disabled children: A replication. *Journal of Learning Disabilities, 9,* 307–311.

Bryan, T. H. (1977). Children's comprehension of non-verbal communication. *Journal of Learning Disabilities, 10,* 501–506.

Bryan, T., and Bryan, J. (1978). Social interactions of learning disabled children. *Learning Disability Quarterly, 1,* 33–38.

Bryan, T., Donahue, M., Pearl, R., and Herzog, A. (1984). Conversational interactions between mothers and learning-disabled or nondisabled children during a problem-solving task. *Journal of Speech and Hearing Disorders, 49,* 64–71.

Bryan, T., Donahue, M., Pearl, R., and Sturm, C. (1981). Learning disabled children's conversational skills. *Learning Disability Quarterly, 4,* 250–259.

Bryan, T., and McGrady, H. (1972). Use of a teacher rating scale. *Journal of Learning Disabilities, 5,* 199–206.

Bryan, T., and Pflaum, S. (1978). Linguistic, cognitive and social analyses of learning disabled children's interactions. *Learning Disability Quarterly, 1,* 70–79.

Bryan, T., and Wheeler, R. (1972). Perception of learning disabled children: The eye of the observer. *Journal of Learning Disabilities, 5,* 484–488.

Bryan, T. H., Wheeler, R., Felcan, J., and Henek, T. (1976). "Come on dummy": An observational study of children's communications. *Journal of Learning Disabilities, 9,* 661–669.

Caro, D., and Schneider, P. (1983). Creating referents in text: A comparison of learning disabled and normal adolescents' texts. *Proceedings of the Wisconsin Symposium for Research in Child Language Disorders.* Madison: University of Wisconsin.

Chapman, R. B., Larsen, S. C., and Parker, R. M. (1979). Interactions of first-grade teachers with learning disordered children. *Journal of Learning Disabilities, 12,* 225–230.

Cicourel, A., Jennings, K., Jennings, S., Leiter K., MacKay, R., Mehan, M., and Roth, D. (1974). *Language use and school performance.* New York: Academic Press.

Clark, H., and Clark, E. (1977). *Psychology and language.* New York: Harcourt Brace Jovanovich.

Cohen, E. (1984). Talking and working together: Status, interaction and learning. In P. Petersen, L. C. Wilkinson, and M. Hallinan (Eds.), *The social context of instruction.* Orlando, FL: Academic Press.

Cooper, C., Marquis, A., and Ayers-Lopez, S. (1982). Peer learning in the classroom: Tracing developmental patterns and consequences of children's spontaneous interactions. In L. C. Wilkinson (Ed.), *Communicating in the classroom.* New York: Academic Press.

Cosgrove, J., and Patterson, C. (1977). Plans and the development of listener skills. *Developmental Psychology, 13,* 557–564.

Denckla, M., and Rudel, R. (1976). Naming of object drawings of dyslexic and other learning disabled children. *Brain and Language, 3,* 1–16.

Deutsch, F. (1974). Observational and sociometric measures of peer popularity and their relationship to egocentric communication in female preschoolers. *Developmental Psychology, 10*, 745–747.

Dickson, W. P. (1982). Creating communication-rich classrooms: Insights from the sociolinguistic and referential traditions. In L. C. Wilkinson (Ed.), *Communicating in the classroom.* New York: Academic Press.

Dickstein, E. B., and Warren, D. R. (1980). Role taking deficits in learning disabled children. *Journal of Learning Disabilities, 13*, 378–382.

Donahue, M. (1981). Requesting strategies of learning disabled children. *Applied Psycholinguistics, 2*, 213–234.

Donahue, M. (1984a). Learning disabled children's comprehension and production of syntactic devices for marking given versus new information. *Applied Psycholinguistics, 5*, 101–116.

Donahue, M. (1984b). Learning disabled children's conversational competence: An attempt to activate the inactive listener. *Applied Psycholinguistics, 5*, 21–35.

Donahue, M. and Bryan, T. (1983). Conversational skills and modeling in learning disabled boys. *Applied Psycholinguistics, 4*, 251–278.

Donahue, M., Pearl, R., and Bryan T. (1980). Conversational competence in learning disabled children: Responses to inadequate messages. *Applied Psycholinguistics, 1*, 387–403.

Donahue, M., Pearl, R., and Bryan, T. (1982). Learning disabled children's syntactic proficiency during a communicative task. *Journal of Speech and Hearing Disorders, 47*, 397–403.

Donahue, M., and Prescott, B. (1983). *Young learning disabled children's conversational participation in dispute episodes with peers.* Chicago: Institute for the Study of Learning Disabilities.

Dorval, B., McKinney, J. D., and Feagans, L. (1982). Teachers' interactions with learning disabled children and average achievers. *Journal of Pediatric Psychology, 17*, 317–330.

Duncan, S., and Fiske, D. (1977). *Face-to-face interaction: Research, methods, and theory.* Hillsdale, NJ: Erlbaum Associates.

Eder, D. (1982). Differences in communicative styles across ability groups. In L. C. Wilkinson (Ed.), *Communicating in the classroom.* New York: Academic Press.

Ervin-Tripp, S. (1977). Wait for me, roller-skate. In S. Ervin-Tripp and C. Mitchell-Kernan (Eds.), *Child discourse.* New York: Academic Press.

Feagans, L., and McKinney, J. D. (1981). The pattern of exceptionality across domains in learning disabled children. *Journal of Applied Developmental Psychology, 1*, 313–328.

Feagans, L., and McKinney, J. D. (1982). *Longitudinal studies of learning disabled children.* Paper presented to the Association for Children with Learning Disabilities, Chicago.

Feagans, L., and Short, E. (1984). Developmental differences in the comprehension and production of narratives by reading disabled and normally achieving children. *Child Development, 55*, 1727–1736.

Fletcher, J., Satz, P., and Scholes, R. (1981). Developmental changes in the linguistic performance correlates of reading achievement. *Brain and Language, 13*, 78–90.

Forness, S. R., and Esveldt, K. C. (1975). Classroom observations of children with learning and behavior problems. *Journal of Learning Disabilities, 8,* 382–385.

Garvey, C. (1977). The contingent query: A dependent act in conversation. In M. Lewis and L. Rosenblum (Eds.), *Interaction, conversation, and the development of language.* New York: John Wiley.

Genishi, C., and DiPaolo, M. (1982). Learning through argument in a preschool. In L. C. Wilkinson (Ed.), *Communicating in the classroom* (pp. 49–68). New York: Academic Press.

Gettinger, M., and Fayne, J. R. (1982). Classroom behaviors during small group instruction and learning performance in learning disabled and nondisabled children. *Journal of Educational Research, 75,* 182–187.

Gottman, J. (1983). How children become friends. *Monographs of the Society for Research in Child Development, 48* (Serial No. 201).

Gottman, J., Gonso, J., and Rasmussen, B. (1975). Social interaction, social competence, and friendship in children. *Child Development, 46,* 709–718.

Grice, H. (1975). Logic and conversation. In P. Cole and J. Morgan (Eds.), *Syntax and semantics; Vol. 3: Speech acts.* New York: Seminar Press.

Gumperz, J., and Tannen, D. (1979). Individual and social differences in language use. In C. Fillmore, D. Kempler, and W. Wang (Eds.), *Individual differences in language ability and language behavior* (pp. 305–325). New York: Academic Press.

Hallahan, D. P., and Reeve, R. E. (1979). Selective attention and distractibility. In B. K. Keogh (Ed.), *Advances in Special Education* (Vol 1). Greenwich, CT: J. A. I. Press.

Hood, L., McDermott, R., and Cole, M. (1980). "Let's try to make it a good day"—some not so simple ways. *Discourse Processes, 1,* 155–168.

Hornby, P. (1971). Surface structure and the topic-comment distinction: A developmental study. *Child Development, 42,* 1975–1988.

Idol-Maestas, L. (1980). Oral language responses of children with reading difficulties. *Journal of Special Education, 14,* 385–404.

Ironsmith, M., and Whitehurst, G. (1978). The development of listener skills in communication: How children deal with ambiguous information. *Child Development, 49,* 348–352.

James, S. (1978). Effect of listener age and situation on the politeness of children's directives. *Journal of Psycholinguistic Research, 7,* 307–317.

Keenan, E., and Schieffelin, B. (1976). Topic as a discourse notion: A study of topic in the conversations of children and adults. In C. Li (Ed.), *Subject and topic.* New York: Academic Press.

Kotsonis, M. E., and Patterson, C. J. (1980). Comprehension-monitoring skills in learning disabled children. *Developmental Psychology, 16,* 541–542.

McKinney, J. D., McClure, S., and Feagans, L. (1982). Classroom behavior of learning disabled children. *Learning Disability Quarterly, 5,* 45–52.

Mehan, H. (1979). *Learning lessons: Social organization in the classroom.* Cambridge, MA: Harvard University Press.

Merritt, M. (1982). Distributing and directing attention in primary classrooms. In L. C. Wilkinson (Ed.), *Communicating in the classroom.* New York: Academic Press.

Noel, N. M. (1980). Referential communication abilities of learning disabled children. *Learning Disability Quarterly, 3,* 70–75.

Pearl, R., and Cosden, M. (1982). Sizing up a situation: Learning disabled children's understanding of social interactions. *Learning Disability Quarterly, 5,* 371–373.

Pearl, R., Donahue, M., and Bryan, T. (1981). Learning disabled and normal children's responses to non-explicit requests for clarification. *Perceptual and Motor Skills, 53*, 919–925.

Pearl, R., Donahue, M., and Bryan, T. (in press). The development of tact: Children's strategies for delivering bad news. *Journal of Applied Developmental Psychology.*

Peterson, P., Wilkinson, L. C., and Hallinan, M. (1984a). *The social context of instruction: Group organization and group processes.* Orlando, FL: Academic Press.

Peterson, P., Wilkinson, L., Spinelli, F., and Swing, S. (1984b). Merging the process-product and the sociolinguistic paradigms: Research on small-group processes. In P. Peterson, L. Wilkinson, and M. Hallinan (Eds.), *The social context of instruction.* Orlando, FL: Academic Press.

Putallaz, M., and Gottman, J. (1981). An interactional model of children's entry into peer groups. *Child Development, 52*, 986–994.

Renshaw, P., and Asher, S. (1982). Social competence and peer status: The distinction between goals and strategies. In K. Rubin and H. Ross (Eds.), *Peer relationships and social skills in childhood.* New York: Springer-Verlag.

Richey, D. D., and McKinney, J. D. (1978). Classroom behavioral styles of learning disabled children. *Journal of Learning Disabilities, 11*, 297–302.

Rubin, K. H. (1972). Relationship between egocentric communication and popularity among peers. *Developmental Psychology, 2*, 364.

Schneider, P. (1982). Formal operations skills vs. explanations. *Psycholinguistics Newsletter, Northwestern University, 8*, 16–23.

Schultz, J. (1979). It's not whether you win or lose, it's how you play the game. In O. Garnica and M. King (Eds.), *Language, children, and society: The effect of social factors on children learning to communicate.* Oxford: Pergamon Press.

Schumaker, J. B., Hazel, J. S., Sherman, J. A., and Sheldon, J. (1982). Social skills performances of learning disabled, non-learning disabled, and delinquent adolescents. *Learning Disability Quarterly, 5*, 388–397.

Schumaker, J. B., Wildgen, J. S., and Sherman, J. A. (1982). Social interaction of learning disabled junior high students in their regular classrooms: An observational analysis. *Journal of Learning Disabilities, 15*, 355–358.

Scranton, T., and Ryckman, D. (1979). Sociometric status of learning disabled children in an integrative program. *Journal of Learning Disabilities, 12*, 402–407.

Shatz, M., and Gelman, R. (1973). The development of communication skills: Modifications in the speech of young children as a function of the listener. *Monographs of the Society for Research in Child Development, 38* (5, Serial No. 152).

Silliman, E. (1984). Interactional competencies in the instructional context: The role of teaching discourse in learning. In G. Wallach and K. Butler (Eds.), *Language learning disabilities in school-age children.* Baltimore: Williams & Wilkins.

Silverman, I., and Geiringer, E. (1973). Dyadic interaction and conservation induction: A test of Piaget's equilibration model. *Child Development, 44*, 815–820.

Silverman, I., and Stone, J. (1972). Modifying cognitive functioning through participation in a problem-solving group. *Journal of Educational Psychology, 63*, 603–608.

Siperstein, G. N., Bopp, M. J., and Bak, J. J. (1978). Social status of learning disabled children. *Journal of Learning Disabilities, 11*, 98–102.

Spekman, N. (1981). A study of the dyadic verbal communication abilities of learning disabled and normally achieving fourth and fifth grade boys. *Learning Disability Quarterly, 4*, 139–151.

Spivack, G., and Shure, M. B. (1974). *Social adjustment of young children: A cognitive approach to solving real-life problems*. San Francisco: Jossey-Bass.

Stone, C., and Selman, R. (1982). A structural approach to research on the development of interpersonal behavior among grade school children. In K. Rubin and H. Ross (Eds.), *Peer relationships and social skills in childhood*. New York: Springer-Verlag.

Vogel, S. (1975). *Syntactic abilities in normal and dyslexic children*. Baltimore: University Park Press.

Webb, N., and Kenderski, C. (1984). Student interaction and learning in small-group and whole-class settings. In P. Peterson, L. C. Wilkinson, and M. Hallinan (Eds.), *The social context of instruction: Group organization and group processes*. Orlando, FL: Academic Press.

Whitehurst, G., and Sonnenschein, S. (1981). The development of informative messages in referential communication: Knowing when vs. knowing how. In W. P. Dickson (Ed.), *Children's oral communication skills*. New York: Academic Press.

Wiig, E., and Semel, E. (1980). *Language assessment and intervention for the learning disabled*. Columbus, OH: Charles E. Merrill.

Wilkinson, L. C., (Ed.). (1982). *Communicating in the classroom*. New York: Academic Press.

Wilkinson, L. C., and Spinelli, F. (1982). Conclusion: Applications for education. In L. C. Wilkinson (Ed.), *Communicating in the classroom*. New York: Academic Press.

Ysseldyke, J., Algozzine, B., Shinn, M., and McGue, M. (1982). Similarities and differences between underachievers and students classified learning disabled. *Journal of Special Education, 16*, 73–85.

Chapter 7

Describing and Treating Discourse Problems in Mentally Retarded Children: The Myth of Mental Retardese

Stephen N. Calculator

OVERVIEW

This chapter discusses discourse problems that have been observed in mentally retarded children. The discussion focuses on those children who fall in the more severe ranges of retardation. These children are migrating from institutional facilities to public school classrooms with increased frequency. The author discusses several problems that arise when these children generalize discourse behaviors found successful in their residential settings to a setting in which discourse expectations are dramatically different (i.e., the classroom). This section concludes by reviewing specific aspects of discourse, perhaps idiosyncratic to self-contained classrooms, that further reinforce these children's deviant discourse behaviors.

Next, the author discusses the joint contributions of various cognitive and noncognitive factors in relation to these children's discourse competencies. Data demonstrating the heterogeneity of communicative functioning among mentally retarded children are discussed. Whereas children's levels of intellectual functioning appear to set a prognostic ceiling upon the form, content, and uses of language they are capable of, noncognitive factors, particularly those related to children's experiences and current discourse demands and opportunities associated with their classroom and residential settings, often determine their actual discourse.

The chapter concludes with a discussion of various training programs and techniques that have been applied to remediation of these children's discourse deficiencies.

MENTALLY RETARDED CHILDREN IN THE CLASSROOM: MAINSTREAMING AND NORMALIZATION

Since the enactment of Public Law 94–142, which assures all handicapped children the right to a free and appropriate public education in the least restrictive setting possible, we have witnessed increasing social commitments to the principles of normalization and mainstreaming. These latter terms are often used synonymously in educational settings. However, the transition severely and profoundly mentally retarded children undergo in moving from an institutional to a public school classroom may not be actualized as a step towards normality. Problems may arise when these children's social and communicative expectations differ significantly from those of their teachers, nonretarded peers, and others.

According to Graham (1976), the discourse needs of some institutionalized mentally retarded children may be limited to finding efficient mechanisms for satisfying their immediate needs. The quality of their social interactions may be of little interest or concern to them. The extent of this indifference is related not only to these children's corresponding degrees of mental retardation but also to the types of social experiences they have previously participated in, as suggested further on.

The mentally retarded child, like his nonretarded peers, is expected by his teacher to display socially appropriate communicative behavior in the classroom. Frequently, this requires timing and tuning the quality with which he conveys his communicative needs and demands to that dictated by the classroom context. Such expectations often diverge from those of the residential environment, where the child may have learned to repress such discourse in order to comply with the regimented scheduling of his institutional environment. The child who enters school having had few previous opportunities to make choices, whose interactions with adults have been confined to activities directly related to his self-care, and whose interactions with peers have been severely restricted since they also had retreated to their own private social spaces, might be expected to encounter problems adjusting to the discourse demands of the classroom environment.

According to the discourse dimensions earlier described in Chapter 1, the severely or profoundly mentally retarded child may lack several content-based skills deemed necessary for successfully participating in classroom discourse. For example, a perusal of the many operant programs designed to accelerate these children's communicative functioning often reveals a common starting point—the establishment of attending behavior. Similarly, analyses of teachers' lesson plans often reveal activities designed for remediation of attentional deficits in these children. Children are taught to stay on task, to initiate and maintain eye contact with speakers, to emit verbal behaviors (e.g., on-topic responses and acknowledgments) that suggest they have been paying attention. The act of addressing a child who shows little acknowledgment of their presence nor desire to reciprocate by returning their discourse appears to be frustrating enough for educators that they have often delayed introducing academic training until these attentional deficits (often regarded as learning prerequisites) are firmly established. Recalling Graham's previous comment, we should not find it surprising that a child with little interest in events having no immediate tangible value for him might display such indifference in the form of attentional deficits. Such problems might better be regarded as reflecting idiosyncratic discourse preferences rather than true information processing dysfunctions.

Moving to some of the other aspects of discourse, the severely or profoundly mentally retarded child may often be quiet, or even passive, until a need arises. At that point, he or she may fail to time appropriately the expression of his or her need. For example, in the middle of a classroom lesson on the weather, the child spots a bag of cookies placed on a shelf that is out of his reach. He wants those cookies *now*, and indicates so, with little concern for the interruption he is causing. The teacher, wanting to maintain topic control (i.e., the weather) may censor the child in various ways (e.g., reprimand him for having interrupted her or ignore the behavior in hopes of extinguishing it). These strategies operate under the assumption that the child embraces the same set of discourse rules and obligations that she does. Unfortunately, this may not be the case. The child's earlier social experiences may have taught him that children who rely on polite request forms often fail to secure their listeners' compliance; as he judiciously selects a progressively more aggressive, impolite, and inconveniencing request form, the likelihood of gaining compliance increases.

To continue with this theme of stylistic variation (or, more accurately, its absence), it should be pointed out that these children are usually placed in self-contained classrooms. By segregating them from their nonretarded peers we are depriving them of the opportunity to observe politer, more appropriate discourse styles. This is particularly true when their classmates have severely limited comprehension abilities. The child *knows*, for example, that to obtain a jar of paint from a student seated next to him it will not help his cause to rely upon a polite request form (e.g., "Please") that neither he nor his listener actually understand. Experience has taught him that the best way to obtain such an object is simply to grab it.

How many of these children have we seen who may have expressive vocabularies of less than 25 words, yet included in their repertoires are the words *please* and *thank you*. For many of these children, the issuance of the various articulatory gestures accompanying these words may be nothing more than that, gestures which, when paired with the expression of a need, increase the likelihood of gaining teachers' compliance during training.

The lack of social conventions characterizing some of these children's discourse appears to be part of a more general lack of interest in engaging in interaction. Wing (1975) noted a strong relationship between these children's language and social abilities. The more severely language-impaired children in her study displayed less awareness of, or interest in, others; greater aloofness; poorer attending skills; and other socially limiting behaviors. Although not addressed by Wing, we might expect such children to display various corresponding discourse problems. For example, a lack of interest in others might take such forms as the child's seeking out a limited number of discourse partners (e.g., teachers and peers). The child might reserve his communicative behavior for those persons who are most likely to be in the position to satisfy his wants and needs. In addition, the child may be uninterested in or unable to maintain conversations about listener-initiated topics that have little potential reward value for him.

To return to the original topic of this section, mainstreaming, speculation exists that the various social deficiencies noted might jeopardize these children's abilities to gain their nonretarded peers' acceptance. This prediction has been borne out in several investigations (see Taylor, 1982, for a review of these findings). Taylor noted that school-aged nonretarded children were less likely to accept children who had been mainstreamed than those who had been relegated to self-contained classrooms. Similarly, preschoolers have been observed to avoid their retarded classmates when selecting seats, playmates, and conversational partners (Gampel, Harrison, and Budoff, 1972; Hartup, 1975).

EXPERIENCIAL FACTORS INFLUENCING TEACHER-CHILD DISCOURSE

These findings suggest that the discourse competencies of mentally retarded children are directly related to the quality of social interactions they experience. The nature and direction of this relationship has been a frequently probed area (Halle, Baer, and Spradlin, 1981; Hubbell, 1981; Mittler and Berry, 1977; Shane, Lipschultz, and Shane, 1982; Silverman, 1980).

Hubbell (1981) indicated that the communicative interactions mentally retarded children engage in may differ from those experienced by nonretarded children. Such differences may impede these children's acquisition and demonstration of discourse competence. For example, Mittler and Berry (1977) alluded to the prevalence of communicative *underfunctioning* among mentally retarded children. They attributed many of the discourse problems of these children to their listeners' failures to provide settings in which the listeners expected and demanded that they use communicative behaviors appropriate to their levels of cognitive and language functioning. Thus, children capable of verbally requesting classroom objects might convey these intents by simply tugging at their listeners' shirt sleeves and gesturing in the direction of the desired item. Similarly, when they do verbalize, these children often use simpler propositions than they are capable of. Once again, it is often the forms with the greatest history of success in keeping them on the winning end of discourse (e.g., having their wants and needs met), with the greatest economy of effort, that these children often select. Frequently, the success of classroom exchanges is not contingent on their use of polite or propositionally complex speaking turns.

TAKING INSTITUTIONAL LIVING INTO THE CLASSROOM

Mittler and Berry (1977) advocated the need for persons interacting with mentally retarded children, whether in the classroom or elsewhere, to create opportunities for them to engage in more complex conversational exchanges. However, the results of several investigations of adult-child interactions in residential settings suggest this does not happen. Silverman (1980) noted that severely handicapped persons who are receiving residential care may actually be discouraged from communicating, since such behavior makes their care more time consuming. The passive child who does not make requests and requires that choices be presented to him or her, requires less staff time than his or her more communicatively assertive peers. This preoccupation with discourse efficiency (i.e., silence, whenever possible) may be attributed, in part, to the various staffing problems that often plague residential facilities. For example, Shane, Lipschultz, and Shane (1982) pointed to factors such as the high rates of turnover and low staff-to-client ratios as key barriers to discourse. Because our motivation to engage in discourse is dependent on the existence of listeners we wish to converse with, the frequent exitings of these children's conversational partners would be expected to discourage such interactions. Similarly, the greater the number of children any one caregiver is responsible for, the fewer the opportunities any one child has to engage her in discourse.

The roles these staffing problems play in children's classroom discourse have not been examined. However, this author's own experiences as a staff speech-language pathologist and consultant for several school systems servicing mentally retarded children lead me to suggest several possible implications. To begin with, many of the more severely and profoundly retarded children rely upon idiosyncratic vocal and gestural communicative modes, either alone or in combination with speech. As staff depart, the meanings of these behaviors often go with them. With their informants gone, teacher-child interactions become riddled with conversational breakdowns. The children, unable to have their needs met, may react aggressively to this situation of conversational disrepair. They may cease attempting to communicate and assume a passive communication role.

As was suggested earlier, many of these children's participation in discourse is predicated on their teacher's introducing topics that are of immediate, personal interest to them. The existence of a caregiver with a lengthy history of contact with a child can serve as a valuable resource who can relate information regarding the child's interests, likes, and dislikes. By judiciously selecting her topics, a teacher can increase the likelihood of engaging, and then maintaining, discourse over larger numbers of speaking turns.

A second discourse-inhibiting feature of residential settings is their predictability (i.e., lack of novel activities or experiences). The child whose day-to-day experiences are highly similar has little information to share with others and, thus, one less reason to communicate. Thus, when their teacher arranges them in a semicircle, systematically making her way from one child to the next, asking each child to relate what he did at "home," the activity terminates quickly. Paucity of experience may also contribute to some of these children's inappropriately recounting old information, over and over, to the same listener. Despite listener feedback, which often becomes increasingly direct (e.g., "Tom, I know, I know. You've told me that a thousand times"), the child may persist at his listener's expense. Some may argue that such problems relate to mentally retarded children's inabilities to distinguish old versus new information or to a lack of linguistic knowledge. However, I have seen several of these children whose demonstrations of such irrelevant discourse diminished radically upon becoming involved in various field trips and related experiences. Noninformativeness gave way to relevant discourse as a by-product of providing them with novel experiences to relate to their listeners. For these children, the act of conversing (even without exchanging information) was socially rewarding to the point of overriding concerns regarding the irrelevance of their conversations.

DISCOURSE UNDERFUNCTIONING IN THE CLASSROOM

The preceding discussion suggested several ways in which mentally retarded children's classroom discourse problems might be related to aspects of their residential living. An examination of how the classroom experiences of these children may further reinforce (and induce) discourse incompetencies is warranted.

Calculator and Dollaghan (1982) investigated the discourse of seven severely handicapped children and their teachers in their respective residential classrooms. These teachers frequently were observed to constrain the children's opportunities to converse with them. For example, they often anticipated their children's needs, obviating any need for the children to initiate discourse. Teachers phrased their messages in forms that restricted the complexity of their students' responses, relying primarily on yes and no question forms and messages dictating gestural responses (e.g., pointing to or touching correct answers).

The children in Calculator and Dollaghan's study rarely initiated topics. Instead, the bulk of their speaking turns consisted of simple contingent replies to their teacher's requests. Teachers did not differentially reinforce or acknowledge children's messages according to their propositional complexity. Instead, they were as likely to respond to these children's unintelligible (outside of context) vocalizations and gestures as to their multiword phrases. The latter were conveyed using communication boards.

One plausible explanation for why these teachers were precipitating and apparently perpetuating their children's passive discourse styles was uncovered following the investigators' examination of the nature of conversational repairs in these dyads. Teachers requested clarification following 28 per cent of their students' topic initiations. Conversely, when the latter occupied the respondent role, teachers' needs to request clarification diminished to 13 per cent.

Additional evidence of teachers impeding children's discourse was provided by Halle, Baer, and Spradlin (1981). These investigators described the classrooms of their six mentally retarded subjects as *benevolent* environments comprised of *benevolent* adults who often preempted children's opportunities to engage in discourse. Before a student could express a need, his teacher would often anticipate his request by asking, "What do you need?" Similarly, coats were zipped and buttoned without any need for the children to verbally solicit their teacher's help. In effect, naturally arising opportunities to engage children in discourse were sacrificed for the sake of greater efficiency in moving these children from one academic-related task to the next.

These investigations suggest a general lack of synchrony between some mentally retarded children's discourse abilities and the concurrent communicative demands their teachers place upon them. These findings support the efficacy of an environmental model of training (Owings and Guyette, 1982). Using this approach, an attempt can be made to align teacher's discourse expectations with their respective students' discourse competencies. This, and other programming issues, will be discussed later in this chapter.

The remainder of this chapter begins by describing the communicative deficiencies of mentally retarded children in greater detail. Arguments are presented in opposition to the notion that mentally retarded children's discourse can be viewed as representing a distinct clinical entity. This discussion rekindles the frequently raised dispute of whether these children's communication problems are more accurately viewed as quantitatively versus qualitatively different from their nonretarded peers. Owing to the paucity of research related specifically to these children's discourse abilities, implications drawn in this area are the author's. Next, we explore some of the interrelationships among these childrens' respective levels of social, cognitive, and discourse functioning. For example, how does knowledge about these children's severity of intellectual impairment assist us in predicting, and then addressing (i.e., treating), their discourse skills and needs? What other factors must be considered in evaluating and treating these children's discourse problems? Therapy programs representing various applications of these data are presented along with several general training principles.

MENTAL RETARDESE:
MYTH OR REALITY?

If There Is a John Doe Will He Please Stand Up!

Zigler (1970) used the term *modal man* to depict the image lay persons associate with the term mentally retarded. The mentally retarded are often erroneously viewed as a homogeneous population, all of whose members share an identical set of attributes. MacMillan (1982), in a comprehensive review of public attitudes toward the mentally retarded, presented several findings that indicate the continuing persistence of these misconceptions. According to MacMillan, the typical referent attached to the label mentally retarded is that of a diseased, biologically impaired, severely or profoundly retarded person whose condition offers a poor prognosis. This tendency to stereotype may partially account for teachers employing discourse styles that delimit their children's communicative repertoires, irrespective of the latters' varying levels of discourse competence (as previously described).

Contrary to the preceding notions of homogeneous functioning among the mentally retarded, several investigators (Bloom and Lahey, 1978; Chapman and Nation, 1981; Miller, 1981) have pointed out the diversity of communication problems evidenced in this population. Chapman and Nation identified six distinct patterns of language dysfunction in their painstakingly derived homogeneous group of 41 educable mentally retarded (EMR) children. These patterns represented different combinations of difficulty with semantic comprehension, semantic formulation, syntax comprehension, syntax formulation, syntax repetition, phonologic comprehension, phonologic formulation, and phonologic repetition. These findings were presented in support of the argument that there are homogeneous subgroups within the EMR population, each displaying comparable linguistic strengths and weaknesses within, but not across, subgroups. However, an examination of the individual performances of children falling into each of Chapman and Nation's purportedly discrete subgroups (e.g., an analysis of the specific types of syntax formulation problems displayed by similarly classified children) might reveal not 6 but 41 distinct patterns. Such a finding would support the present author's contention that the mentally retarded represent a heterogeneous aggregate of communication subgroups, each with a population of one.

Other examinations of these children's linguistic abilities have generally found them to be consistent with those expected of nonretarded children of comparable mental ages (Coggins, 1979; Gordon and

Panagos, 1976; Keane, 1972; Lackner, 1968; Semmel and Dolley, 1971; Yoder and Calculator, 1981; Yoder and Miller, 1972). Kamhi and Johnston (1982) recently summarized the nature of this relationship between mentally retarded and nonretarded children's communicative abilities. According to these investigators, the linguistic complexity (i.e., qualitative aspects) of mentally retarded children's language is largely determined by their corresponding levels of intellectual functioning. In other words, the higher a child's mental age, the greater the propositional complexity of his discourse. Conversely, noncognitive factors (e.g., motivation, listener feedback, prior experience) are purportedly responsible for the frequencies (i.e., quantitative aspects) with which these children actually use the various forms and contents in their communicative repertoires. This would help to explain why a child who is capable of formulating a variety of question forms fails to do so in a classroom setting that preempts such requests.

Relationship Between Communication Skills and Intellectual Ability

Unlike Kamhi and Johnston, other investigators have failed to observe such a close fit between these children's levels of cognitive and communicative functioning. Miller, Chapman, and Bedrosian (1978) examined the language of 82 mentally retarded children, whose cognitive abilities ranged between Sensorimotor Stage IV and late preoperations. Eight of these children were found to display language abilities in excess of that predicted by their corresponding mental ages. Of these children, all displayed superior vocabulary comprehension and three displayed advanced syntactic abilities.

Miller and coworkers' findings indicate that noncognitive factors may not only account for these children's acquisition of the various quantitative aspects of language but account for some qualitative aspects as well. This contention has been expressed by several previous investigators (e.g., Bowerman, 1983; Cromer, 1976; Schlesinger, 1977; and Slobin, 1979) who point out the numerous conventions of language that require the learning of specific surface rules (e.g., how to mark possession, irregular plurals, and person-number agreement). According to these investigators, such conventions do not relate to any corresponding cognitive abilities. Instead, their learning is contingent on the nature of verbal input to which children are exposed. By employing a simplified, redundant style of discourse (i.e., motherese, or baby talk), adults can highlight these forms when addressing their children. Additional learning occurs as adults provide feedback and modeling contingent upon their children's uses of these forms.

The mentally retarded child who is placed in a self-contained classroom may not be exposed to the quantity, nor quality, of verbal input received by his nonretarded peers. Opportunities for teacher feedback regarding the correctness of his utterances may not be forthcoming in an environment that discourages discourse or expects little from the child with respect to the linguistic complexity of his messages.

IMPLICATIONS FOR
CLASSROOM DISCOURSE

In summary, the label mental retardation does not, in itself, assist the teacher or clinician in predicting a child's communicative abilities or needs. Such an outcome necessitates a detailed description of each individual child's relative proficiencies across the various phonologic, syntactic, semantic, and pragmatic dimensions of language. Even then, a child's possession of a given linguistic skill provides no assurance that such a skill will actually be used. For example, Kamhi and Johnston's retarded subjects were observed using fewer question forms and marking most utterances in the present progressive tense despite their abilities to issue a greater number and variety of these forms.

Earlier, the highly structured, preempting nature of teacher's discourse as one possible explanation for these children's infrequency of question asking was implicated. Efficient teaching often seems to be equated with low frequencies of children's question asking. In Calculator and Dollaghan's (1982) earlier described study, the children were not found to issue *any* requests for clarification, despite their cognitive abilities to do so. Whether this finding reflects an unusually clear discourse style being employed by the teachers, a relative absence of this speech act from the children's discourse repertoires, or a lack of motivation to convey such requests (e.g., why should a child seek clarification of information he is not interested in to begin with?) is unknown. The more general lack of question asking evidenced in these particular children might also be explained, in part, as an artifact of their rarely occupying the role of initiator.

One might also look to environmental variables as a possible source for explaining why a disproportionate number of mentally retarded children's references are to ongoing events (e.g., present-progressive). The child with a dearth of experiences to relate may see little use for forms of the past tense; the child whose future experiences often represent repetitions of what he has already experienced will have little reason to relate such upcoming events; the child whose primary source of experiences is the classroom will be verbally preoccupied with present ongoing events.

Thus, noncognitive factors partially explain how these children will use language in their classrooms. Cognitive factors (i.e., a child's mental age), in turn, offer a prognostic ceiling as to the level of linguistic complexity, and discourse, that can be expected of a child. For example, like nonretarded children, retarded children are not expected to be capable of using symbolic language before attaining various problem-solving abilities commensurate with Sensorimotor Stage V (Chapman and Miller, 1980; Owens and House, 1984; Shane and Bashir, 1980). Thus, while children not yet operating at this level might be trained to use a small lexicon, their ability to appropriately *use* such words in meaningful dialogues with their teachers is doubtful. Aside from their abilities to label some immediate objects, their range of speech acts would be limited. Also, teachers' references to objects or events that were spatially or temporally removed from the immediate classroom setting would be expected to be ignored or else incorrectly responded to. A teacher wishing to successfully engage such a child in discourse would have to combine her judicious selection of immediate-centered topics with various conversational repair strategies (e.g., answering for the child).

Similarly, prior to Sensorimotor Stage VI (MA 18 to 24 months), the child is still not expected to be capable of engaging in discourse focusing upon nonimmediate referents. Failure to initiate or maintain such topics is not viewed as reflecting an attentional deficit or aloofness but is instead viewed as reflecting the child's inability to conceptualize events outside his immediate classroom setting.

SOCIAL FACTORS AND DISCOURSE TRAINING

The preceding discussion should not be interpreted as an admonishment against early intervention but as a warning to adjust such programs to children's developmental capabilities. By introducing discourse training to presymbolic mentally retarded children, we can begin instilling in them an understanding of the rules and purposes of discourse as a social tool. Such learning has been viewed by some investigators as forming a basis from which subsequent, more elaborate discourse skills can evolve (Bricker and Bricker, 1974; Calculator, 1984; Harris and Vanderheiden, 1980).

Calculator's (1984) prelinguistic training program illustrates the social foci of such training. He provides a series of procedures designed to manipulate the interactional behaviors of profoundly mentally retarded children *and* their teachers. The goal of this program is for the children to begin inducing the social and communicative value of their behavior. This is accomplished, in part, by expanding children's prelinguistic discourse repertoires (e.g., smiling, vocalizing, reaching, and mutual gazing) while simultaneously teaching their teachers to respond to these behaviors in a protoconversational format. During this process, children are purportedly learning the rules of turn-taking. More importantly, they are gaining an understanding of how they can control teachers' discourse behaviors (e.g., attending, smiling, and verbalizing) through their own vocal and gestural behaviors.

This program represents a departure from clinical procedures aimed at increasing children's frequency or types of vocalizations, contending that such changes do not signal an increased ability to participate in discourse. It is only when children's communicative acts are appropriately timed and then contingently responded to by their teachers that a true progression in discourse is acknowledged.

INFLUENCE OF SETTING ON CHILDREN'S DISCOURSE SKILLS

No child can be expected to initiate or participate in classroom discourse, regardless of his developmental readiness, unless he or she feels a need to do so. Such a need arises once the child views discourse as a necessary and efficient vehicle for conveying and fulfilling his or her wants, needs, and feelings. This outcome is fostered by a responsive environment that continuously creates the need for, and then contingently responds to, the child's spontaneous communicative attempts.

The setting described contrasts greatly with that experienced by many severely handicapped children. As noted earlier, adults (e.g., teachers) often preclude their children's discourse opportunities by providing objects, materials, and activities in response to predetermined schedules rather than supplying their students' conveyed wants. Many of these children enter school with the expectation that all necessary goods and services will be provided to them without any need for imput on their parts. These hypotheses are then borne out in the classroom.

In observing lunch or snacktime in many of these children's classrooms, an institution-like quality to the ongoing exchanges is often present. Food is doled out in compliance with each child's dietary restrictions; the menu and amount are all determined prior to the child's sitting down at the table. Conversation is secondary to consumption. Conversely, many teachers use mealtime as a setting in which they can encourage children's initiations and maintenance of discourse. For example, while the "powers above" may have decided that Jill will have two ounces of green vegetable with her lunch, Jill's teachers may (1) give her a choice of two vegetables; (2) purposely give her a vegetable she dislikes that, upon Jill's conveying her dissatisfaction, is replaced with an alternative; (3) place a bowl of vegetables in Jill's sight, but out of her reach, in front of a classmate. Jill would thus be prompted to initiate discourse with her peer.

Each of these procedures represent different ways in which teachers can sabotage their children's environments to create needs to communicate. Halle and colleagues (1981) demonstrated that when severely handicapped children are suddenly confronted with a need to participate in discourse, they do so with surprising regularity. They trained teachers to implement a delay procedure in which they paused 5 seconds before preempting their students' messages. These delays served as nonverbal cues to the children to initiate discourse. As simple as this procedure was, its introduction resulted in sharp increases in the frequency of children's topic initiations. In addition, teachers spontaneously generalized their uses of this discourse-elicitation procedure beyond the original three contexts of interest (i.e., free play, snack, and lunchtime).

USE OF DISCOURSE AS A NATURAL CONTINGENT REINFORCER

McCormick and Goldman (1984) suggested that in order to design a teaching environment that maximizes opportunities for discourse, teachers should base their selections of materials and program content on their children's interests and needs. They stress the need to respond contingently to children's spontaneous communicative attempts in order to reinforce the functional value of discourse. The Halle and associates procedure assures the teacher of selecting naturally occurring, child-centered events to precipitate discourse, since delays are applied to events initiated by the children themselves. Furthermore, teachers' responses are directly related to their children's conveyed needs, assuring coherent, topic-relevant discourse traversing a minimum of three speaking turns (e.g., teacher sets up the need for a child to communicate in order to have a want satisfied; the child initiates a contextually appropriate message; the teacher responds on topic).

Children have been found to be more likely to repeat discourse behaviors that have previously elicited natural consequences from their listeners (e.g., Meline, 1980; Sailor, Goetz, Schuler, Utley, and Baldwin, 1980). It would thus appear more logical to respond to a child's use of a targeted request form (e.g., "me go out") by opening a door for him than by praising him or rewarding him with a token.

Natural reinforcers (e.g., contingent responding) enhance the child's likelihood of generalizing discourse behaviors to other settings. Furthermore, these responses promote discourse coherence (e.g., as in the Halle et al. procedure). Conversely, teachers who respond to their students' messages with clinical reinforcers (e.g., raisins, M&Ms, and social praise) terminate discourse all together or preclude the need for further discussion. It is difficult for a child to converse with a full mouth.

Two negative outcomes of noncontingent responding were recently observed by the author. Joanie, a nonspeaking, severely mentally retarded 10 year old, often interrupted classroom activities by wetting her pants. Her teacher instituted a toileting program. Joanie was to learn that by tapping a picture of a toilet, prior to wetting, she would be taken to the bathroom and provided with her favorite toy, a Slinky. Cognitively, Joanie was unable to see the symbolic relationship between the picture of the toilet and its referent in the bathroom. Also, she was confused as to the way in which this picture could serve as a discriminant means (by tapping) to an end (being taken to the bathroom). What Joanie was observed doing over the next several weeks was tapping on all types of objects around her, then waiting expectantly for her Slinky. Frequently, these gestures arose simultaneously with her wetting.

Sally, a seven year old severely retarded child had supposedly been taught to use a communication board containing approximately 100 pictures to supplement her often unintelligible speech. One hot summer day, I entered Sally's classroom with a frosty Coke. Sally drooled, stared, vocalized, became progressively distressed, and did everything but point to the picture on her board, connoting that she wanted a drink. Sally's teacher had taught her to *identify* all the pictures, assuming this alone would assure her functional use of such pictures in conveying various other communicative intents besides labeling. In "learning" the pictures, Sally was reinforced with tokens. It was thus little wonder why she lacked an understanding of how her pictures could serve as aids for engaging in discourse (e.g., requesting Coke when she was thirsty).

PROGRAMS FOR TRAINING FUNCTIONAL DISCOURSE

As suggested, the role of social variables in discourse acquisition and training has been addressed primarily in relation to the environmental contexts of these children. Investigators have stressed the need to provide settings that necessitate, and then naturally reinforce, children's spontaneous discourse (Gullo and Gullo, 1984; Halle et al., 1981; Hart and Risely, 1975; Hart and Rogers-Warren, 1978; Mahoney and Weller, 1980; Spradlin and Siegel, 1982). Other areas that these investigators agree upon include (1) training discourse in natural or simulated classroom contexts, as opposed to laboratory settings; (2) involving teachers, classmates, and others as primary discourse models; and (3) involving the child as an active discourse partner through various types of environmental manipulation and prompting.

Several programs related to classroom discourse have evolved from these concepts of functional communication. These procedures represent a shifting of speech-language and related professionals' interests from the surface forms their children produce (e.g., relative mastery of a grammatic morpheme) and understand, to the actual success and efficiency of these children as conversational participants. As indicated in the following paragraphs, these programs differ significantly with respect to what they interpret as being attainable, and functional, for given individuals.

Chronologic Age-Appropriate Programming

Brown and coworkers (1979) discussed the need to provide chronologic age-appropriate programming for retarded individuals. Their program begins by identifying the specific discourse skills necessary for the child to function independently in his various classroom and other settings. These skills are then taught, irrespective of the child's cognitive abilities, using a task analysis procedure.

If we were to apply Brown and colleagues' program to classroom discourse, the trainer's task would begin by his elucidating what discourse demands were associated with each of the child's various settings (e.g., mathematics, reading, art, music, lunch, and recess). Children would then be taught vocabulary items that frequently occurred in each respective setting. Similarly, high-incidence commands and directions would be introduced in conjunction with the appropriate ways of responding to such exchanges. For example, the child's opportunities to participate in recess might be predicted to increase if he were able to conform to the discourse rules governing a particular playground game. The child might be taught to (1) sit passively in a circle with his peers, (2) ignore the verbalizations of game players other than the girl who is "it," (3) respond discriminately to the latter person's patting him on the head, depending on whether this gesture is paired with the word "duck" (in which case he is to ignore her) or "goose" (in which case he is to chase her around the circle). At the conclusion of training, the child would be expected to be capable of participating in a game of "Duck-duck-goose."

Advocates of Brown and colleagues' program see no necessary correlation between the sequence and system of discourse skill acquisition in normal children with that followed by mentally retarded children. Not only do they reject entities such as cognitive or linguistic prerequisites but they discard the feasibility of applying a model based on normal children to children they say are not developing normally.

Developmentally Appropriate Programming

Unlike Brown and colleagues' procedure, Owings and Guyette's (1982) environmental approach bases its program content not only on the chronologic but also on the developmental appropriateness of activities. After determining the discourse demands of a particular classroom activity, for example, the trainer would then design objectives that would be developmentally appropriate (i.e., skills expected of the child would entail comparable linguistic complexity to that displayed by younger, nonretarded children at a comparable mental age). A second major difference between these two approaches relates to their respective foci of training.

Whereas Brown and colleagues attempt to resolve discrepancies between environmental demands and children's abilities by concentrating exclusively upon the child, Owings and Guyette take a more reciprocal approach. The latter investigators note situations in which listeners' discourse demands significantly exceed the cognitive or communicative abilities of their children. They advocate remediating such discrepancies by directing treatment towards the listeners (rather than the children), teaching them to simplify their discourse demands. Such programming may involve encouraging teachers to tune the complexity of their language (syntactically, semantically, or pragmatically) to their children's developmental levels. This enhances the likelihood that children will derive meaning from their teachers' discourse acts, increasing the likelihood of their responding on topic and extending discourse over increasing numbers of turns.

Context Sensitive Programming

Whereas the two preceding approaches apply to the immediate discourse needs of mentally retarded children, Gullo and Gullo (1984) also prepare these children to participate in future discourse settings. Their program for mentally retarded adolescents employs a combination of modeling, role play, and practice. Activity-specific language is introduced in contexts designed to simulate natural settings. Upon demonstrating their classroom mastery of those discourse behaviors felt to be prerequisite to their effectively conversing in a specific outside setting, children are then given the opportunity to put their teachers' hypotheses to the test in subsequent field experiences.

This program appears to address a pervasive problem among mentally retarded children—their inability to generalize classroom learning to other settings. As Spradlin and Siegel (1982) pointed out, some of this may result from the insufficient opportunities these children have to engage in discourse outside the classroom. As indicated above, Gullo and Gullo's program directly addresses this issue. Also, by bringing in extraclassroom experiences, teachers can expand their children's discourse repertoires (e.g., breadth of topics), increase their motivations and reasons to communicate (as novel experiences are encountered), and broaden their uses of discourse. Following a field trip, children have embodied experiences and reactions that can subsequently be shared with classmates as well as naive listeners.

Other Discourse Training Strategies

Each of the preceding programs can address children's discourse problems by providing them with setting-specific communicative behaviors that, when emitted in the appropriate classroom context, enhances their likelihood of successfully participating in classroom discourse. These procedures can be supplemented with other techniques that attempt to increase the frequency with which these children engage in discourse, particularly in the role of topic initiator. Lucas (1980) contended that children will not acquire discourse skills unless they have sufficient opportunities to use them. By implementing the following techniques, the underfunctioning (or otherwise noncommunicative) child learns to associate discourse with the satisfaction of his or her personal wants and needs.

The first strategy, environmental sabotage, appears to capitalize on the premise that a sadist lies deep in the hearts of all of us. This technique can involve such pleasantries as taping scissors together, plugging glue bottles, breaking points off pencils, cutting holes into the bottoms of cups, providing interesting-looking games without any directions as to how they are played, and so on. These situations are carefully woven into unsuspecting children's natural classroom routines. By responding appropriately (either spontaneously, or with the help of varying levels of prompting and modeling) the child earns immediate, natural payoffs for his or her having communicated.

Sam, a 12 year old severely retarded child, was approximately 50 per cent intelligible to his teachers. He thus used a combination of speaking and pointing to photographs to engage in discourse. One socialization goal for Sam was that he seek out friends among his peers. This was initially addressed by training him to point to the correct children's photographs in response to his teacher's going through the morning roll call.

One day, Sam's teacher accidentally (on purpose) sat him next to a student she knew he disliked. As Sam whined, his teacher asked what was wrong. Sam spontaneously pointed to the photograph of another classmate, looked in her direction, and said, "There." His teacher quickly relocated him. This simple act of environmental sabotage encouraged Sam to initiate a meaningful discourse sequence that, at the same time, reinforced his program goals.

A second frequently used technique for providing children with opportunities to engage in classroom discourse is referred to as mand-modeling (Rogers-Warren and Warren, 1980). This strategy commences with the teacher's attracting or directing her child's attention to a desirable object or event. As the child attempts to approach the material, or participate in the event, the teacher blocks his access and mands (e.g., "Tell me what you want"). The mand serves as an overt signal to the child that it is necessary that he verbalize his request, if he is to have it fulfilled. If the child fails to issue his request, the teacher then models the desired response. Once again, the response itself is one that the child is developmentally capable of producing and is functional insofar as its production results in the immediate satisfaction of a need. Upon his imitation of his teacher's model, the desired object or event is provided.

Recall the earlier case of Sally, who was unable to convey her request for a Coke. Let's now examine the finale to this incident. Sally's teacher instructed her to show the visitor (me) what she wanted, using her communication board (the mand). When Sally did not respond, the teacher pointed to the "drink" symbol (the model) and quickly obtained a cup of Coke from me. This sequence was repeated several times, while Sally grew progressively more upset. Her teacher then physically prompted Sally to point to the designated symbol. Sally quickly caught on, smiling as her thirsty visitor departed.

Environmental sabotage, mand-modeling, and delays (previously discussed) have several features in common. Each requires momentary, one-to-one interactions between teachers and children; all occur in the natural classroom setting; all base their selection of activities upon individual children's likes and dislikes; and all terminate with natural reinforcement. In practice, these techniques are often applied in combinations with one another.

FINAL NOTE

The discourse problems of mentally retarded children are as diverse as the children themselves. Although discourse competency corresponds greatly to children's respective levels of intellectual functioning, alternate factors (e.g., social variables) often have an important bearing on the quality and quantity of mentally retarded children's classroom discourse. Still, numerous questions remain. For example, what are the effects of institutionalization and deinstitutionalization, mainstreaming, and normalization on these children's discourse skills? Do certain situational variables reinforce appropriate versus inappropriate discourse skill acquisition and performance? To what extent can these children's discourse differences be attributed to their developmental delays versus other ill-defined variables (e.g., illusive artifacts of syndromes, residues of nonfunctional treatment approaches, products of communicatively stifling environments)? As we attempt to answer these and other questions we must not become sidetracked from our primary objective, providing improved strategies for facilitating functional, socially appropriate interactions between these children and their *special needs* listeners.

REFERENCES

Bloom, L., and Lahey, M. (1978). *Language development and language disorders*. New York: John Wiley and Sons.

Bowerman, M. (1983). Reorganizational processes in language development. In L. Gleitman and E. Wanner (Eds.), *Language acquisition: The state of the art*. New York: Cambridge University Press.

Bricker, W., and Bricker, D. (1974). An early language training strategy. In R. Schiefelbusch and L. Lloyd (Eds.), *Language perspectives: Acquisition, retardation and intervention*. Baltimore: University Park Press.

Brown, L., Branston, M., Hamre-Nietupski, S., Pumpian, I., Certo, N., and Gruenwald, L. (1979) A strategy for developing chronological age appropriate and functional curricular content for severely handicapped adolescents and young adults. *Journal of Special Education, 13*, 81–90.

Calculator, S. (1984). Prelinguistic development. In W. Perkins (Ed.), *Language handicaps in children*. New York: Thieme-Stratton.

Calculator, S., and Dollaghan, C. (1982). The use of communication boards in a residential setting. *Journal of Speech and Hearing Disorders, 47*, 281–287.

Chapman, D., and Nation, J. (1981). Patterns of language performance in educable mentally retarded children. *Journal of Communication Disorders, 14*, 245–254.

Chapman, R., and Miller, J. (1980). Analyzing language and communication in the child. In R. Schiefelbusch (Ed.), *Nonspeech language and communication: Analysis and intervention*. Baltimore: University Park Press.

Coggins, T. (1979). Relational meanings encoded in the two-word utterances of

Stage 1 Down's syndrome children. *Journal of Speech and Hearing Research,* *22,* 166–178.

Cromer, R. (1976). The cognitive hypothesis of language acquisition and its implications for child language deficiency. In D. Morehead and A. Morehead (Eds.), *Directions in normal and deficient child language.* Baltimore: University Park Press.

Gampel, D., Harrison, R., and Budoff, M. (1972). *An observational study of segregated and integrated EMR children and their nonretarded peers: Can we tell the difference by looking?* Cambridge, MA: Research Institute for Educational Problems.

Gordon, W., and Panagos, J. (1976). Developmental transformational capacity of children with Down's syndrome. *Perceptual-Motor Skills, 43,* 967–973.

Graham, L. (1976). Language programming and intervention. In L. Lloyd (Ed.), *Communication assessment and intervention strategies.* Baltimore: University Park Press.

Gullo, D., and Gullo, J. (1984). An ecological language intervention approach with mentally retarded adolescents. *Language, Speech and Hearing Services in Schools, 15,* 182–191.

Halle, J., Baer, D., and Spradlin, J. (1981). Teachers' generalized use of delay as a stimulus control procedure to increase language use in handicapped children. *Journal of Applied Behavior Analysis, 14,* 389–409.

Harris, D., and Vanderheiden, G. (1980). Augmentative communication techniques. In R. Schiefelbusch (Ed.), *Nonspeech language and communication.* Baltimore: University Park Press.

Hart, B., and Risely, T. (1975). Incidental teaching of language in the preschool. *Journal of Applied Behavior Analysis, 8,* 411–420.

Hart, B., and Rogers-Warren, A. (1978). A milieu approach to teaching language. In R. Schiefelbusch (Ed.), *Language intervention strategies.* Baltimore: University Park Press.

Hartup, W. (1975). The origins of friendships. In M. Lewis and L. Rosenblum (Eds.), *Friendship and peer relations.* New York: John Wiley and Sons.

Hubbell, R. (1981). *Children's language disorders. An integrated approach.* Englewood Cliffs, NJ: Prentice-Hall.

Kamhi, A., and Johnston, J. (1982). Towards an understanding of retarded children's linguistic deficiencies. *Journal of Speech and Hearing Research, 25,* 435–445.

Keane, V. (1972). The incidence of speech and language problems in the mentally retarded. *Mental Retardation, 10,* 3–5.

Lackner, J. (1968). A developmental study of language behavior in retarded children. *Neuropsychologia, 6,* 301–320.

Lucas, E. (1980). *Semantic and pragmatic language disorders.* Rockville, MD: Aspen.

MacMillan, D. (1982). *Mental retardation in school and society.* Boston: Little, Brown and Company.

Mahoney, G., and Weller, E. (1980). An ecological approach to language intervention. In D. Bricker (Ed.), *New directions for exceptional children: Language intervention with children, 2,* 17–32.

McCormick, L., and Goldman, R. (1984). Designing an optimal learning program. In L. McCormick and R. Schiefelbusch (Eds.), *Early language intervention.* Columbus, OH: Charles E. Merrill.

Meline, T. (1980). The application of reinforcement in language intervention. *Language, Speech and Hearing Services in Schools, 11*, 95-101.

Miller, J. (1981). *Assessing language production in children: Experimental procedures*. Baltimore: University Park Press.

Miller, J., Chapman, R., and Bedrosian, J. (1978). Defining developmentally disabled subjects for research: The relationship between etiology, cognitive development, and language and communicative performance. *New Zealand Speech Therapists Journal, 33*, 2-19.

Mittler, P., and Berry, P. (1977). Demanding language. In P. Mittler (Ed.), *Research to practice in mental retardation. Vol. II, Education and Training*. Baltimore: University Park Press.

Owens, R., and House, L. (1984). Decision making processes in augmentative communication. *Journal of Speech and Hearing Disorders, 49*, 18-25.

Owings, N., and Guyette, T. (1982). Communication behavior assessment and treatment with the adult retarded: An approach. In N. Lass (Ed.), *Speech and language. Advances in basic research and practice* (Vol. 7). New York: Academic Press.

Rogers-Warren, A., and Warren, S. (1980). Mands for verbalization: Facilitating the display of newly trained language in children. *Behavior Modification, 4*, 361-382.

Sailor, W., Goetz, L., Schuler, A., Utley, B., and Baldwin, M. (1980). Language and the severely handicapped. Deciding what to teach to whom. In D. Bricker (Ed.), *New Developments in Special Education*. New York: Jossey-Bass.

Schlesinger, I. (1977). The role of cognitive development and linguistic input in language acquisition. *Journal of Child Language, 4*, 153-169.

Semmel, M., and Dolley, D. (1971). Comprehension and imitation of sentences by Down's Syndrome children as a function of transformational complexity. *American Journal of Mental Deficiency, 75*, 739-745.

Shane, H., and Bashir, A. (1980). Election criteria for the adoption of an augmentative communication system: Preliminary considerations. *Journal of Speech and Hearing Disorders, 45*, 408-414.

Shane, H., Lipschultz, R., and Shane, C. (1982). Facilitating the communicative interaction of nonspeaking persons in large residential settings. In D. Yoder (Ed.), *Topics in language disorders: Communication interaction strategies for the severely communicatively impaired* (pp. 73-84). Rockville, MD: Aspen.

Silverman, F. (1980). *Communication for the speechless*. Englewood Cliffs, NJ: Prentice-Hall.

Slobin, D. (1979). *Psycholinguistics* (2nd ed). Glenview, IL: Scott, Foresman.

Spradlin, J., and Siegel, G. (1982). Language training in natural and clinical environments. *Journal of Speech and Hearing Disorders, 47*, 2-6.

Taylor, A. (1982). Social competence and interpersonal relations between retarded and nonretarded children. In N. Ellis (Ed.), *International review of research in mental retardation*. New York: Academic Press.

Wing, L. (1975). A study of language impairments in severely retarded children. In N. O'Connor (Ed.), *Language, cognitive deficits, and retardation*. Boston: Butterworth and Company.

Yoder, D., and Calculator (1981). Some perspectives on intervention strategies for persons with developmental disorders. *Journal of Autism and Developmental Disorders, 11*, 107-123.

Yoder, D., and Miller, J. (1972). What we may know and what we can do: Input toward a system. In J. McLean, D. Yoder, and R. Schiefelbusch (Eds.), *Language intervention with the retarded: Developing strategies*. Baltimore: University Park Press.

Zigler, E. (1970). Social class and the socialization process. *Review of Educational Research, 40*, 87–110.

Chapter 8

If Teaching Is Conversation, Can Conversation Be Taught?: Discourse Abilities in Hearing Impaired Children

Penny L. Griffith
Harold A. Johnson
Sondra L. Dastoli

Whether at home or at school, the adult communication partner has been found to play a major role in the language acquisition of the child. For most children, the parent is the primary source of language modeling, and for most children, language acquisition is close to being complete by the time school age arrives. For these children, language is a means of gaining access to and participating in the academic setting (Green and Harker, 1982). For these children, school is a place where language is refined, and conversational sophistication, already acquired, is extended to reading and writing modes. In school these children learn how to manipulate their language, and together with their teacher, use language to construct and complete the tasks of learning (Green and Wallat, 1981; Mehan, 1979).

Sociolinguistic research, however, has shown that for many children, the process of conversational interaction as well as of academic learning is not as straightforward as just suggested. The social interaction demands of the classroom are very complex (Green and Harker, 1982; Green and Wallat, 1980), and for children who are at a disadvantage, whether linguistically, culturally, or academically, the role of the teacher as a communication facilitator becomes crucial. Cultural incongruence between the classroom participation structure and that of the home may disrupt or prevent lessons from progressing (Au and Mason, 1983). Social participation, if restricted by language differences, can be a major factor in failure to learn academic lessons (DeStefano, Pepinsky, and Sanders, 1982; Eder, 1982; Fillmore, 1982). Teacher's decisions at the general level of classroom organization, and at the specific level of microinteraction have been found to affect the opportunities students have to develop academic and interpersonal communication competencies (Wilkinson, 1982).

In classrooms for hearing impaired students the same factors— complexity of social structures, diversity of student background and cognitive abilities, incongruence between home and school cultures, and the interaction decisions made by the teacher—exist as influences on the student's ability to gain access to learning. Beyond those factors that affect the culturally different students or the minority language–speaking student, however, the hearing impaired student and his teacher have additional communication obstacles to overcome.

That the hearing impaired child is restricted in his access to verbal information presented in the classroom is obvious. Regardless of oral or total communication methodology, the greater the hearing loss, the more likely it will be that the child will depend upon the visual channel for communication. More significant than the restriction placed on the sensory channels for reception of communication, however, is the resulting implication that, without hearing, most children arrive at school age with very limited language ability. For most hearing impaired children, school is a place where language, including conversational skills as well as academic lessons, remains to be learned. The hearing impaired students and their teacher, then, must not only construct lessons, but must also construct the medium through which formal learning will be communicated.

The purpose of this chapter will be to review the literature that describes the abilities of hearing impaired children as conversational participants. Although the foci of this book, and of the majority of studies presented in this chapter are on communication between students and teachers in the classroom setting, literature in two other areas provides insight into the global difficulty facing a hearing impaired child in conversing with any communication partner. Therefore, information concerning the development of conversational skills between hearing impaired children and their mothers and hearing impaired children and their hearing and deaf peers is presented first. The problems encountered in these two situations have significant implications for what is done in the classroom. Following the review of mother-child, peer, and classroom discourse studies, a discussion of strategies for intervention at the conversational level is presented.

DEAF CHILDREN OF DEAF PARENTS

Before beginning the discussion of conversational abilities, a short exception is presented concerning one group of deaf children. Because the nature of this book is sociolinguistic, which includes the area of cultural and language minorities, it is necessary to separate for the reader the small percentage of genetically deaf children with deaf parents from the majority of hearing impaired children. It is widely accepted by linguists and sociologists that children learning American Sign Language from birth constitute a linguistic and cultural subgroup in this country (Bellugi and Klima, 1972; Erting, 1981; Schlesinger and Meadow, 1972). These children may have some difficulty learning English in school; however, the vast majority are thought to develop language at a rate comparable with hearing children learning spoken English, tend to achieve in social areas, have a positive self-concept, and have higher academic achievement scores than other groups of hearing impaired students (Erting, 1981; Schien and Delk, 1974; Schlesinger and Meadow, 1972; Vernon and Koh, 1970). Studies concerning the conversational abilities of this group of children are not presented in this chapter, except in those instances in which deaf children–deaf mother dyads were compared with other groups or investigators did not report the parental hearing status of their subjects.

DISCOURSE ABILITIES OF HEARING IMPAIRED CHILDREN AND THEIR MOTHERS

Hearing impaired infants and their mothers are at high risk in terms of the development of successful conversational interaction. From the very beginning the two partners are relying on different channels of communication. In early infancy, when normally much of the mother-child interaction is face to face, deaf children and their hearing mothers may experience relative success in their communicative exchanges. However, as the mother begins to expect vocal interactions, problems are very likely to occur. Deafness naturally causes the child to appear less responsive. Until the hearing problem is diagnosed, the mother may interpret the child's reduced responsiveness as an unwillingness to participate and as a rejection of her attempts to interact. Jones (1977) states that the most disastrous kind of communication breakdown is the apparent nonresponsiveness of one of the participants.

A very limited amount of research has been carried out on the interactions between hearing mothers and their hearing impaired children. The information presented here is divided according to whether the mother-child dyads were interacting through the oral-aural mode or through the simultaneous mode (sign and speech).

Oral-Aural Discourse

Descriptions of mother-child interactions in which an aural-oral approach was used have substantiated theoretical concerns regarding the potential for communication breakdowns between mothers and children. Mothers of deaf children between the ages of one and two years do use a simplified, concrete, and grammatical register of language that is very similar to that used with hearing children of the same age (Cheskin, 1981; Gregory, Mogford, and Bishop, 1978; Wedell-Monnig and Westerman, 1977). The children, however, are passive participants who respond to nonverbal stimuli rather than verbal stimuli. Cheskin points out that the simplified language register is inappropriate for children who are not indicating comprehension of verbal language or not beginning to express themselves verbally. Interaction on a nonverbal basis utilizing gaze and facial expression would appear appropriate. Probably in reaction to the child's nonresponsiveness the language of these mothers remained simplified over time, in contrast to the language mothers address to hearing children, which becomes more complex over time (Gregory, Mogford, and Bishop, 1978).

Mothers using oral-aural communication characteristically appear to dominate the conversation (Cheskin, 1981; Schlesinger and Meadow, 1972; Wedell-Monnig and Lumley, 1980). Mothers were observed to initiate interactions on an average of 21.8 times per 20 minute sessions, whereas the hearing impaired children initiated interactions only about 2.3 times. Initiations by hearing children and their mothers were more equitable, with the average mother initiation equaling about 9.6 times and children 12.7 times per observation. Conversational bouts between hearing mothers and deaf infants were awkward, in that responses to one another were often not contingent. Children appeared to be unaffected by their mothers' utterances. Mothers often interpreted their children's communicative acts as attempts to label objects rather than as conversation starters. Mothers often missed or did not respond to their children's efforts to initiate interaction. Much of the nonresponsiveness and misinterpretation on behalf of the mother was attributable to the unintelligibility of the child's speech and to the mother's failure to pick up on existing nonverbal clues that might have aided her in understanding the child's utterance. There were more vocal clashes (talking at the same time) between hearing mothers and deaf children than between hearing mothers and hearing children (Gregory, Mogford, and Bishop, 1978).

Wedell-Monnig and Lumley (1980) found that the amount of interaction between hearing mothers and deaf children decreased over time. The lack of success that mothers of deaf children using aural-oral communication experience may cause frustration, which leads to fewer attempts at communication, thereby reducing the experience of communication breakdowns and miscommunications.

Discourse Using Simultaneous Communication

Interactions between hearing mothers and deaf children using simultaneous communication present a more positive tone. The interactions are generally described as comfortable and stimulating (Gardner and Zorfass, 1983; Meadow, Greenberg, Erting, and Carmichael, 1981; Preisler, 1981). Dialogues presented by Schlesinger and Meadow (1972) and Preisler (1981) indicated that mothers' and children's responses to one another were contingent and that dyads were able to maintain topics through second and third turns.

Direct comparisons of dyads showed that hearing mothers using simultaneous communication were much more successful interactors than mothers using speech alone. Shafer and Lynch (1981) studied the linguistic growth of six deaf children, between 15 and 34 months of age, who used simultaneous communication with their mothers. Their subjects consistently demonstrated larger expressive vocabularies and higher mean length of utterances (MLUs) than children using aural-oral communication. These children were also able to repair communication breakdowns when the listener appeared not to understand their speech.

Greenberg (1980) compared the social interaction skills of 14 aural-oral and 14 simultaneous communication mother-child dyads. The children were between the ages of three and five years. Mothers and children in both groups were able to initiate interactions on an equitable basis, and no differences were found between the dyads in terms of topic selection. Simultaneous communication dyads, however, were found to conduct interactions that were significantly longer and more complex than those conducted by the aural-oral dyads. Meadow and colleagues (1981) elaborated upon Greenberg's study by adding two additional classifications of dyads. These included one in which both partners had hearing and one in which both partners were deaf. The results indicated no significant differences between the interaction of hearing-hearing dyads and the deaf-deaf dyads. Both of these groups were able to carry on conversation about each other and nonpresent objects and events. Deaf-hearing dyads using simultaneous communication were found to be functioning at a level in between the oral dyads and the other two groups. Hearing dyads using oral-only communication spent significantly less time engaged in interaction than did the other three groups. These dyads also had the least number of child-initiated bouts and the highest proportion of nonelaborated bouts.

These studies point out the necessity of close monitoring of the quality and development of communicative interaction between hearing mothers and deaf children. Ideally, the mother should become sensitive to the dyadic interactional abilities and be able to adjust her communicative behavior as required. In order to do this, mothers need to be in contact with professionals who are supportive and open and who can provide guidance relative to all aspects of communication. Successful mother-child communication is crucial if the deaf child is to enter school with any of the discourse abilities needed to participate in learning. Meadow and colleagues (1981) point out that deafness in and of itself does not preclude the development of positive mother-child interaction. A match between the communication style of the mother and the child is what seems to be important in order for interactions to be successful.

DISCOURSE ABILITIES WITH PEERS

Several groups of investigators have found that hearing impaired children interact more with their teachers than they do with their peers (Anitia, 1982; Brackett and Henniges, 1976; Kennedy, Northcott, McCauley, and Williams, 1976; McCauley and Bruininks, 1976). This seems to be the case regardless of age, setting, oral communication ability, or hearing status of peers. In observations of preschool hearing and hearing impaired children, McCauley and Bruininks (1976) found that hearing preschoolers interacted with a greater number of peers and to a greater extent than did hearing impaired children. Interactions between the hearing children and their teachers were significantly fewer than those of hearing impaired children and their teachers.

Types of communication interactions and the conditions that influenced them were described by Brackett and Henniges (1976). More peer interactions occurred during free play than during structured language time. Hearing impaired children also initiated more peer interactions during free play than during structured lessons. However, the number of responses to initiations of others were about the same in both settings. Those with higher linguistic ability interacted more often with hearing children than did hearing impaired children with a low linguistic level; however, all hearing impaired children spent more time with other hearing impaired children than they did with hearing children. In at least one study, interactions between hearing and hearing impaired preschoolers increased over a two year observation period (Craig and Douglas, 1976); nevertheless, even in this instance the deaf children tended to interact with one another more than with hearing peers.

Anitia (1982) studied deaf students in grades 1 through 6 who were partially integrated into mainstreamed settings and compared social interactions in each setting. As with the younger children, most hearing impaired children spent a large proportion of time interacting with their teachers, even in the mainstream classes. The total amount of communication between hearing impaired children and peers was about equal in integrated and special classes. Anitia concluded either that the special class environment was not any more conducive to student communication than was the integrated setting or that very few of the 32 children studied had the social skills necessary to initiate or continue a conversation even with other hearing impaired children.

Results on mode of communication indicated that these students used less rather than more oral communication in the integrated settings than in the special setting. Hearing impaired children may be embarrassed about speaking in front of hearing peers, or it may be that teachers in the hearing impaired class require more communication than the student would produce under voluntary conditions. At any rate, simply placing the hearing impaired student in a mainstream class does not ensure that his or her conversational ability will increase.

In a national survey of 557 hearing impaired adolescents between 11 and 16 years of age, a number of communication practices of students in the mainstream were reported (Libbey and Pronovost, 1980). About one half of the students had been mainstreamed for seven years or more. In a self-report the students stated that their mode of communication differed according to the situation. Although most said that they spoke to the majority of hearing people, many also said that they used writing as a major means of communicating to hearing peers. Most said that they used signing with their deaf friends, and about one fourth used interpreters to interact with mainstream teachers. In reporting "self-perceptions" of communication style only about 38 per cent of the students said that they often started conversations with others.

Major communication problems stated were related to the adolescents' feeling uncomfortable talking with hearing peers and teachers and not being able to comprehend what was said during a conversation. The students felt that most hearing people wanted to communicate with deaf people, but that their interactions often were plagued by inability to understand one another. The biggest school problem was that of joining in a class discussion with over 25 per cent reporting that they never joined in.

Brackett and Donnelly (1982) studied the abilities of hearing and hearing impaired students to identify junctures in conversations at which it would be possible for them to insert a comment. They found that visual and paralinguistic cues were all that were necessary for both hearing and hearing impaired adolescents to determine where various junctures in videotaped conversations were located. Paralinguistic conversational cues that are redundant with linguistic cues are available to hearing impaired persons with hearing below 250 Hertz. However, hearing impaired individuals generally have fewer linguistic cues available to them and are at a particular disadvantage in group situations with multiple speakers. In adult situations a hearing friend often will facilitate the participation of a hearing impaired member by pointing to the current speaker or by repeating what was said if a speaker is out of visual range. Brackett (1982) found that this was not likely to happen in groups of adolescents. Hearing peers are less likely to play the role of facilitator for a deaf student. In at attitude sampling of deaf mainstreamed adolescents, 48 per cent of the students indicated that they felt left out of peer conversations and tended not to participate in conversations that involved more than one other person.

Thus it appears that being able to perform academically, or even having knowledge of the linguistic content necessary for participating in a conversation, is not enough. Even the most successful hearing impaired students may not be able to take part in the classroom structure of a mainstream class placement. Nor can it be taken for granted that the student will improve his social or conversational skills simply by being integrated with hearing students.

Brackett and Maxon (1978) investigated one hearing impaired child's ability to adapt messages to listeners varying in knowledge, visual acuity, and age. The eight year old child was able to adapt her language appropriately to an 18 month old by using higher pitch and exaggerated duration in speaking. However, she was not able to adapt her language to help adults complete a task until specific information was requested ("I can't see; which one is it?"). Brackett concluded that hearing impaired children may possess some of the pragmatic skills needed for adapting communication according to the listener's needs but may be unaware of the need or of the situations in which to do so. The importance of training communicative functions along with language structure cannot be overlooked if the hearing impaired student is going to be able to communicate with his peers and people outside the classroom setting.

Interaction Process Analysis (IPA) (Bales, 1950) was used to study problem-solving skills of hearing impaired students during small group interactions (Pendergrass and Hodges, 1976). The adapted Bales system included 12 categories related to group interaction that reflected (1) positive reactions, (2) negative reactions, (3) attempted answers, and (4) questions. Groups of six hearing impaired students using total communication were observed and behaviors coded. The results showed that students were not able to ask for information, ask for suggestions, or ask for others' opinions. They were able to make statements, give information and directions, agree or disagree, and show friendship or antagonism. Communications that indicated positive social-emotional problem-solving development were more evident in groups of older students, suggesting that deaf children tend to become more socially positive toward accepting ideas from others as they mature. Questioning strategies, however, remained a major difficulty for even older students.

Hearing impaired students in both speaker and listener roles were studied during communication breakdowns (Donnelly and Brackett, 1982). Hearing impaired listeners were able to give the forms of feedback listed in the literature as being indicative of their not understanding. However, explicit feedback such as "What?" occurred most often. Speakers responded most often by giving exact repetitions of utterances or by repetition of the operative word in an utterance. This study suggested that hearing impaired students are able to use pragmatic skills similar to those used by hearing persons in daily conversation; however, because their repertoire of skills may be limited, they may often be perceived as changing the topic abruptly or appear rude by using one type of explicit feedback ("What?") when a more polite or subtle form would be called for ("Pardon me, what did you say?").

The studies on discourse abilities with peers point out the importance of careful and strategic planning on the part of the classroom teacher to ensure that situations exist within lessons for hearing impaired students to communicate with one another.

DISCOURSE ABILITIES AND THE TEACHER

Many investigations have focused on communication that occurs in the classroom between the teacher and hearing impaired students. During the 1970s these studies were called "classroom interaction studies" and were conducted by placing live observers in the classroom who recorded communication behaviors on some time interval basis. Predetermined category systems were employed to keep track of the types of behaviors that occurred. Finally, observations were quantified and results reported in regard to the amount and type of communication that occurred in classrooms for the hearing impaired.

More recently these studies of classroom communication have been focused on pragmatic skills of students, and the teacher has been viewed as a facilitator of language use. These "discourse" studies have been carried out with the use of videotape and transcription methods derived from the field of linguistics. Findings from these studies have been much more descriptive than quantitative and have resulted in conclusions regarding the social structure of the classroom and the students' abilities as conversational participants.

Both interaction and discourse studies have provided us with an insight into the difficulties that face the hearing impaired child who is dependent on the classroom environment for a major portion of his or her language exposure. In application of these methodologies the language of the teacher has been described in much greater detail than that of the students. By understanding the teacher as speaker, model, listener, critic, and major source of language input, researchers can shed light on the needs of the hearing impaired student in the areas of conversational and social interaction skills.

In this section findings from classroom interaction studies are presented first, followed by studies of discourse abilities of hearing impaired students with their teachers.

Classroom Interaction Studies

For the most part investigators of communication behaviors of teachers and hearing impaired students have employed a version of the Flanders (1960, 1965) interaction analysis system to quantify observations. This system has been recognized as one of the most sophisticated techniques for this purpose and was first adapted for use with hearing impaired students by Craig and Collins (1970). In the Flanders procedure emphasis is on the verbal communication between the teacher and student with direct-indirect teacher influence as the primary dimension of interest. Craig and Collins extended the Flanders system from 10 to 20 categories, including 9 categories for teacher talk, 9 categories for student talk, and 2 categories for lack of communication. Observers were trained to use this system by recording communication behaviors at 3 second intervals.

Craig and Collins used their system to study the classrooms of hearing impaired students at the primary, intermediate, and high school level. Communication at all levels was found to be teacher dominated, with the most frequently used types of communications being "questioning" and "informing." Very little student-initiated talk occurred, especially during language-dependent academic lessons.

Craig and Holman (1973) and Collins and Rose (1976) observed communication behaviors of hearing impaired students in "open" classroom environments. Observers used the Craig and Collins adaptation of the Flanders system to observe teacher-initiated communication, and used the Pittsburgh Revised Interaction Analysis system (Craig and Holman, 1973) to observe individual student communication behaviors. Students were found to initiate and influence more communication than those who had been studied in traditional classroom settings (Craig and Collins, 1970). Craig and Holman concluded that open classroom environments were more conducive to active student participation than were traditional settings. Therefore, it seems that the free play situation that was found to be facilitative for peer interaction at the preschool level might well be extended to a less-structured class environment for older hearing impaired children.

Wolff (1977) compared the Flanders observational system used by Craig and Collins (1970) to the Cognitive Verbal-Nonverbal Observation System (CVNC). The CVNC included categories for communication intent, four levels of cognitive implications, and categories for mode of communication. Observers coded behaviors at 6 second intervals. The CVNC indicated four times more student communication than did the Flanders system (Craig and Collins, 1970), since the Flanders system allowed only for coding of verbal interactions. Wolff found that deaf students used formal language only 20 to 30 per cent of the time in their classroom communication and nonverbal or gestural communication the rest of the time. Wolff pointed out that the sole use of verbal categories without examination of gestural communication would result in invalid results regarding the communication of hearing impaired students. In a comparison of teachers of the deaf with other public school teachers, the teachers of the deaf were found to be less directive; that is, hearing impaired students were allowed more communication time by their teachers than were students in public school classes. However, at all grade levels and across oral and total communication settings the vast majority of communications were at the lowest cognitive (memory) level. Inference questions occurred, on the average, for less than 1 minute of an entire academic period in hearing impaired classrooms.

Lawson (1978) used the Craig and Collins (1970) adaptation of the Flanders system as well as a compliant versus self-directive measure (Parker and French, 1971) to determine whether intermediate-level hearing impaired students spent more classroom communication time on compliant communication or on self-directive communication. No differences were found between the percentage of compliant and self-directive sign-speech communications of students; however, students in this study were found to be communicating 62 per cent of the time and teachers only 34 per cent of the time. The categories of self-directive communications used most often by the students were asking questions and informing. It is interesting to note that no students used the category "development of another person's idea."

Results of interaction studies suggest a number of patterns regarding the classroom communication of hearing impaired students and the classroom as a language-learning environment. As a language-learning environment, it appears that a self-contained setting is more facilitating than is a mainstream setting. In a special class there are fewer students, and the teachers were found to allow more student talk than were teachers in regular public school classes. Open classrooms appear to be even more facilitative, since students take more responsibility for obtaining information about their work, and lessons are not presented by a teacher to the group.

Results of these studies also suggest that hearing impaired students have a limited repertoire of language structures to draw upon in conversing during lessons. There was general agreement among investigators that students used informing as their main category of communication. Although they were able to ask questions to obtain information from the teacher, they were not able to employ conversational strategies needed for small group interaction. Finally, communication in virtually all classrooms remained at the lowest cognitive level, that of memory. It may be that hearing impaired students are adept at giving information and asking for information because that is the type of communication interaction in which they are usually involved. Do teachers reduce their language to the most basic level in order to maintain the flow of the lesson, or are students unable to employ conversational strategies simply because of lack of exposure? The evidence is inconclusive. However, some of the more recent studies of conversational discourse support the findings presented here and provide more detail regarding the kinds of problems exhibited by hearing impaired students in conversing.

Studies of Classroom Discourse

In looking at classroom conversations between hearing impaired students and their teachers, investigators have drawn upon methods from the field of sociolinguistics for obtaining conversational samples and for analyzing them. Classroom conversations have been contrasted to naturally occurring conversations in the literature dealing with normally hearing children (Green and Wallat, 1981; Mehan, 1979). Investigators looking at hearing impaired students have related their findings to this literature.

For instance, Wood, McMahon, and Cranstoun (1980) found that in naturally occurring conversations, speakers negotiated the conditions under which they were willing to answer questions. For example:

Question: Do you enjoy teaching?
Response: "Yes, very much."
                         or
                "Why do you ask?"

Children in regular preschool classes, however, did not use these options. They tended to answer a question, when asked, but then they stopped talking. The teacher used a variety of options in responding to questions posed, but the students considered response a requirement when a question was addressed to them. In studying deaf preschoolers Wood and coworkers hypothesized that the children would make frequent mistakes in attempting to understand what kind of move the teacher was making. Preschool teachers are more likely to veer from the very structured question, answer, and follow-up sequence identified as typical of classroom conversation. Perhaps this variation is an attempt to make learning interesting and to keep the children motivated (Mehan, 1979). However, the deaf children performed very much like the hearing children. For example, they never confused an open-ended question with a closed-response question, nor did they treat a contribution made by the teacher as a question.

Through further analysis Wood and colleagues found that the adult style of conversational control greatly influenced the deaf child's contributions to classroom conversations. Teachers who exerted a high degree of control by asking questions were less likely to receive answers and were less likely to get double turns or elaborations from the students. Students were also much less spontaneous in their conversations. The more controlling the teacher, the more passive the children. Teachers who simply told the preschoolers what they thought about things, who showed reactions of disbelief, surprise, and so forth, received more questions from the children, and more frequent spontaneous contributions as well. The longest utterances by the children, in terms of MLU, came after comments made by the teacher, whereas the shortest utterances came after questions. In virtually all aspects of discourse studied the deaf children performed very similarly to hearing children. However, a major difference was found between teachers of hearing preschoolers and teachers of deaf preschoolers. In hearing classrooms no attempts were made to teach children how to express themselves better. Similar to adults at home, these teachers attended to the meaning of what was said. In classrooms of deaf children, however, teachers made the children very much aware of what was said, how they said it, and how it could be said more intelligibly.

Repair Strategies

Teachers of the hearing impaired use a number of repair strategies when miscommunications occur. Erber and Greer (1973) observed ten teachers at the Central Institute for the Deaf, and found four main repair strategies in use. Teachers repeated all or a selected part of an utterance. They emphasized certain parts of utterances through facial or acoustic stress. They altered an utterance through structural change, such as change in vocabulary or syntax. Finally, they used supplementary information in the form of cues or prompts within the context of an utterance. Emphasis and repetition were the most frequently used strategies.

Wood (1980) found wide variation in the use of repairs by teachers of the hearing impaired. Some teachers used as many as 70 per cent repair moves during a lesson. Other teachers used as few as 14 per cent repair moves. Wood noted that repair moves caused the conversation to backtrack. Repairs often caused a child and teacher to become mired in the speech correction exchange, so that the goal of the original exchange was lost.

Griffith, Panagos, and Ripich (1982) studied repair sequences in third, fourth, and fifth grade oral classes for the purpose of generating social participation rules in teacher-student exchanges. They found that teachers varied in their correction of speech errors across students. Some students were corrected much more often than others, and some students never received correction, even though speech errors were evident on the videotape. Although the cause of selective correction was not traced in this study, Wood (1980) found that the degree of hearing loss correlated highly with the degree of correction received. Griffith and colleagues did find that the students who received the greatest amount of speech correction offered the fewest spontaneous contributions to the lesson. They were more likely to say "I don't know" when responses were elicited by the teacher, and they were more passive than students who were rarely corrected.

Analysis of correction sequences revealed an underlying social participation rule employed by one teacher, as follows: When a speech error is made, the student is not rewarded for the content answer, even if it is correct. The following sequences illustrate this rule:

T   How many doors do you see?
S   Two door. (correct answer)
T   I see... (Begins repair.)
S   I see.
T   Two doorsss. (Stresses /s/.)
S   Two doors.
T   The whole thing.
S   I see two door.
T   doorsss.
S   doors.
T   So, how many doors are there? Bill. (Calls on different student.)
B   There are two doors.
T   Very good, right! (Rewards second student.)

Although the first student gave the correct content answer, he did not receive positive feedback for this answer from the teacher. Instead, he received correction of the form of his utterance. This pattern occurred for 42 per cent of the exchange sequences in which speech correction was used. In 35 per cent of the correction exchanges between another teacher and her students, positive feedback for a correct content answer was delayed until after the speech correction sequence occurred.

T   Do you think this sentence is complete or incomplete?
S   Ingomblede.
T   Let's try that word again.
S   Icomplede
T   That's better, watch your speech.
T   Okay, you are right, it is incomplete. Why do you think it is incomplete?

In none of the four classrooms studied did students consistently receive positive feedback for correct content answers before having their speech corrected. Based on this evidence Griffith and coworkers concluded that a second social participation rule deduced by students would be: The form of the answer is as important as the content of the answer. If this in fact is the message imparted to hearing impaired students, it is not surprising to find that they rarely initiate conversation in or out of the classroom.

Other Discourse Areas

Griffith and associates found, as did Wood and colleagues, that deaf children were basically competent at several discourse strategies in classroom conversations with their teacher. For instance, students were able to follow various surface forms used to indicate turn allocation. They responded to (1) their name only, when the task involved taking the next question in a series, or reading in turn; (2) boundary markers, including eye-gaze from the teacher and the words, "Okay, next"; and (3) requests for bids from the teacher ("Okay, who can tell me what that word means?") as well as many other common turn-allocation techniques used in the classroom. There were instances of miscommunication when students responded to a gestural cue rather than a verbal one. For instance, students had been reading as a group from a chart and then discussing the story. At one point, the teacher asked, "Who do you think this person is?" and pointed to the name in the story. In response to her gesture toward the chart the class immediately began to read again as a group. These instances of miscue were not frequent, however, and overall students were able to participate at the interaction level.

Students were able to tell the difference between a teacher repetition that served as a correction and one that served as acceptance of an answer, even though the content of the teacher's utterances were exactly the same:

1. Acceptance	T	How are these alike?
	S	Both are mammals.
	T	Both are mammals. (Falling intonation at the end indicating an acceptance.)
	S	(Student does not speak.)
2. Correction	T	Okay, M, did you hear that? How are these alike?
	M	Bo ah mammal.
	T	Both are mammalsss. (Louder and stress on /th/ and /s/, indicating a correction.)
	M	Bot ah mammas. (Student responds to correction.)

Even though the content of the teacher's two utterances was exactly the same, the two students knew what kind of response was required of them. Whether, as suggested by Brackett (1980), the students are able to attend to the paralinguistic information available below 250 hertz, or whether the facial expression of the teacher gives them a clue, they are obviously not relying on lipreading alone to follow the conversation.

Students were also found to be able to follow lesson activities and to change activities without explicit verbal instruction from the teacher.

S	The cat's got your tongue. (Students read together.)
T	What's the verb in that sentence?
S	students raise hands
T	B (Calls on student.)
B	Got
T	Got. Okay.
T	Okay, M (Looks at M, and then at the board.)
M	She is always beating around the bush."

In this example, M knew that she was supposed to read the next sentence, even though this was a departure from the pattern the lesson had taken earlier. Up to this point, the class had been reading each sentence as a group. It appears on the basis of the two discourse studies presented so far that hearing impaired students are able to participate in the conversational sequences that occur during lessons. At least this is the case within the special class setting and in conjunction with the teacher as the main conversational partner.

Focusing more on the teacher's style of communication, Kluwin (1981, 1983) conducted two discourse studies in secondary classrooms for hearing impaired students. Attention-getting devices were examined in the first study as well as attention maintenance. The problems of attending during group discussions for hearing impaired students (Lawson, 1978; Pendergrass and Hodges, 1976) were discussed previously in the chapter. Attention-getting devices of teachers using total communication were found to be very similar to those used by deaf adults in gaining the attention of a potential addressee. The strategies involved increasing proximity until the person responded. The teachers used hand waves or "R" handshapes to signal ready (if at least one student was looking). If this was unsuccessful, the teacher tapped on one or more students' desks. If still unsuccessful, the teacher would touch one or more students on the arm or shoulder.

Maintaining attention during instruction was very difficult. Kluwin described problems that occurred when one student did not see a response given by another student. Erber and Zeizer (1974) found that the most convenient attending strategy for the deaf student is to continue looking at the teacher, even when someone else is talking. This caused problems for the students, if they were called upon to contribute following the contribution of a peer. They were able to see what the teacher's follow-up to a response was but they did not know what the first student's response had been.

Kluwin also found that students were not always able to tell when a teacher was marking a speaking-turn. Teachers using total communication were found to mark a turn in the oral mode without marking it in the manual mode. The result was often a lapse in the flow of the lesson. Because the students did not respond, the teacher waited and then had to repeat or modify her message. Kluwin concluded that interaction used by hearing teachers in secondary level total communication classes was functional but inefficient for maintaining the flow of the lesson.

In a second discourse study Kluwin (1983) described teaching episodes in four total communication classes at the secondary level. In this study differences in hearing and deaf teacher style was discussed.

Kluwin outlined two types of instructional strategies employed by teachers. Procedural episodes were employed to review material or reinforce something already presented. Topical episodes involved the development of a complex idea or an abstract concept. Procedural episodes were easier for students to follow. In analyzing topical episodes, differences were found between the strategies the hearing and the deaf teachers used to get through the episode. Deaf teachers had much longer topical episodes with their students that ended more often with the deaf student arriving at the right answer. Hearing teachers tended to give the deaf students the correct answer after only a few conversational exchanges. The deaf teachers also began the questioning of students with higher cognitive level questions. Kluwin found that this strategy allowed for more flexibility, since it allowed the teacher the option of shifting down if the students were unable to answer. Using lower demand questions to initiate an instructional sequence reduced the teachers' alternatives either to repeating the question another way or to giving the answer. Kluwin also found that language facility between the teacher and the students in this case (sign language) was related to the instructional success of the teacher. Johnson and Griffith (1985) compared teaching episodes in a self-contained class for hearing impaired students and a class of hearing students. Two of the hearing impaired students were going to be mainstreamed. The two fourth grade classes were videotaped during a spelling lesson. The lessons were analyzed using Sinclair and Coulthard's (1975) system for analyzing classroom discourse.

The structure of teaching episodes was found to be very different in the two classes. Episodes in the general education class, although patterned, were marked by variety of language structures and complexity in form. In the hearing impaired class episodes were found to be constructed of very simple language forms and were much more redundant in function. The spelling lesson in the general education class included three very different academic tasks, reflected in the patterns of teaching episodes within each task. These tasks moved from several episodes related to the spelling list to individual seatwork and checking the workbooks to work at the blackboard. Each academic task was clearly discernible from the others, according to the types of interactions that occurred between the teacher and the students.

In the hearing impaired class, only one continuous academic task could be identified. The entire lesson focused on the spelling list. Episodes revolved around single words. The pattern of exchanges between teacher and students consisted of sets of five different utterances: (1) utterances by the teacher asking the students to say the word, (2) utterances asking the students to sign the word, (3) utterances asking the students to use the word in a sentence, (4) utterances asking students to tell the meaning of the word, and (5) utterances asking the students to find the key word, which explained how the spelling word should be pronounced. The use of one or more of these utterances accounted for all instructional exchanges within the lesson.

Just as a point of contrast, the teacher in the general education class used a total of 32 different utterances in requesting information from her students. This difference in the variety of language used exemplifies differences found at all levels of the lesson analyses.

These authors concluded that closer examination of teacher style, complexity of information, and teacher-student discourse of the self-contained setting and the prospective mainstream setting are necessary before placing hearing impaired students. In this study, being able to spell fourth grade spelling words would not be enough to ensure successful achievement in the mainstream class.

The discourse analysis studies suggest that hearing impaired students are able to interact with their teachers and do seem to be able to apply at least some basic pragmatic skills during instruction. Although results are far from conclusive, students appeared to have fewer discourse ambiguities when they were able to rely on their residual hearing for some of their conversational cues. Students in total communication classes, at least at the secondary level, experienced some difficulty when the discourse demands depended upon visual cues. Although there are only a few studies available that employ discourse analysis techniques, these few represent well the specific information concerning teacher-student conversations that can be obtained. Information such as that described here can be of great value in determining the conversational abilities of hearing impaired students and in examining the intervention strategies currently in use.

STRATEGIES FOR IMPROVING DISCOURSE ABILITIES IN HEARING IMPAIRED CHILDREN

Parent Training Strategies

Professionals working in the field of hearing impairment realized the need for early intervention long before legislation mandated it. Preschool programs for the hearing impaired have existed for many years; however, until the last decade most programs offered only the aural-oral approach to language intervention. Intervention techniques followed those in the mainstream of language disorders, and parents were taught to focus on having the child speak in complete sentences. Parents were encouraged to talk to their hearing impaired children and to disregard any kind of gestural communication used by their children. Forms of manual communication were thought to hinder the development of speech, and speech was equated with language. The more current perspective toward early intervention proposed by many professionals (Champie, 1981; Clark and Watkins, 1978) focuses on the needs of the individual child. This view includes the determination for each child of the mode of communication that will be most facilitative to the development of communication. Several programs available for parent-infant training provide procedures for determining communication prescriptions, including the Texas Curriculum (Champie, 1981) and the Sky-High program (Clark and Watkins, 1978). Procedures similar to those included in these two programs were devised by Dastoli (1981) for making communication prescriptions for hearing impaired children. The procedures were based primarily on the child's aided auditory threshold and information regarding speechreading ability and reliance on the visual channel for communication. By entering data from these areas along with other information about hearing status of the parents, intelligence, motor skills, visual acuity, and socioemotional development into a flow chart, one of five communication prescriptions would be selected for use with the child. The communication prescriptions were as follows:

1. Aural communication: The child should be able to acquire language through the auditory channel when fitted with an appropriate hearing aid.
2. Aural-oral, Style A: The child should be able to acquire language through the combined use of the aided auditory channel and speechreading.
3. Aural-oral, Style B: The child should be able to acquire language through the combined use of aided hearing, speechreading, and fingerspelling when needed to clarify consonant sound confusion.
4. Total communication, Style A: The child should be able to acquire language through the combined use of aided hearing, speechreading, and fingerspelling. Sign language would be used to supplement these modes when needed.
5. Total Communication, Style B: The child should be able to acquire language through the combined use of all modes mentioned in Numbers 1 through 4; however, aided hearing and speechreading would be supplemental to sign language and fingerspelling.

Implementation of communication prescriptions according to most parent-infant programs is not fixed but can be changed as the child's communication skills develop or as the parents' communication skills develop. The most important component of early intervention is the instruction of the parents regarding communication strategies to be used with their hearing impaired child. Successful communication with significant others in the environment may be the crucial factor in determining the child's final level of language development. As indicated by the literature reviewed in this chapter, classroom and clinical approaches to language intervention to date have been only minimally successful with hearing impaired children.

The shift to total communication during the last few years in the majority of school programs should not be viewed as a panacea. Layton, Holmes, and Bradley (1979) found that preschoolers instructed through the total communication method were not developing language in a sequence comparable with that measured in normally hearing infants. Expressive language was categorized according to the semantic system devised by Bloom, Lightbown, and Hood (1975). Layton and colleagues attributed this language variance to the idea that the hearing impaired children were "instructed" in language in a school setting. The language of the hearing impaired children was stilted and was absent of semantic categories needed for conversing. Layton and colleagues pointed out the importance of appropriate parent training. The parents in their study signed very little with their children at home.

Parents who opt for a total communication placement for their child need to be instructed not only in the sign system being used by the school but also in those aspects of caregiver-child interaction that have been found to be facilitative in studies of language acquisition. For instance, question forms and expansions of child utterances have been found to be positively correlated to language growth in the child, (Newport, Gleitman, and Gleitman, 1977) whereas imperatives, self-repetitions, negation of child actions, monologuing, and frequent topic changes have been found to be negatively correlated with language growth in the child (Bradley, Caldwell, and Elardo, 1977; McDonald and Pien, 1982).

Many teachers as well as parents must become more attuned to the level of the child's communicative skill. In instances in which parents or teachers are just learning how to sign, the adult communication partner may be too concerned with signing each and every morpheme and not be aware of the limits of the child's attention span or interests. In many cases the structure of the message is far above the child's current comprehension level. Instructing parents to focus on the meaning and the purpose of the message will undoubtedly prove more successful than attending to the form alone. Studies of mother-infant interaction suggest that early mother communication is simpler in structure and more redundant than that addressed to older children and adults (Cross, 1978; McDonald and Pien, 1982). It may be that parent trainers should stress sign vocabulary acquisition, so that parents will have a large cadre of signs to choose from in communicating with their children. Parents should also be encouraged to fingerspell short words or meanings for which they have not yet learned a sign. This not only reduces frustration on the part of the parent in trying to converse but enhances speech sound recognition in the child. Establishing successful parent-child communication as early as possible is paramount to the development of all other aspects of learning in the hearing impaired child.

Classroom Techniques

With the application of sociolinguistic approaches to the study of classroom interaction and the emphasis upon the instructional conversation as a message unit, there has been a shift in perspective concerning the communication skills needed by the child and the means through which he or she can best acquire them. The literature presented throughout this book is one form of evidence that language learning is most likely to occur in the context of conversations. The child who can fulfill the responsibilities of being a conversational participant will be the most successful language learner. Strategies that provide children with the opportunity to be successful as a communication partner can be said to be the most facilitative. Language instruction that falls short of providing the child with such strategies, and the opportunities to employ them, is inefficient at best.

Several authors provided suggestions for improving the conversational and interactional skills of hearing impaired students. Strategies fell into two broad areas: (1) those that assisted the student in gaining access to classroom information, and (2) those that assisted the child in participating in group conversation. Four main areas, including skills of attending, skills for spontaneous interaction, strategies for clarifying one's communication, and social skills were outlined by Duffield (1980) as necessary for group participation. Skills of attending could be modeled by the teacher, who would attend to a speaker for an entire statement. Hearing impaired students are notorious for not attending to one another's statements, responses, questions, and comments. Teachers could assist in developing this skill by pointing out who is talking and waiting for students to focus on that person.

Spontaneous interaction was listed as one of the most difficult areas for hearing impaired adolescents in their self-reports (Brackett, 1983).

Facilitation of peer communication could be accomplished by mediation on the teacher's part, such as reporting what kinds of communication were occurring (e.g., "Mike, John asked you a question"). The teacher could also incorporate attending skills and spontaneous interaction by asking questions such as, "Mike, what do you think of John's idea?" Teachers might also assist students in contributing ideas to a conversation by helping them build a repertoire of possible comments or by giving them a list of comments that would continue a conversation. Later, students might be asked to decide if sample comments were appropriate or inappropriate for various conversations.

Duffield pointed out that students who are unable to follow peer comments in a self-contained class cannot be expected to contribute appropriately in a mainstream setting. Since it is not likely that language lessons in self-contained classrooms for deaf students have focused on conversational interaction among group members in the past, it is not surprising that so many mainstreamed adolescents reported that they never participated in class discussions or initiated conversations with their peers.

Students could also be positively reinforced for using a strategy not previously in their repertoires. For instance, a student might be rewarded for maintaining eye contact during conversation, first with close friends, and then with other classmates, other teachers, and so forth.

Several other techniques that Duffield suggested included modeling, rehearsal, and feedback. Modeling involves the students' observation of others. Teachers could set up situations in which the students could observe two adults or other students engaged in the use of a particular conversational skill, from beginning to end. A videotape strategy such as that used by Brackett and Maxon (1978) for research purposes could be used for training students to identify junctures in conversations in which interruptions could occur, and then students could be asked to insert a real message.

Rehearsal is currently considered a negative language intervention strategy in the education of hearing impaired students, since emphasis upon it in the past has resulted in stilted language use and rote sentence patterns by deaf students. However, rehearsal of conversation situations would assist the student in assimilating the discourse and behavioral requirements of various conversational roles. Conversations can be practiced for situations that are significant to the student, such as interviewing for a job or asking someone for a date.

Feedback is providing the student, as a conversational partner, information as to the current status of the conversation. Rather than correcting a speech error, a teacher might say, "Pardon me, I don't know what you said." By incorporating the rehearsal strategy and the feedback strategy, the hearing impaired student could better learn to ask for clarification and not assume that a communication breakdown is totally the result of their handicap. Hearing impaired students should also be given information concerning communication breakdowns, as experienced by hearing persons. The research suggests that hearing impaired students are very self-conscious about the possibility of misunderstanding or being misunderstood. It is very likely that many students are unaware that hearing speakers also experience communication breakdowns and also experience miscommunication. Upon realizing that the responsibility for communicating is shared by both conversants, some students may feel more confident about attempting to interact.

One technique, developed at the National Technical Institute for the Deaf (NTID), employed the use of videotapes of succesful conversations. Students viewed the tapes, analyzed the conversations, and then role-played specific communicative situations before the camera. Participants as well as their peers analyzed the resultant tapes. This interpersonal skills course employed role-playing, third-party appraisal, and confrontation training. Confrontation training informs the student about the difference between the speaker's message and the listener's needs and the relationship between the message and how the listener performs. By observing the relationship as a third party, the students are able to notice the causal aspect of a listener's confusion if the speaker's message is ambiguous.

Johnson and Griffith (1982) developed a videotape strategy for preparing hearing impaired students to be mainstreamed. Regular class teachers were videotaped during typical lessons with hearing students. These tapes were analyzed for nonverbal and verbal clues that signalled the various juncture points in the lesson. Teacher style of presentation was also analyzed. Teachers were found to have very predictable communication patterns. For instance, when one teacher was presenting information to be given on a test, he wrote the information on an overhead. When he was opening the floor to discussion of material that would not be on the test he stood out to the side of his desk. These tapes were used as a preparation technique for hearing impaired adolescents. The students viewed the tapes, and were instructed in the information about the teacher. The tapes were also used for speechreading practice for the students. When actually mainstreamed into the classrooms, students appeared to adjust more quickly in the classes in which they were familiar with the teacher's communication patterns.

Emphasizing conversational skills does not necessarily mean that students are adept at all other levels of language use. However, language intervention can be carried out in an interactive framework from the very early stages. Gawlik, McAleer, and Ozer (1976) developed an intervention strategy used at Kendall Elementary School called Adaptive Dialogue. Gawlik and associates found that hearing impaired students did not have a way of signaling when they did not understand what had been said by the teacher. Children rarely admitted to not understanding but often either failed to comply with requests or made inappropriate responses. Students rarely requested a repetition of the teacher's utterance or asked the teacher to slow down. Through implementation of the Adaptive Dialogue, students were taught to use interactive phrases to signal their need for help. The simplest interactive phrase was, "I don't know." Teachers were taught to respond with facilitative phrases such as, "How can I help you?" Then strategy phrases that represented a means of control for the student in maintaining the conversation were introduced to students. These phrases included:

"Again, please."
"Again, slow."
"Write, please."
"Show me."
"Do it with me."
"Talk loud."
"Help me."

Students who functioned at a higher linguistic level were taught to use more sophisticated phrases. In implementing this Adaptive Dialogue, Gawlik and coworkers found that teachers rated it as very useful, and at least one half of the students could use most of the phrases. All students were able to use at least the interactive phrase which signaled the need for help.

CONCLUSION

The information presented in this chapter leaves no doubt that intervention strategies to date have failed to provide the hearing impaired child with the skills needed to be a successful conversational participant. The literature presented on interactions with mothers, peers, and teachers indicates that mere exposure to communication partners will not lead to the development of interactional strategies. Although it appears that children of hearing mothers who use total communication have an advantage over profoundly deaf children who communicate with their mothers through the oral method, there are very few of these students who have completed an educational program as of yet. The evidence regarding total communication remains inconclusive. The studies by Kluwin (1981, 1983) point out the pitfalls of teachers, who are not fluent signers themselves, in trying to implement such a communication approach. At least for now, communication mode alone cannot resolve the problem. A positive approach to the conversational difficulties faced by the hearing impaired populations seems to lie in a combination of new research techniques that analyze the conversation as it occurs and involve strategic planning on the part of professionals. Conversation should no longer be thought of as simply the medium through which lessons are accomplished. Conversational skills must be incorporated into the goals of the lesson. Most especially, language time in classrooms for hearing impaired students must focus on dialogue. Teaching syntactic skills may have to be postponed until students are able to master the interactive requirements of their language. Teachers can become aware of the conversational abilities of their students and of their own teaching styles by videotaping any lesson and then observing how many turns are given to each student. What are the typical topics introduced during classtime? Are students allowed or encouraged to use phrases that they might need outside of the academic lessons? Are students allowed to introduce their own topics of conversation? Do they know how to initiate conversation? These questions are crucial to the language development of any hearing impaired student, because for many students school is the main source of social communication, or any communication, each day. If teaching and learning occur through conversations, then perhaps conversing can be taught.

REFERENCES

Anitia, S. D. (1982). Social interaction of partially mainstreamed hearing-impaired children. *American Annals of the Deaf, 127*, 18–25.

Au, K., and Mason, J. (1983). Cultural congruence in classroom participation structures: Achieving a balance of rights. *Discourse Processes, 6*, 145–167.

Bales, R. F. (1950). *Interaction process analysis*. Reading, MA: Addison-Wesley Press.

Bellugi, U., and Klima, E. (1972). The roots of language in the sign talk of the deaf, *Psychology Today, 6*, 61–76.

Bloom, L., Lightbown, P., and Hood, L. (1975). Structure and variation in child language. *Monographs of the Society for Research in Child Development, 40*(2).

Bradley, R. H., Caldwell, B., and Elardo, R. (1977). Home environment social status and mental test performance. *Journal of Educational Psychology, 69*, 697–701.

Brackett, D. (1983). Group communication strategies for the hearing impaired. *Volta Review, 85*(5), 116–128.

Brackett, D., and Donnelly, J. (1982). *Hearing impaired adolescents' judgment of appropriate conversational entry points.* Paper presented at the American Speech-Language-Hearing Association Convention, Toronto.

Brackett, D., and Henniges, M. (1976). Communicative interaction of preschool hearing impaired children in an integrated setting. *Volta Review, 78*(6), 276–285.

Brackett, D., and Maxon, A. (1978). Oral habilitation update. Unpublished working papers. University of Connecticut, Storrs.

Cheskin, A. (1981). The verbal environment provided by hearing mothers for their young deaf children. *Journal of Communication Disorders, 14,* 485–496.

Clark, T. C., and Watkins, C. (1978). *The sky high model: A comprehensive model for identification, language facilitation, and family support for hearing handicapped children through home management ages birth through six.* Logan: Utah State University Department of Communication Disorders. (ERIC Document Reproduction Service No. ED 162 451).

Collins, J. L., and Rose, S. (1976). Communicative interaction patterns in an open environment for deaf high school students. *American Annals of the Deaf, 121,* 497–501.

Craig, W., and Collins, J. (1970). Analysis of communicative interaction in classes for deaf children. *American Annals of the Deaf, 115,* 79–85.

Craig, H., and Douglas, C. L. (1976). *Aural alternatives for deaf students.* Pittsburgh: Western Pennsylvania School for the Deaf.

Craig, H., and Holman, G. (1973). The "open classroom" in a school for the deaf. *American Annals of the Deaf, 118,* 675–685.

Cross, T. (1978). Mothers' speech and its association with rate of linguistic development in young children. In N. Waterson, and C. Snow (Eds.), *The Development of Communication.* New York: John Wiley.

Dastoli S. (1981). *Assessment of communication potential of hearing impaired children in the Warren-Champion schools.* Unpublished document, Kent State University, Department of Special Education, Kent, OH.

DeStefano, J., Pepinsky, H., and Sanders, T. (1982). Discourse rules for literacy learning in a classroom. In L. C. Wilkinson. (Ed.), *Communicating in the Classroom.* New York: Academic Press.

Donnelly, J., and Brackett, D. (1982, November). *Conversational skills of hearing impaired adolescents: a simulated TV interview.* A paper presented at the American Speech-Language-Hearing Association Convention, Toronto, Canada.

Duffield, J. (1980). Skills and strategies for preparing a hearing impaired child for participation in a group. *Volta Review, 84,* 45–51.

Eder, D. (1982). Differences in communicative styles across ability groups. In L. C. Wilkinson (Ed.), *Communicating in the Classroom.* New York: Academic Press.

Erber, P., and Greer, C. (1973). Communication strategies used by teachers at an oral school for the deaf. *Volta Review, 9,* 480–485.

Erber, P., and Zeiser, M. (1974). Classroom observation under conditions of simulated profound deafness. *Volta Review, 76,* 352–360.

Erting, C. (1981). An anthropological approach to the study of the communicative competence of deaf children. *Sign Language Studies, 32,* 221–237.

Fillmore, L. (1982). Instructional language as linguistic input: Second language learning in classrooms. In L. C. Wilkinson (Ed.), *Communicating in the Classroom.* New York: Academic Press.

Flanders, N. (1960; 1965). *Teacher influence: Pupil attitudes and achievement.*

Research Manual, University of Minnesota, Minneapolis.

Gardner, J., and Zorfass, J. (1983). From sign to speech: The language development of hearing impaired children. *American Annals of the Deaf, 128*(1), 20–24.

Gawlik, R., McAleer, M., and Ozer, M. N. (1976). Language for adaptive interaction. *American Annals of the Deaf, 121*, 556–559.

Green, J. L., and Harker, J. O. (1982). Gaining access to Learning: Conversational, social, and cognitive demands of group participation. In L. C. Wilkinson (Ed.), *Communicating in the classroom*. New York: Academic Press.

Green J., and Wallat, C. (Eds.), (1981). *Ethnography and language in educational settings*. Norwood, NJ: Ablex.

Greenberg, M. T. (1980). Social interaction between deaf preschoolers and their mothers: The effects of communication method and communication competence. *Developmental Psychology, 10*(5), 465–474.

Gregory, S., Mogford, K., and Bishop, J. (1978). Mothers' speech to young hearing impaired children. *Journal of the British Association of Teachers of the Deaf, 3*(2), 42.

Griffith, P., Panagos, J., and Ripich, D. (1982, November). *Classroom discourse: Speech-context and socialization rules*. Paper presented at the American Speech-Language-Hearing Association Convention, Toronto, Canada.

Johnson, H., and Griffith, P. (1982, June). *A videotape protocol for analyzing teacher communication: A mainstreaming preparation strategy*. Paper presented at the Alexander Graham Bell Convention, Toronto, Canada.

Johnson, H., and Griffith, P. (1985). The spelling class as a context: Classroom interaction in mainstream and special education settings. Manuscript submitted for publication.

Jones, O. H. (1977). Mother-child communication with pre-linguistic Down's syndrome and normal infants. In H. R. Schaffer (Ed.), *Studies in Mother-Infant Interaction*. New York: Academic Press.

Kennedy, P., Northcott, W., McCauley, R., and Williams, S. (1976). Longitudinal sociometric and cross sectional data on mainstreamed hearing impaired children: Implications for the school planning. *Volta Review, 78*, 71–81.

Kluwin, T. (1981). A preliminary description of the control of interaction in classrooms using manual communication. *American Annals of the Deaf, 126*, 510–514.

Kluwin, T. (1983). Discourse in deaf classrooms: The structure of teaching episodes. *Discourse Processes, 6*, 275–293.

Lawson, C. (1978). Patterns of communication in intermediate level classrooms of the deaf. *Audiology and Hearing Education, 4*, 19–36.

Layton, T., Holmes, D., and Bradley, P. (1979). A description of pedagogically imposed signed semantic-syntactic relationships in deaf children. *Sign Language Studies, 23*, 137–160.

Libbey, S., and Pronovost, W. (1980). Communication practices of mainstreamed hearing impaired adolescents. *Volta Review, 82*, 197–213.

McCauley, R. W., and Bruininks, R. H. (1976). Behavior interactions of hearing impaired children in regular classrooms. *Journal of Special Education, 10*, 277–284.

McDonald, L., and Pien D. (1982). Mother conversational behavior as a function of interactional intent. *Journal of Child Language, 9*, 337–358.

Meadow, K. P., Greenberg, M. T., Erting, C., and Carmichael, H. (1981). Interactions of deaf mothers and deaf preschool children: Comparisons with three other groups of deaf and hearing dyads. *American Annals of the Deaf, 126*(4), 454–468.

Mehan, H. (1979). *Learning lessons: Social organization in the classroom.* Cambridge: Harvard University Press.

Newport, E., Gleitman, H., and Gleitman, L. (1977). Mother, I'd rather do it myself: Some effects and non-effects of maternal speech style. In C. Snow and C. Ferguson (Eds.), *Talking to Children: Language Input and Acquisition.* Cambridge: Cambridge University Press.

Parker, L., and French, R. (1971). A description of student behavior: Verbal and nonverbal. *Theory Into Practice, 10*(4), 276–281.

Pendergrass, R. A., and Hodges, M. (1976). Deaf students in group problem solving situations: A study of the interactive process. *American Annals of the Deaf, 121*, 327–330.

Preisler, G. (1981). Modifications of communication by a small deaf girl. *American Annals of the Deaf, 126*(4), 411–416.

Schein, J., and Delk, M. (1974). *The deaf population of the United States.* Silver Springs, MD: The National Association of the Deaf.

Schlesinger, H., and Meadow, K. (1972). *Sound and Sign: Childhood deafness and mental health.* Berkeley: University of California Press.

Shafer, D., and Lynch, J. (1981). Emerging language of six prelingually deaf children. *Journal of British Association of Teachers of the Deaf, 5*(4), 94–111.

Sinclair, J. M., and Coulthard, R. M. (1975). *Toward an analysis of discourse: The English used by teachers and pupils.* Oxford: Oxford University Press.

Vernon, M., and Koh, S. (1970). Effects of manual communication on deaf children's educational achievement, linguistic competence, oral skills, and psychological development. *American Annals of the Deaf. 115*(5), 527–536.

Wedell-Monnig, J., and Lumley, J. M. (1980). Child deafness and mother-child interactions. *Child Development, 51*, 766–774.

Wedell-Monnig, M., and Westerman, T. B. (1977). *Mother's language to deaf and hearing children.* Paper presented at the Boston University Conference on Language Development, Boston.

Wilkinson, L. C. (Ed.), (1982). *Communicating in the classroom.* New York: Academic Press.

Wolff, S. (1977). Cognition and communication patterns in classrooms for deaf students. *American Annals of the Deaf, 122*(3), 319–327.

Wood, D. J. (1980). The structure of conversations between teachers of the deaf and their children. In *Report of proceedings of the conference for heads of schools and services for hearing impaired children.* University of Manchester, England: John Rylands University Library of Manchester Printing Department. Department.

Wood, D. J., McMahon, L., and Cranstoun, Y. (1980). *Working with under-fives.* London: McIntyre.

Chapter 9

A Comparison of Classroom and Clinical Discourse

Francesca M. Spinelli
Danielle N. Ripich

The chapters in the first section of this book demonstrate that children master a set of discourse rules for conversational interaction prior to entering school. Upon arrival they learn another set of rules appropriate for that context. Although there is similarity between these two sets of rules, there is also substantial disparity. For children who receive special assistance outside the classroom context, there is an additional set of discourse rules to be learned. The purpose of this chapter is to examine one of these contexts, the speech therapy room, and compare it with the typical primary grade classroom. This comparison and a discussion of implications for communication-impaired children will be organized according to the five discourse content areas introduced in the first chapter of this volume: attention, turn-taking, topic, repair, and role adjustment.

CLASSROOM DISCOURSE

Attention

Attention is essential for any communication interaction. In the classroom children's mastery of discourse rules relating to attention requires knowledge in two areas. The first concerns attending to speakers in the classroom and responding to implied or stated requests for attention. The second involves obtaining the attention of teachers and peers.

Listener Attentional Skills. Visits to a variety of classrooms reveal that teachers employ some common strategies to elicit students' attention.

For example, they may speak louder or use a marker with a term of address (e.g., "Okay, class" or "All right, boys and girls") (Merritt, 1982). Children likely learn these rules from one teacher and then apply them to other teachers. Teachers also use idiosyncratic attentional devices such as flashing classroom lights, striking a piano chord, or shouting, "Heads up" (Merritt, 1982). There is little opportunity to generalize these rules to other classrooms.

Once attention is obtained it must be maintained. The frequency of requests by teachers such as "Look at me" and "Listen carefully" suggest this is not an easy task. In a study examining two first grade teachers' instructions, Spinelli and Wilkinson (1973) found that 15 per cent of teachers' utterances consisted of requests to attend or improve behavior.

However, it may be that children are attending better than they appear to be. Teachers use many cues as signs of attentiveness, including maintaining eye contact, asking questions, and not talking (Steinberg and Cazden, 1979). Although children may be attending without exhibiting overt signs, teachers may require attentional cues because they cannot be certain children are attending otherwise. Support for this comes from an observation by Steinberg and Cazden (1979) of a child teaching another child. The child-teacher was observed to exhibit many stereotypic teaching behaviors, such as use of an "expectation" voice and nonverbal gestures. In one instance she demanded that the listeners demonstrate attention by looking at her as she spoke. Steinberg and Cazden suggest that classroom teachers may make similar requests because of the difficulty in knowing whether a student is really listening.

It appears that subgroups of children within classrooms may use differering sets of attentional rules and that these rules may be associated with teacher reinforcement. Eder and Felmlee (1984) examined teacher behavior according to four levels of reading groups: high, medium high, medium low, and low. Based on teacher responses, it appeared that teachers were less accepting of inattentiveness in the higher reading groups and more accepting of this behavior in lower reading groups. By the end of the year the behavior of the lower reading groups was characterized by more attention disruptions. Furthermore, the teachers were reprimanding these children more often but for greater offenses than those of the higher groups. It appears that the low and high reading groups were operating under a different set of attentional rules. The children in the lower reading groups may have learned that a greater degree of inattention was acceptable. This is supported by Eder and Felmlee's observation that children in the higher groups were more likely to note and reprimand inattention in their peers.

In addition to attending to the teacher, children must also learn to determine *when* to attend. Often when talking to a group, a teacher will interrupt the lesson to focus on specific needs of individual children (e.g., providing a pencil, permitting a child to leave for the restroom). During this time the other children need not show evidence of attending. However, following this interruption, the child must demonstrate attention again. The following example illustrates the changing attentional demands during an instructional sequence to a first grade reading group: "Look at the first line on your worksheet. Robert, where's your pencil? Read the sentence, then choose the word that finishes the sentence." In this example the child must attend to the teacher, then reattend to the instructions following the request directed to Robert.

SPEAKER ATTENTIONAL SKILLS

A common primary classroom need is obtaining the teacher's attention. This is often difficult for children entering school from the home environment because they are accustomed to fewer competitors vying for the adult's attention.

Merritt (1982) and Merritt and Humphrey (1979) have described a set of discourse rules that appear to operate in a primary classroom when a teacher is working with a group of children and a child outside the group desires the teacher's attention. She has found that the kind of message (content) determines if the interruption will be accepted. First greetings of the day, emergencies, and an inability to continue an assignment without the teacher's help generally result in an acceptable response from the teacher. Timing also influences the likelihood of a response. Interruptions during a teacher's pause in instruction, for example, when children are writing, are more likely to receive a response. Nonverbal approaches, which allow the teacher to initiate the interaction, also increase the likelihood of a positive response. Additionally, a response is more likely if the request is one the teacher can satisfy nonverbally (e.g., a headnod to signal yes or no). Merritt also found that teachers are less likely to respond if there have been many previous interruptions. There is also one notable exception to these rules exhibited by teachers and very persistent children. Persistent children get a response following repeated requests and appear to have used the rule, "If at first you can't obtain the teacher's attention, try, try again."

Requests to peers for attention are also important in the classroom. Wilkinson and her colleagues (Wilkinson and Calculator, 1982; Wilkinson and Spinelli, 1983) found that designation of a listener prior to making a request was one of several communication variables associated with successfully soliciting a response from a peer. Cooper, Marquis, and Ayers-Lopez (1982) found that kindergarteners and second graders used attentional bids such as saying "Hey" or calling the listener's name to peers when making requests with mixed success. The second graders went one step further and paired their bid with a specific request, which led to much greater success. It appears that obtaining the peer's attention was important but not sufficient for obtaining a successful response.

Turn-Taking

In a classroom an organization for taking turns must exist or chaos would prevail. Thus, turn-taking rules are learned early in the school process and are often highly formalized, with control of turn initiation given to the teacher (DeStephano, Pepinsky, and Sanders, 1982).

A common turn-taking sequence described by Mehan (1979) is three part: initiation-reply-evaluation. Here the teacher initiates the sequence with a request or question, the child replies, and the teacher evaluates the response. Thus the teacher has the first turn, the child the second, and the teacher the third. The particular child speaker may be determined in several ways. The teacher may call on a student randomly or in response to a raised hand, open the question to the class (e.g., "Who knows what this is?"), or use a predetermined response pattern such as sequential seating order.

Mehan points out that the three-part sequence can be extended to include corrections, revisions, or follow-up questions. This occurs when students provide incorrect responses or distractions occur. Whether the sequence is three part or extended, Mehan found that the ending is usually marked by a positive evaluation, a slowing of the teacher's speaking rate, and a possible manipulation of materials. This signals to the children that a new turn-taking sequence may begin.

This sequence suggests that children have little opportunity to initiate turns in a classroom setting. Indeed, Mehan noted that if a child wished to initiate a turn the only appropriate time was at the end of a sequence. Furthermore, the information must be topically appropriate in order to be acknowledged.

Additional sets of turn-taking rules are utilized with various activities. For example, Green and Wallat (1979) described a set of rules during one kindergarten classroom's circle time. In this activity it was very clear whose turn it was to speak. Turns were taken sequentially around the circle with additional indication by the teacher who called out each speaker's name. Specific rules allowed turn initiation out of sequence. Listeners could initiate speaking out of turn with nonverbal indicators such as making eye contact with the teacher or the present child speaker. In addition, the comment made by the out-of-turn speaker had to be topically relevant in order to be acceptable. Thus, acquisition of these subtle turn-taking rules was complicated by the accompaniment of a developing awareness of topic continuation.

Classroom turn-taking rules are not as routinized as the previous discussion may imply. Rather they provide a basic structure that allows flexibility, exceptions, variations, and inconsistencies. Erickson (1982) pointed out that many factors, including accuracy of answers and number of participants, may interfere with specific rules. He suggested that teachers and students adapt to the immediate situation by improvising on the basic rule structure. Although this flexibility allows a free flowing interaction, it also presents opportunities for turn disruption.

Another reason that turn-taking can be confusing is that teachers are not always consistent in their expectations with all children. As with teacher attentional demands discussed earlier, Eder (1982) reports that teachers may have differential acceptance of one type of inappropriate turn, interruptions, for different ability levels.

Eder examined teacher-student interactions in high, medium high, medium low, and low reading groups. She found that children in the lower reading groups initiated fewer speaking turns at the beginning of the year. As the year progressed these less advanced children produced topically relevant interruptions with greater frequency. In contrast, the children in the higher reading groups reduced the frequency of their topically appropriate interruptions. Eder observed that the teachers responded differently to interruptions by children in high and low reading groups. The teachers discouraged interrruptions from children in the higher groups by ignoring, interrupting, or reprimanding this behavior, whereas they tolerated topically appropriate interruptions by the other children. Eder suggested that the teachers responded this way to encourage the children in the lower groups to talk more during the academic lesson and to maintain student interest during long and laborious reading turns. Consequently, children in the lower reading groups were using a discourse rule that differed from that used by higher-ability children. Although the children in the lower reading groups used a rule that was accepted in the classroom, they may be penalized if they generalize this rule to other contexts in which they may be judged inappropriate and poor communicators.

Topic

The previous section suggested that turn-taking skills cannot be considered independently of topic continuation abilities. Topically appropriate comments are encouraged early in the educational process, with teacher reinforcement evident at the preschool (Merritt and Humphrey, 1979) and primary (Eder, 1982) levels. Eder found that teachers encouraged topical comments and discouraged nontopical comments for all levels of first grade reading groups. This is in contrast to her findings that acceptance of interruptions and attention varied with the reading abilities of the children.

Learning what is topically appropriate is a process that begins long before children enter school (Bloom, Rocissano, and Hood, 1976; Terrell, this volume). This ability continues to be refined during the school years through both teacher and peer support. Eder (1982) found that first grade teachers were more than three times as likely to acknowledge topically appropriate comments than inappropriate ones. Wilkinson and Spinelli (1983) found that second and third grade children produced task-appropriate comments to peers about 90 per cent of the time. However, they noted that some children fell far below this level and were at times reprimanded by their peers. Eder (1982) found that children in first grade reading groups also varied in their ability to provide topically appropriate comments, with children in higher-ability reading groups producing more topically appropriate comments. She observed that these children assisted other children in returning to the appropriate topic.

Another area of topical knowledge is organization of information in a topically cohesive manner. Teachers devote direct attention to assisting children in producing well-organized written and oral narratives as well as in understanding the organization of academic materials. One of the earliest vehicles for teaching children to produce topically organized narratives is "Show and Tell." Michaels and Cook-Gumperz (1979) examined first graders' narratives in this type of activity. They found that the children used either a topic-centered organized narrative with the narrative built around a central theme or a topic-linking organization with loosely related ideas strung together. The former organization was preferred and encouraged, whereas the second was shaped to become more topic centered. The teacher encouraged topic elaboration through the use of comments, questions, and reactions. The teacher simplified the task for the students, which allowed the children to focus on topical organization without the need to devote attention to other discourse areas. For example, the teacher often held the floor for the speaking child and did not require the child to tie the narrative to a larger whole such as the previous topic of discussion. Continued development of topical organization skills is encouraged throughout the school years. Evidence for this is provided by the inclusion of story telling, other narrative skills, and organizational abilities in school curricula. For example, Boyce and Larson (1983) note that the Minnesota Department of Education lists creating stories, summarizing and organizing information, and choosing and introducing appropriate topics among target communication skills for fifth to eighth graders.

Knowledge of the topical organization structure of a passage is thought to assist the comprehension and recall of information (Kintsch and Kozminsky, 1977; Meyer, 1981; Waters, 1981). Based on this premise many academic tasks require the student to identify or use passage structure through such tasks as finding main ideas, organizing disorganized passages, excluding ideas that do not belong, selecting ideas that support a major theme, and identifying causal and sequential relations (Pearson and Johnson, 1972). In classroom learning materials various kinds of organizational structures may be found. An organizational structure used in primary grade materials is story grammars that identify the major divisions of a story (e.g., Mandler and Johnson, 1977). Later, other organizational structures are introduced with factual expository information. Organizational frameworks commonly found in educational materials include collections, which are main ideas with related supporting details; comparison-contrasts; and problem-solutions (Meyer, 1981). In each of these, knowledge of the structure of the text enables the reader or listener to better anticipate subsequent information and to systematically store the information. Although knowledge about organizational structures is just beginning to have an impact on educational learning materials, teachers have long emphasized the development of these organizational skills (Pearson and Johnson, 1972).

Repair

Requests for clarification are used frequently by both teachers and students. It is clear that this would be the case in a learning situation involving a number of participants. New information brings many opportunities for misunderstanding, and the presence of several children can produce interferences and interruptions. Furthermore, the children in the classroom possess differing abilities and levels of knowledge, so that some children may need additional clarification of the classroom lesson. Following is a discussion of teacher and peer requests for clarification.

Teacher Requests for Clarification. Mehan (1979) described three ways that teachers use requests for clarification as formal teaching devices when children provide incorrect answers: prompts, repetitions, and simplifications of the original request. These clarification requests may be directed to the child who answered incorrectly or another child. Prompts are hints used to assist performance. In the following example the teacher uses a series of prompts to elicit a correct response to her initial question:

Teacher   Where did the clown hide?
Tom   Umm. I forgot.
Teacher   Did he hide under the table?
Tom   No.
Teacher   Did he hide behind the plant?
Tom   No.
Teacher   Where did he hide?
Tom   In the closet.
Teacher   Yes, in the closet.

Repetitions are simply the reasking of a question. The wording may be exactly the same or imply the same meaning, as the next example shows.

Teacher   What time is it?
Susan   Eleven o'clock?
Teacher   No. Jeff, can you tell me?
Jeff   Eleven thirty.
Teacher   That's right, eleven thirty.

When simplifying an elicitation, the teacher asks an easier question to lead the student to the correct response.

Teacher   What color is this design?
Sarah   Blue.
Teacher   It's like an apple. What color are apples?
Sarah   Red.
Teacher   Yes, red.

Desired forms of response to request for clarification in the teaching context are not difficult for students to determine, as the structure of the teacher's request makes the form of the desired response clear. Thus, the child can focus on lesson content rather than language form.

Student Requests for Clarification. Children direct a wide variety of clarification request types to both teachers and peers. Christian (cited in Shuy and Griffin, 1981), in a study of preschool through third grade children, identified eight types: repetition, partial repetition, specification, and elaboration, each with a confirmatory and nonconfirmatory form. These are similar to the clarification types identified by Garvey (1977) as used by preschool children. Christian reported that the children directed requests to both teachers and peers but were more likely to ask peers for clairification in the higher grades. One reason for this may be teacher encouragement, as the study found that teachers rated children as smarter if they requested clarification from peers rather than the teacher. Another reason for the shift may be that as children advance in school they are better able to provide clarification to peers. Furthermore, peers may be more accessible than teachers. Christian found that the form of responses to requests for clarification also changed with school advancement.

Children in the early grades were more likely to respond by repeating an utterance, and older children were more likely to elaborate on the original utterance. Interestingly, teacher ratings of communicative effectiveness did not correlate with the types of clarification responses used by the students.

In contrast to these teacher ratings Wilkinson and her colleagues (Wilkinson and Calculator, 1982; Wilkinson and Spinelli, 1983) found that requests for clarification were among variables associated with communication effectiveness in first, second, and third grade classrooms. They found that several characteristics were associated with obtaining an appropriate response to a request from a peer, including using a direct request form (e.g., "What's the first answer?") and repeating or revising unsuccessful requests. Cooper, Marquis, and Ayers-Lopez (1982) also reported that requests for repetitions and revisions often resulted in successful responses for kindergarten and second grade children. They observed that children revised requests in a variety of ways, including repeating, specifying, bargaining, shaming, pleading, and threatening. They noted that the kindergarteners tended to revise requests to more direct forms, whereas the second graders changed to more indirect (polite) ones. It appears, then, that primary grade children have mastered a variety of request forms and are learning to use them effectively.

Role Adjustment

Studies of children's role-taking activities demonstrate a clear differentiation of teacher and student roles. Steinberg and Cazden (1979) reported that elementary school children assigned as peer teachers used many teacherlike behaviors, including intonation, gesture, and language forms that indicated the higher teacher status. Ervin-Tripp (1982) observed that an eight year old English-speaking child who had been speaking French for three months adopted teacherlike intonation and positioning patterns while "playing school" in French. In addition, these researchers noted that children in the student role exhibited different, more student-like behaviors, including occasional uncooperativeness.

Children's knowledge of the differences between student and teacher roles is demonstrated further in their talk to teachers and peers. Teachers are addressed with a title and last name, whereas peers are addressed with first names only. This reflects knowledge of status and appropriate forms of address (Ervin-Tripp, 1971). It is reasonable to expect that children might also use more polite request forms with teachers than with peers based on findings that preschool children are typically more polite with adults than peers (Bates, 1976; James, 1978). However, in a study by

Wilkinson, Wilkinson, Spinelli, and Chiang (1984) utilizing elementary school children in judgment and role-playing tasks, only minimal differences in the politeness of request forms to teachers and peers were found.

This study revealed that other role-related variations were more dominant in the communication patterns of these first, second, and third graders. When taking the requester role, these children showed an increased use of indirect forms with age and a developing awareness of the appropriateness of direct and indirect forms. These results are consistent with actual request use. Classroom findings indicate that primary grade children are likely to use direct forms when making requests and that direct forms are more likely to achieve the desired results (Cooper, Marquis, and Ayers-Lopez, 1982; Wilkinson and Calculator, 1982; Wilkinson and Spinelli, 1983). This is in contrast to adult requests, which are characterized by the use of indirect forms as an indication of politeness (Ervin-Tripp, 1971). It may be that primary grade children are moving towards the use of adultlike rules when taking the requester role.

CLINICAL DISCOURSE

Ripich   What's the most important thing your teacher in your class wants you to do?
Child   Be quiet and listen.
Ripich   How about your speech teacher? What's the most important thing she wants you to do?
Child   Oh, she wants me to talk.

This conversation between one of the authors and a child enrolled in speech remediation reveals differences between classroom and clinical discourse as perceived by a young participant in both settings. It suggests that there are variations in the expectations and purposes of communication interactions in different school settings. This section of the chapter will consider some of the differences between discourse styles in these settings as well as some of the similarities these two learning contexts reveal. This will be accomplished by a review of relevant clinical discourse followed by a discussion of classroom and clinical discourse.

Although there is a fairly substantial body of research documenting classroom interaction, there are few studies of clinical interaction and even fewer that make reference to ties between intervention and classroom discourse. The following studies investigated features of clinical discourse with children.

Prutting, Bagshaw, Goldstein, Juskowitz, and Umen (1978) analyzed audiotaped clinical language lessons contributed by eight public school speech and language pathologists for communicative acts and topic usage. They found that the clinicians controlled the lesson discourse by talking more, introducing topics, requesting responses, and evading the children's requests. In contrast, the children produced many responses and rarely made requests of the clinicians. The roles of the clinicians and clients appeared to reflect relative differences in power between adults and children.

Silliman, Gams-Golub, and Chizzik (1980) reported similar findings for four clinician-child dyads. Additionally, they isolated three instructional strategies by which therapy discourse was sustained: (1) initiating therapy through task introduction; (2) focusing attention by keeping the child on the task and the topic; (3) sequencing requests for information to promote continuous performance. The three strategies had the overriding function of maintaining the dominant role of the clinician, although she adapted her speech style to the children's linguistic levels.

Bobkoff (1982) analyzed videotapes of six school clinicians conducting routine language lessons by considering multiple levels of discourse, including the nonverbal level. The patterns of conversational control were present and traceable to higher levels of organization, such as sequencing lesson tasks, initiating tasks, and regulating instructional sequences. Leaning, pointing, holding, touching, and eye gaze were nonverbal behaviors whose functions were tied to verbal components. Bobkoff suggested that clinician-child discourse is similar to the teacher-child discourse observed in school classrooms. Both classroom and clinical lessons are teacher controlled, hierarchically organized, and integrative with respect to the components of social roles, instructional tasks, topics, and communicative acts.

The findings of these contemporary studies of clinical discourse are consistent but do not take into account the child's perspective as a participant in the clinical lesson. Ripich (1982) used a role-play method to study children's perceptions of intervention rules. Eight dyads of speech impaired school children enrolled in speech remediation programs were videotaped while role-playing 5 minute articulation lessons. Analyses of lesson transcripts were carried out at selected levels. The children acting as "clinicians" controlled the lesson tasks and topics and used communicative acts in a manner typical of adult clinicians. The children as "clients" role-played cooperatively and displayed the response patterns of children receiving remedial lessons. Hierarchical relationships among the selected levels of analysis suggested the use of a cohesive register appropriate for clinical teaching.

Clinical discourse studies having been reviewed, traditional clinical discourse will be examined in terms of the five areas of discourse discussed previously. It will become evident that some clinical interaction patterns may be efficacious across clinical and classroom settings, whereas some clinical interaction patterns may interfere with learning in settings outside the therapy room.

Attention

The first point to be raised is that it is relatively easy to gain and maintain attention in the clinical setting. One reason for this is the physical context of the therapy room. The room is typically small, and the clinician and student(s) are seated around a single table so that there is a closely shared space and accompanying shared materials. In this situation clinicians or students can speak softly and be heard. Furthermore, eye contact is easily maintained. In this context the clinician or the child can attain and maintain attention relatively easily. The clinician's attention is generally focused on the child, and she typically anticipates any needs the child may have in this setting.

This ease of attention attainment and maintenance is in contrast to the classroom setting where the number of participants and the capacity for potential disruptions is much greater. It appears that the clinical setting can be useful for establishing basic attending behavior in children. However, generalization to the classroom may be difficult because of the previously noted differences.

A second point about attention relates to the use of attentional devices in the therapy room setting. Clinicians use a high number of these forms (Ripich, Hambrecht, Panagos, and Prelock, 1984). The use of these conversational devices by clinicians is apparently noted by children receiving intervention. As evidence, the "clinician" children in Ripich's (1982) role-play study used 90 per cent of all attentionals. A high use of attentionals is also found in the classroom setting. Becoming attuned to attentional devices within the clinical context may assist the child in understanding classroom attention rules.

Turn-Taking

Turn-taking in the therapy room differs from the classroom in two important ways and can be more or less complex depending on the area of focus. It seems quite evident that turn-taking in the small group setting would be less complex than in a larger group because of the fewer number of potential participants. Indeed, there is greater opportunity to take turns in therapy, and there is greater processing time before a turn must be taken. It would appear that monitoring turns in dyads is less demanding than in large groups. Thus the complex monitoring demands of the classroom may affect learning for communication impaired children, although they may appear competent in the clinical setting.

It also appears that clinical turn-taking can be more complex in the clinical setting in some ways. This complexity is the result of the clinician's focus on both form and content of children's responses. The initiation-reply-evaluation sequence identified by Mehan (1979) and discussed previously becomes more complex, as shown in the following exchange with a hearing impaired child in a group language lesson (Griffith, Panagos, and Ripich, 1982).

Clinician	What can we walk through to go into a house?
Child	Winow.
Clinician	Window?
Child	Window.
Clinician	Can we walk through a window to go into a house?
Child	Sidewalk.
Clinician	Sidewalk?
Child	Oh, door.
Clinician	Okay.

The children in this group appeared to differentiate a request for a correction of form from a request for correction of content with 90 per cent accuracy. A question of how the children knew the type of correction being made arose. Repeated reviews of the lessons on tape revealed that the clinician requested correction of form first. In addition, it appeared that when the clinician corrected form there was less than a second's delay in the evaluation, whereas for content there was a least a one second latency. Exaggerated prosodic cues were also present in the clinician's form corrections. The children's accuracy in choosing the type of correction suggests that they had internalized at least one of these signals for use in structuring appropriate responses. These hearing impaired children were employing a sophisticated system of rules in regard to appropriate response turns. Children involved in regular classroom correction exchanges are rarely required to determine the type of correction, as it is nearly always focused on content.

Topic

Prutting and colleagues (1978) documented topic continuation in clinical interaction. As noted earlier, they found that topic was controlled by clinicians, much as it is controlled by classroom teachers. Ripich (1982) in her role-playing task found that topic shifts by the child "clinician" were tied to the academic lesson; for example, as in the introduction of a new language task. In contrast, the "child" topic shifts were tied to nonacademic conversational topics such as, "I lost my sweater." In these instances the child "clinician" immediately reintroduced an academic topic, as in "Um-hum, let's do these cards now." These children appeared to realize that the clinician has the role obligation of maintaining instructional topics, and children have the right to attempt to redirect the topic to more conversational areas. In an examination of syntax and articulation lessons, Ripich, Hambrecht, Panagos, and Prelock (1984) confirmed this pattern of topic introduction between clinicians and children.

One important function of topic continuation is to keep the conversation flowing. This can be accomplished by the use of an organized narrative and through a continuous cohesive linking of ideas. Clinical discourse style is sometimes inconsistent with these two objectives. Although organized narratives are encouraged in the classroom, and at times are specific therapy objectives, children are sometimes encouraged to violate rules for producing good narrative structure. Children may be encouraged to talk just for the sake of producing long narratives. Repeated requests to "tell me more" often result in lengthy chains of ideas without a central topic. Clinicians may not even be aware of the content of the child's utterances if they are listening for specific syntactic forms or counting the number of utterances to ensure that a minimum 50 or 100 were obtained. The child learns that the clinician values the amount of talk rather than the content. This is in contrast to the classroom, where succinct speech is rewarded and lengthy or redundant utterances are discouraged.

Repair

In the area of repair two differences between classrooms and therapy rooms are evident: opportunity for self-repair and degree of peer assistance. In the classroom the child has limited opportunity for self-repair. An incorrect response frequently results in the forfeiture of a turn. However, in the clinical setting there is more opportunity for self-repair. The clinician prompts the child or modifies the request to facilitate a correct response and reinforces spontaneous self-correction by the child. A second difference between the therapy and classroom settings is found in the amount of peer clarification. In the classroom the child may request clarification from the teacher or peers. However, in the clinical setting there is little opportunity to request clarification from peers because there are few peers available. Furthermore, there is little need, as the clinician is generally present to resolve questions.

Role Adjustment

Children clearly perceive differences between clinician's and student's roles. This is illustrated in an example from a study by Ripich (1982) in which she asked children about therapy room roles.

Ripich	What's different about what you do in speech therapy and what Mrs. Michael does?
Amy	Mrs. Michael makes good "r's". I make bad "r's".
Ripich	Don't you ever make good "r's", Amy?
Amy	No, I supposed to make the bad "r's".

Although all children receiving speech therapy may not perceive themselves as Amy does, this illustration suggests an implied social contract. Children are in therapy because something is wrong; the clinician's role is to be right. Persistence of such a belief could interfere with remediation of the problem.

Chidren's knowledge of role differences between clinicians and students is apparent in other areas as well. The study of child language intervention sessions by Prutting and colleagues (1978), discussed earlier, reported that clinicians, but not children, evaded or ignored requests. The authors speculated that ignoring requests may be a sophisticated discourse feature not present in the repertoire of the children. However, the role-play study by Ripich (1982) demonstrated that children acting as clinicians frequently ignored requests from children acting as clients. These findings indicate that ignoring is a role-related feature that is seen as being appropriate for clinicians but not for children. The higher status person has more rights and privileges and the lower status person has more obligations, for example, to always answer. Children, then, far from being unsophisticated communicators, are making discourse decisions that take into account the status and role features of the listener.

The goals of clinical discourse result in a set of discourse rules that are used with the clinician but not with other listeners. One of these, the production of long narratives with less regard for content, was discussed earlier. Another example is the use of the clinical prompt "Tell me the whole thing" when an abbreviated response would be more correct. For example:

Clinician	Who is eating soup?
Child	The boy is.
Clinician	Tell me the whole thing.
Child	The boy is eating soup.
Clinician	Good, the boy is eating soup.

In using this expanded form the child achieves practice of specific linguistic structures but uses a discourse style that is inappropriate in other contexts. Elliptical speech is a more acceptable conversational style outside of the clinical context. Thus clinical discourse may be encouraging speech that is inappropriate in classroom discussions and on the playground.

CONCLUSION

This chapter has described discourse characteristics of classrooms and therapy rooms. There are similarities in these two teaching contexts as well as differences.

The similarities exist because both are teaching contexts with an adult providing direction to child learners. Thus, there is a continuity between the two settings. It may be that specific language structures and forms associated with certain discourse characteristics of the clinical setting may be better generalized to settings that share discourse rules of the first learning context. Thus, the similarities of the two settings may provide an opportunity for knowledge mastered in one setting to be generalized to the other.

In contrast, the differences between the clinical and classroom settings could interfere with comunicative effectiveness. The differences may require that the communicatively different child learn a new set of discourse rules that has limited relevance to other settings. For the linguistically impaired child, who has difficulty mastering communicative rules, this may create a burden that interferes with learning of more generally used rules.

Clearly, some differences between the two settings must remain as the purposes of the two differ. Although both involve learning, the clinical setting intends to teach specific linguistic skills that have not been learned in other settings. This necessitates a teaching approach that can maximize learning of this information. However, it may be advisable to consider the differences in classroom and clinical rules when structuring remediation procedures. It may be possible to minimize the differences by using some classroom rules in a clinical setting. This may be especially effective during transitional (better known as carryover) periods of remediation. The rule differences also highlight the need to involve the classroom and the classroom teacher in the intervention process. Mutual involvement can affect goal selection, clinical teaching techniques, and teacher involvement and support. Discussion of means for doing this are presented in Chapter 10. By understanding the communicative demands of the classroom, speech and language pathologists can capitalize on the similarities and differences between the classroom and the therapy room to create remediation programs that support communication success in the classroom.

REFERENCES

Bates, E. (1976). Pragmatics and sociolinguistics in child language. In D. M. Morehead and A. E. Morehead (Eds.), *Normal and deficient child language*, pp. 411–463. Baltimore: University Park Press.

Bloom, L., Rocissano, L., and Hood, L. (1976). Adult-child discourse: Developmental interaction between information processing and linguistic knowledge. *Cognitive Psychology, 8*, 521–552.

Bobkoff, K. (1982). Discourse analysis of client-clinician interaction. Unpublished doctoral dissertation. Kent State University, Kent, OH.

Boyce, N. L., and Larson, V. L. (1983). *Adolescents' communication development and disorders*. Eau Claire, WI: Thinking Ink Publications.

Cooper, C. R., Marquis, A., and Ayers-Lopez, S. (1982). Peer learning in the classroom: Tracing developmental patterns and consequences of children's spontaneous interactions. In L. C. Wilkinson (Ed.), *Communicating in the classroom*. New York: Academic Press.

DeStephano, J. S., Pepinsky, H. B., and Sanders, T. S. (1982). Discourse rules for literacy learning in a classroom. In L. C. Wilkinson (Ed.), *Communicating in the classroom*. New York: Academic Press.

Eder, D. (1982). Differences in communicative styles across ability groups. In L. C. Wilkinson (Ed.), *Communicating in the classroom*. New York: Academic Press.

Eder, D., and Felmlee, D. (1984). The development of attention norms in ability groups. In P. L. Peterson, L. C. Wilkinson, and M. Hallinan (Eds.), *The social context of instruction*. Orlando, FL: Academic Press.

Erickson, F. (1982). Classroom discourse as improvisation: Relationships between academic task structure and social participation structure in lessons. In L. C. Wilkinson (Ed.), *Communicating in the classroom*. New York: Academic Press.

Ervin-Tripp, S. (1971). Sociolinguistics. In J. A. Fishman (Ed.), *Advances in the sociology of language*, Vol. I. The Hague, Netherlands: Mouton.

Ervin-Tripp, S. (1982). Structures of control. In L. C. Wilkinson (Ed.), *Communicating in the classroom*. New York: Academic Press.

Garvey, C. (1977). The contingent query. In M. Lewis and L. Rosenblum (Eds.), *Interaction, conversation, and the development of language*. New York: John Wiley and Sons.

Green, J. L., and Wallat, C. (1979). Social rules and communicative contexts in kindergarten. *Theory into Practice, 18*, 275–284.

Griffith, P., Panagos, J., and Ripich, D. (1982). Classroom discourse: Speech-context and socialization rules. Paper presented at the American Speech-Language-Hearing Association Convention, Toronto, Canada.

James, S. (1978). Effect of listener age and situation on the politeness of children's directives. *Journal of Psycholinguistic Research, 7*, 307–317.

Kintsch, W., and Kozminsky, E. (1977). Summarizing stories after reading and listening. *Journal of Educational Psychology, 69*, 491–499.

Mandler, J. M., and Johnson, N. S. (1977). Remembrance of things parsed. Story structure and recall. *Cognitive Psychology, 9*, 111–151.

Mehan, H. (1979). *Learning lessons*. Cambridge, MA: Harvard University Press.

Merritt, M. (1982). Distributing and directing attention in primary classrooms. In L. C. Wilkinson (Ed.), *Communicating in the classroom*. New York: Academic Press.

Merritt, M., and Humphrey, F. (1979). Teacher, talk and task: Communicative demands during individualized instruction time. *Theory into Practice, 18*, 298-302.

Meyer, B. J. F. (1981). *Prose analysis: Procedures, purposes and problems.* Prose Learning Series, Research Report Number 11. Tempe, AZ: Arizona State University.

Michaels, S., and Cook-Gumperz, J. (1979). A study of sharing time with first grade students' discourse narratives in the classroom. *Proceedings of the Fifth Annual Meeting of the Berkeley Linguistics Society.*

Pearson, P. D., and Johnson, D. D. (1972). *Teaching reading comprehension.* New York: Holt, Rinehart and Winston.

Prutting, C., Bagshaw, N., Goldstein, H., Juskowitz, S., and Umen, I. (1978). Clinician-child discourse: Some preliminary questions. *Journal of Speech and Hearing Disorders, 43*, 123-139.

Ripich, D. (1982). Children's social perception of speech-language lessons: A sociolinguistic analysis of role-play discourse. Unpublished doctoral dissertation, Kent State University, Kent, OH.

Ripich, D., Hambrecht, G., Panagos, J., and Prelock, P. (1984). An analysis of articulation and language discourse patterns. *Journal of Childhood Communication Disorders, 7*(2), 17-26.

Shuy, R. W., and Griffin, P. (1981). What they do at school anyday: Studying functional language. In W. Patrick Dickson (Ed.), *Children's oral communication skills.* New York: Academic Press.

Silliman, E. R., Gams-Golub, S. E., and Chizzik, S. G. (1980). Clinician-child discourse: How accommodating is the clinician? In M. S. Burns, and J. R. Andrews (Eds.), *Current trends in the treatment of language disorders.* Evanston, IL: Institute for Continuing Professional Education.

Spinelli, F. M., and Wilkinson, L. C. (1973). Teachers' instructions to first grade reading groups. Paper presented at the American Speech-Language-Hearing Association, Cincinnati, OH.

Steinberg, Z. D., and Cazden, C. B. (1979). Children as teachers—Of peers and ourselves. *Theory into Practice, 18*, 258-266.

Waters, H. S. (1981). Organizational strategies in memory for prose: A developmental analysis. *Journal of Experimental Child Psychology, 32*, 223-246.

Wilkinson, L. C., and Calculator, S. (1982). Requests and responses in peer-directed reading groups. *Journal of Educational Psychology, 68*, 103-116.

Wilkinson, L. C., and Spinelli, F. (1983). Using requests effectively in peer-directed instructional groups. *American Educational Research Journal, 20*, 479-501.

Wilkinson, L. C., Wilkinson, A. C., Spinelli, F. M., and Chiang, C. P. (1984). Metalinguistic knowledge of pragmatic rules in school-aged children. *Child Development, 55*, 2130-2140.

PART IV

INTERVENTION AND DISCOURSE

Chapter 10

An Ethnographic Approach to Assessment and Intervention

Danielle N. Ripich
Francesca M. Spinelli

The role of the speech-language pathologist in the schools appears to be expanding in a variety of ways. One of the most important changes is the development of intervention beyond linguistic rule training in phonology, syntax, and semantics to discourse skill development in areas such as topic maintenance, turn-taking, and listening. Just as the 1970s saw school clinicians broadening their case loads beyond articulation problems to include children with language disorders, clinicians of the 1980s are opening their case loads to children with pragmatic and discourse problems. The traditional methods of assessment and intervention were amenable to carryover from articulation to language training but do not seem to serve as well in the new area of discourse intervention. This raises the issue of a second major change in school speech-language pathology. The school clinician is leaving the therapy room and venturing out into the milieu of the school to conduct intervention. By becoming a more integral part of the school environment the clinician can better understand the linguistic and discourse demands placed on children in their day-to-day activities.

The following approach is designed to meet the needs of children with discourse problems and to capitalize on the greater mobility of clinicians within the school. It is meant to provide an alternative to traditional assessment and intervention. The approach is based on an established form of description and analysis called ethnography.

WHAT IS ETHNOGRAPHY

Ethnography refers to methods of study of events and persons that enable us to ascertain the underlying rules that operate for the participants. There is increasing interest in the use of ethnographic techniques common to anthropology and sociology to study the unique environment of schools. It is important to note that ethnography has a long tradition in the social sciences but for various reasons has remained outside the mainstream of communication and educational practices (Hymes, 1982; Wilson, 1977). The poverty of ethnographic work in education is a result of both theoretic and methodic limitations.

Traditional assessment and intervention has been developed around deductive reasoning and the premise that measured variables can be manipulated and that regular and universal laws can be developed based on the relationships between the variables across all situations. For example, a standardized test of language abilities will demonstrate the child's level of linguistic competence. This approach, based on the scientific method, has given us a great deal of information. However, there is a growing consensus that something as complex as communication or teaching and learning cannot be studied using only deductive methods.

In order to study the nature of communication and education, we need to examine the quality of interactions as well as the quantity of events. Ethnographies use inductive reasoning and are designed to impose and manipulate persons and events as little as possible. These two approaches, traditional and ethnographic, appear to represent fundamentally different claims about the education process. Traditional assessment and intervention, in some ways, seems reflective of an adult-centered view of education. Children are seen as passive agents to be acted upon by teachers and clinicians within the system. We talk about putting children "into speech therapy" or "through the reading program." Children are the products of the system. In contrast, an ethnographic approach appears to reflect a child-centered, constructionist view of teaching and learning. Here, children and teachers are active participants in the construction and design of the remediation process. This differentiation of perspectives is evidenced in the kind of research questions asked by the two schools of thought. Assessment and intervention traditionally focus on how often children perform a task correctly, whereas an ethnographic perspective generally examines the manner in which children seem to arrive at the correct task performance.

According to Wilson (1977) there are two hypotheses that underlie the rationale of ethnographic study of education. The first is the naturalistic ecological hypothesis; it is essential to study events in their natural settings because of context influences. Simply stated, if we want to learn about how a child is communicating in the classroom, we need to go into that environment and study the communicative demands of that particular context. Two types of competence will be required of the child: linguistic competence, the knowledge of phonologic and grammatical rules of language; and communication competence, the knowledge of social rules of the classroom context.

The second hypothesis supporting educational ethnographies Wilson (1977) terms the qualitative difference hypothesis; it is essential to study behavior within the framework of the ongoing process rather than to focus on the end product. Products provide one type of information about education, but the nature of an event is often not amenable to study by examining the number of items correct or in error. For example, in a study of request behavior, every question (product) that a teacher asks in a lesson may be tallied in the same manner. However, every question may not accomplish the same thing and may not have the same meaning (process) within the lesson. Experimental studies of selected groups of students in controlled settings may not provide generalizable data on the nature of interaction or "what is happening" in the classroom for teachers and students. When ethnographic studies describe the nature of the interaction, they are looking at process rather than product.

In following Wilson's hypotheses, to study natural events and examine the ongoing process, clinicians encounter the problem of gaining access. Gaining access to the classroom and its processes is complex. Physical access—entering the classroom or placing recording devices in the context—often poses problems. As long as the child is clearly identified as the person who has the problem and is removed from the room to learn to participate better during lessons, schools and teachers are cooperative. This pattern of intervention fits with tradition. An ethnographic approach that includes entering the classroom to study the child and the teacher in the teaching-learning environoment challenges the established patterns. Generally, clinicians encounter "gatekeepers" (Corsaro, 1979a) in the form of principals, aides, and teachers who feel obligated to protect the classroom from intrusion. Even though classroom teachers have referred the child for evaluation and identified the problem as related to the classroom, they are cautious about allowing someone into this territory. They understand that classrooms are complicated systems, and outsiders may fail to appreciate the reasons for certain rules and behaviors within this environment.

This brings us to the second type of accessing that must occur, psychological access. The clinician needs an open attitude from the teacher in order to develop a strong assessment and intervention program. Teachers may inadvertently block important information. They may be fearful of criticism. However, if teachers can see themselves as participants in the assessment and intervention process, they are willing to assist the clinician and the child. If they feel the clinician's work is directed toward promoting better communication in the classroom, they are encouraged to cooperate.

Once having gained the cooperation of the teacher, the clinician is faced with accessing the child's perspective in the classroom. Children are also wary of being studied. In addition, they perceive all adults as being aligned together and as having great power and authority. In addition to perceived power and status is the problem of physical size. William "Bill" Corsaro (1981), in an ethnographic study of nursery school classrooms, attempted to act as a participant observer. He encountered some resistance to his participation on the part of the children. A conversation, centered on Bill's size, took place early in the school year between Bill and two 4 year old girls, Betty and Jenny. Betty told Bill he could not play because he was too big. Bill offered to sit down on a chair, but Betty insisted that he was still too big. Bill asked if he might watch, and Jenny agreed but cautioned him to "touch nuthin'." Bill agreed and Betty restated the contract, that he was just to watch. Jenny asked for concurrence by saying, "Okay, Big Bill?" and Bill said, "Okay." Bill was eventually allowed to play and for the remainder of the school year was addressed as "Big Bill." In this way the children gave him access to their play but continually noted his difference in status and physical size.

If the clinician is successful in gaining access to the classroom through the teacher and the children, the third obstacle becomes his or her own internal biases and preconceptions. The ethnographer assumes the position of a naive observer who is seeking to uncover the rules of the context. Just as the anthropologist studies many different cultures and seeks to discern the structure of an alien society by suspending prior knowledge and allowing the cultural rules to emerge from observation of daily life, the clinician studies each classroom as if it operates as a culture within itself and poses the question, "If I had never been in a classroom before, what rules would I need to succeed in this particular context?"

ETHNOGRAPHIC ASSESSMENT

The following section presents a series of ethnographic methods organized into a systematic approach to studying communication breakdown in the classroom. There are a wide range of methodologies applicable to ethnographic work. However, the following system presents the steps generally recognized as necessary in the construction of an ethnography.

Step One: Identify the Child

Teachers are the primary referral source for the identification of children experiencing communication problems in the classroom. Clinicians may contact teachers and ask for the names of children who demonstrate communications problems. Questionnaires and checklists of behaviors are used to further identify communicatively impaired children. Questionnaires are sometimes viewed as having limited use in ethnographic studies, as preselecting questions and rating scales may bias findings. However, as a device for the teacher's identification of communication problems of children in classrooms, questionnaires may prove to be the most efficient tool available. Information provided by the classroom teacher provides a referral base for the clinician and allows the clinician to be viewed as a consultant to the classroom. If teachers identify certain children as having difficulty participating in discussions or interrupting during lessons, the clinician can reasonably suggest a visit to the classroom to observe the children's communication breakdown.

Step Two: Describe the
Communication Breakdown

The clinician develops a description of the child's communication problem based on information collected from a variety of sources. Initially, the clinician records the problem identified by the teacher in the classroom. For example, a teacher may report, "Carrie is mildly hearing impaired. She never seems to follow the topic during a lesson and her comments are off the wall during discussions." This definition of the problem may undergo refinement and even change during the ethnographic assessment process, but it is important to have a clear idea of how the teacher views the communication breakdown in the classroom.

Interviews are another method of obtaining information. Interviews that yield the richest information generally are structured around open questions ("Carrie, why is it hard for some kids to follow the topic of the reading lesson?") and comparison questions ("What's different about what you do in speech therapy and what you do in your classroom?"). Allowing the teacher or the child to speculate about or describe persons and events provides the best opportunity for obtaining the salient points of classroom communication difficulties.

Step Three: Develop a Summary of the Problem

The clinician integrates the preliminary information and develops a summary of the problem. For example, Carrie is demonstrating difficulty in maintaining attention. This may be related to her inability to follow topic shifts appropriately in discussions.

Step Four: Observe Interaction in the Classroom

The clinician gains information about classroom interaction through observation of the process. There are several observation approaches: outside observation, participant observation, and audio- and videotapes. As an outside observer the clinician sits within the classroom, lunch room, and so on and, using a system of field notes and charting, records observations. For example, a clinician observed playground discourse during ball games at an inner city elementary school. She documented the interactions surrounding choosing sides, the self-selection of "captains," and argument negotiation. It is interesting to note that the clinician found the children who demonstrated better skill on language tests were not necessarily the most effective communicators on the playground. This study was conducted using the simplest of research tools—a good eye for details, and paper and pencil.

Participant observation is a second way of gaining information. The clinician in this method becomes part of the context and the group being studied. The clinician might act as "Big Bill" (Corsaro, 1981) did in the nursery classroom or as in the previous example join one of the teams in the ball game. Although participant observation is fraught with difficulties, it is an advantage to become a part of what you try to study. Only by experiencing can we become sensitive to certain elements in a context.

The third type of observation involves audio- and videotapes. These recordings are generally made without the researcher being present. Cazden and associates (Cazden, Cox, Dickinson, Steinberg, and Stone, 1979) reported that chidren became acclimated to the microphone and camera and eventually ignored them altogether. She offered as an example a child who was angry with another student and swore at her. As she began to swear the child covered her mouth and turned away from the teacher but toward the microphone that was part of the recording device. The primary advantage of recording is that the information is available for repeated viewing by the researcher and for multiple viewing by other researchers to determine reliability of charting and coding.

Children's role-play of teaching-learning situations and drawing inferences from behavior to underlying knowledge is an excellent method of gaining insight into the child's world (Cazden et al., 1979; Ripich and Panagos, 1983). It is an indirect observation method of accessing the teaching-learning process. Role-play is a rich source of information regarding the child's perception of a variety of persons and events. It puts on display the knowledge of the child and demonstrates what are the salient points in his or her perspective.

Step Five: Summarize Observations and Identify Patterns of Communication Breakdown

The information obtained in the classroom observation process is examined by the clinician. There are two goals for this step of the assessment: to determine patterns of discourse and perspectives of the participants in the classroom (teachers and children) and to compare observation data with the problem as initially stated in order to revise the problem statement if necessary.

Step Six: Validate Observations

There are numerous ways of confirming the accuracy of observations. One of the most useful is to compare multiple viewpoints. In a study of videotaped lessons collected in two kindergarten classrooms over a period of three years, Green and Harker (1982) used interviews with teachers and children to corroborate their research findings. The investigators solicited information from teachers and children regarding lessons in a variety of ways. Videotapes were reviewed and discussed, children were asked to construct maps of the classroom, and teachers were asked to audiotape their lesson goals for the videotaped lessons. The evidence was laid side by side and examined for consistency. If the researcher's findings were not confirmed by the teacher of the children, then the descriptive analysis was explored to determine the inconsistency. When perceptions of all three persons matched, the results were considered valid. Thus, consideration of multiple viewpoints improved the accuracy of the observations. This method of involving participants in the research process has been termed triangulation (Corsaro, 1979b), in reference to the three persons examining the data base.

In addition to validating the hypotheses of the clinician, the process of examing the lesson behavior can lead to insight on the part of the participants and improve teaching-learning discourse. Such changes have been observed in teachers' attitudes as a result of reviewing the videotapes of their classroom interaction (Steinberg and Cazden, 1979). Although not reported in the literature, it can be speculated that children observing themselves in classroom interaction could also experience new perspectives on their behavior and subsequently improve their communication skills.

Comparison of adult views with those of children is critical to gaining insight into the student view of the classroom. Sociolinguistic research has suggested that children's social culture is organized on its own terms and is not merely a flawed version of adults' social reality. In a review of research of children's understanding of social events Cook-Gumperz (1975) suggested that children place more importance on nonlinguistic variables than do adults, whereas adults use the syntactic-semantic message as the foregrounded interpretive component and as background the manner and physical setting. The child judges the social intent equally by its syntactic-semantic form, manner, and physical setting.

In another study, Yarrow and Campbell (1963) asked children (8 to 13 year olds) in a new social situation (getting settled at camp) to report characteristics of their peers during the first two hours of meeting. Adult observers were asked to record and classify (as friendly, aggressive, assertive, and submissive) the children's behaviors during the same two hours. The descriptions of the child reporters and the adult observers differed markedly. What the adults saw as aggressive behavior was described by the children as being friendly. In addition, the frequency of an event made it more important to adults but not to children. Although methodologic problems (children reported verbally and adults charted and classified in writing) may account for some differences in the descriptions of the participants, such discrepancies may also be the result of differently organized systems of interpretation of social events. Yarrow and Campbell concluded that the adult observer may impute a meaning that is reliable from an adult perspective but is different from the perspective of a child. This implies that there is a clear need for caution in employing adult observer views as "objective" measures of a child's interaction behavior. Results from the Yarrow and Campbell study suggest that it is not only possible but very probable that events and persons are perceived and organized in very different ways by adults and children.

Researchers, educators, and children have their own special perspectives and, within ethno-graphic constructs, they can act as partners in discovering the nature of classroom conversation. Through ethno-graphic investigation we can describe the nature of the complex patterns of classroom interaction and determine the communicative demands placed on children in the school environment.

Ethnographic assessment offers convincing and undeniable evidence because its data base is not constructed in a laboratory but instead arises from the "real world" (Ripich, 1982). It requires good inductive reasoning, keen observation skills, and the ability of the clinician to suspend his or her own judgment and see an event from another perspective. Intervention based on this assessment paradigm has an optimal chance of carrying over into everyday life because the areas of concentration arise directly from the child's communication environment. Ethnographic methodology is rigorous and sytematic, its results are verifiable, and its techniques are in keeping with a generous view of the scientific method (Hymes, 1982). For more detailed presentations of methodology, the reader is referred to Glaser and Strauss, 1967; Green and Wallat, 1980; and Spradley, 1980.

CASE STUDY

The following case study follows the steps outlined in the previous section.

Background Information

Steven is a nine year old fourth grader with a history of communication disorders. He received language and articulation therapy during first, second, and third grades for mild to moderate articulation and syntax disorders. At the current time his speech and language appears appropriate except for occasional syntax errors in verb tense. Results of language testing suggest moderate auditory memory difficulties and comprehension and production skills that are slightly below average. He exhibits a slow response to questions but generally answers appropriately. Steven is receiving assistance from a learning disabilities specialist for reading and spelling.

Step One: Identify the Child

Because of the limited language problems, limited probability of continued improvement, and enrollment in a learning disabilities program, Steven's clinician considered dismissing him from therapy. However, when the teacher was informed of the clinician's plan, she protested. Steven's teacher strongly felt that he was an ineffective communicator in the classroom. Steven was a good candidate for an ethnographic approach for two reasons. First, his primary communication problem was in classroom discourse. Second, his teacher had identified the areas of breakdown and requested assistance from the speech-language pathologist in developing a plan for assessment and intervention. For these reasons the clinician decided to continue to work with Steven, using an ethnographic approach.

Step Two: Describe Communication Problem

The clinician initially obtained a description of Steven's classroom communication by asking the teacher to describe Steven's problem. The teacher replied that Steven was well behaved but did not follow instructions well. To assess performance during a variety of discourse behaviors, the clinician and the teacher evaluated Steven's interactions using the Classroom Communication Checklist (Fig. 10–1). They discussed each of the seven communication areas—participation, soliciting attention, paying attention, questioning, appropriateness, descriptive ability, and general speech and language skills—and assessed Steven's performance relative to his classmates. Steven was reported as being less effective than most children in his class in five of these major areas. Only appropriateness and descriptive ability were judged to be average for the class level.

The areas identified as below the class average were discussed further, using the Communication Probe Sheet (Fig. 10–2) for a guide. A general description of Steven's behavior in each area was recorded. In the area of participation the teacher stated, "Steven almost never raises his hand and when he is called on he gets a look of panic on his face." The clinician probed for specific context information by asking a series of questions. When does Steven volunteer information? Does he ever respond to questions directed to the entire class? Does he participate in reading group discussions? Is he responsive on a one to one basis? The teacher reported that Steven never responded in the general class lessons, seldom participated in reading group work, and, although shy, would interact on a one-to-one basis. The clinician then asked for a description of appropriate classroom behavior in each context. This description guided the clinician in determining the teacher's expectations for Steven. Similar probes were conducted for the remaining four areas in which he was considered below the class level.

Based on the teacher's report, the clinician interviewed Steven. Each area of communication breakdown was discussed. The interview questions were designed to be generic and to allow Steven to reveal possible motivations for his behavior. The following excerpt from the interview question on participation offers insight into Steven's perspective:

Figure 10-1.   Classroom Communication Checklist

Child _____   Speech and Language Pathologist:

Grade _____   _____

Teacher _____   Date _____

Communication Area	Effectiveness Rating*					Comments
	1	2	3	4	5	
Participation						Steven panics when called
Amount					x	upon.
Interruptions			x			
Soliciting Attention						
Manner		x				
Frequency				x		
Paying Attention						Occasional problems re:
Maintaining Attention				x		attending following
Following Instructions				x		interruptions.
Questioning						
Amount				x		
Content Appropriate			x			
Appropriateness						
With Teacher			x			
With Peers			x			
Descriptive Ability						
Amount			x			
Organization			x			
Speech-Language Abilities				x		

* *1*, Excellent; *2*, good; *3*, adequate; *4*, fair; *5*, poor.

Clinician   Why do children not always answer in class?
Steven   They don't know the answer or they don't think fast enough. My mom
            says it's better to listen.
Clinician   So do you try to listen?
Steven   Yeah, that's the best way.

The other areas of communication breakdown were discussed with Steven
but always without direct reference to his behavior.

Step Three: Develop a Summary of the Problem

The clinician used the results of the teacher and student interviews as
well as language test information to construct a summary of the problem.
She concluded that Steven probably does not participate spontaneously
in class. He may participate in a small group setting with prompts, and he
may have overgeneralized the rule that it is important to listen. Steven
exhibits difficulty following classroom instructions. This is possibly
related to processing variables of memory and attention maintenance.

Figure 10-2. Communication Probe Sheet

Child _____   Speech and Language Pathologist:

Grade _____   _____

Teacher _____   Date _____

Ineffective Communication Area: Amount of classroom participation.

General Description: Steven is a reluctant communicator who does not follow
    instructions well.

Specific Contextual Information:

	Description or Example	Desired Behavior
Context 1.	Entire class group: Steven never volunteers information and seldom responds when called on.	Voluntary contribution to class discussion.
Context 2.	Small groups: Steven seldom volunteers information but reluctantly responds when called on.	Voluntary contribution to group discussion.
Context 3.	Teacher-child dyad: The teacher interacts appropriately, but unenthusiastically.	Initiation of questions and elaboration of comments.

Step Four: Observe in Classroom

The clinician observed the class for 1 hour during which Steven participated in an English lesson for the whole class and a reading group for five students. In addition, she asked the teacher to audiotape the reading-group lesson for three days. The clinician's four goals for this step of the assessment were (1) to see when Steven participates, (2) to see how the teacher responds to him, (3) to see how successful Steven is in following instructions, and (4) to see if the form of the teacher's instructions assist or interfere with Steven's processing of information.

Step Five: Summarize Observations and
Determine Pattern of Communication Breakdown

The following information relating to the four goals of assessment was obtained. First, Steven's participation in class is limited. He asks questions only if he is missing a major piece of information. He does not volunteer information if anyone else can provide it. He appears tense when asked to answer questions. Second, the teacher seldom calls on Steven with the complete class present and only occasionally in a small group. Third, Steven experiences difficulty in following instructions.

Fourth, the manner of the teacher's instruction may have contributed to Steven's confusion. The following set of instructions were given to Steven's reading group on one of the days the teacher audiotaped the lesson.

Teacher   Look at page 4. Read the sentences and the words underneath. Find the best words and put them into the sentences. If you have trouble reading any words, ask Mrs. Jackson [the teacher's aide] to help you out. Okay, now let's see, on the worksheet you did yesterday, I mean the day before, you did real well, Kim. Here it is. Everyone else got theirs back yesterday when you were absent. Do the ditto from the workbook first and then the other one, four.

Jimmy   Four?

Teacher   Four. And then the other one. Oh, you haven't got your pencil (to Kim). And page 5 is just like page 4 except it's different words. See if you can pronounce them and make sure you know their meaning. One word that was hard is evacuate. The word evacuate, what do you think that means?

Steven   To leave.

Teacher   What?

Steven   To leave.

Teacher   Well yeah, if a town was evacuated everybody was leaving. Yeah. So find the rest of the words and fill them in. I want your names and dates on all of these please. Okay?

An analysis of this discussion revealed that the children were required to follow nine instructions after the teacher left. Three of the instructions depended on oral information only (e.g., do the ditto first then page 4). Four of the instructions were aided by worksheet cues (fill in the blanks) and two were routine (give name and date). Steven experienced difficulty on the instruction dependent on verbal information only, compared with instructions utilizing contextual cues. He followed the routine instructions well. On this lesson Steven completed the assignment correctly. He asked the teacher one clarification question and a peer one clarification question. However, he was also reminded by a peer to do the ditto sheet first. Distractions appeared to affect Steven. He took an extra moment to get back to task after the discussion of the previous day's worksheet, and he did not appear to attend after the teacher's discussion of "evacuate." The teacher interrupted instruction to discuss materials (Kim's worksheet from yesterday and her pencil) and to introduce new information (definition of evacuate).

In summary Steven is willing to communicate when highly motivated; that is, if he needs information to complete his work. He is not motivated for social communication. Steven's difficulty in following instructions is probably a result of the teacher's presentation of instructions and Steven's processing difficulties. In larger groups these problems are intensified.

Step Six: Validate Observations

The clinician, teacher, and Steven met to talk about the information obtained from the interviews and the classroom observations. Steven and his teacher were shown a transcript of the instructions previously discussed, and both agreed that these were representative of what usually occurred in a reading group. They also agreed with the clinician's summary of the problem. Options for a plan of intervention were discussed. The teacher suggested she needed to be more systematic in giving instructions. Steven said he would like to practice "doing his work right and talking more in class." The clinician took responsibility for developing an intervention approach.

ETHNOGRAPHIC INTERVENTION

When the assessment phase is complete, the next step is to develop an intervention plan that includes the teacher, the child, and the clinician. In some cases the focus of the program will be on teaching discourse rules so that children acquire the skills necessary to participate fully in school activities. The goal is to facilitate their "access to learning," the child's ability to interact in teaching-learning exchanges with teachers and peers. Since an emphasis on teaching rules and skills without accounting for differences in context is inappropriate, discourse rules are taught with academically relevant methods. Often children with poor classroom communication have not tuned in to the discourse rules operating in this context at a time when most of their peers are competently managing these rule. For these children a direct, structured, and intensive approach to discourse rule acquisition is warranted. This is not necessarily a fixed program, however. The intervention should be dynamic and allow for continuous reassessment and adjustment. There are numerous ways of designing programs that consider discourse rules. A single type of remediation may be used, or a combination of several approaches may be developed. There are four main types of intervention plans to consider: (1) traditional individual therapy, (2) construction of a miniclassroom, (3) entrance to the classroom, and (4) consultation with teacher and child in an advisory role.

Within the parameters of traditional therapy children can be instructed regarding communication rules for gaining attention, paying attention, and so on. A formal approach to discourse rule learning is likely to be of value as a first step to developing the student's self-awareness of inappropriate interaction behavior. The formal training can be quickly followed with activities that are directly tied to the context of concern (classroom, reading group, and so on). In combination with the other three approaches to be discussed, this method is likely to facilitate generalization of discourse rule knowledge.

The second plan, a miniclassroom, offers the opportunity to move beyond instruction in discourse rules to practice of the communication skills in a group situation. It provides a meaningful context for using group interaction skills. This method can serve to bridge the gap from therapy room to classroom. In this approach the clinician assumes a classroom teacher–like role and uses traditional classroom discourse rules as outlined in Chapters 3, 4, 6, 8, and 9. For example, children may be required to raise their hands to gain a speaking turn. At various times the children in the group can alternate in a teaching role and experience a different status and role in the interaction (e.g., asking questions to which they already know the answer, a common teaching ploy).

One of the authors (F.M.S.) developed a miniclassroom for learning-disabled fourth and fifth grade children. Following interviews with parents and teachers, group intervention objectives were established, including participating in classroom discussions, reporting school experiences, attending to speakers, and requesting clarification. A 30 minute classroom format was used in which children raised their hand to participate or took turns in a sequential order. Each session began with the children describing past or future school events. The descriptions became increasingly lengthy and complex as the year progressed. The next segment of the miniclassroom involved an academic task such as worksheets, listening activities, or group-participation projects. The clinician purposefully left out critical information regarding the academic task and so indirectly the children were prompted to request clarification. The program was successful in a number of ways. The children's discourse skills improved in the miniclassroom context. Teachers and parents gave unsolicited reports that the children were participating more fully in classroom interactions. Clinician observation of these children in their regular classroom supported the reports.

The third type of intervention, entrance into the classroom, has become very popular with some school clinicians. The clinician works with the child in the classroom and prompts the use of appropriate communication behaviors. This approach includes a range of clinician involvement, from the clinician as one of two team teachers to the clinician sitting beside the child in the classroom once a week to reinforce the therapy objectives. By moving into the classroom the clinician can see the communication demands placed on the child, evaluate the child's competence, and "fine tune" remediation objectives. Some speech and language pathologists have used this as their primary intervention approach with children experiencing difficulties in the classroom. These clinicians work closely with the teachers and develop language lessons that incorporate academic materials in the classroom.

The fourth approach involves meeting with the teacher and the child to discuss the communication breakdown and steps necessary for changing this pattern. This is often considered a "classroom consultation" approach. Here assistance is provided to structure class activities to accommodate the student's limitations and needs. The emphasis is placed on assisting teacher and child rather than on criticizing the current practices. In this approach, it is critical to treat the classroom teacher with regard and respect. Taking the role of "communication expert" can block any opportunity for obtaining access to a teacher or a classroom in the future.

A combination approach means not only a mixing of intervention contexts but a plan that involves all three participants. This may call for shifts in behavior for the classroom teacher (itemizing instructions rather than giving them in narrative form), for the child (learning to request clarification when he or she fails to understand), and for the clinician (developing small groups for focus on turn-taking and attention issues and incorporating typical classroom communication breakdowns into clinical intervention sessions).

Which approach is used or how approaches are combined depends on several factors. First, the appropriateness of the approach to the child's needs are of primary concern. For example, if the child needs help in turn-taking skills, individual therapy is obviously a poor context for work in this area. Next, the availability of the approach must be taken into account. If the classroom teacher is not amenable to classroom intervention, that approach may have to be discarded. Finally, the personal preferences of the clinician are accounted for. A clinician with strong counseling orientation might choose individual therapy, initially, in order to further explore causes underlying the child's poor communication in the classroom. Another clinician, in the same situation, might opt for a small group approach and begin working on shaping the behavior rather than attempting to discover its origins.

There is no single approach or combination of approaches that is best for children with poor communication skills. Each child, each teacher, and each clinician forming the triad brings his or her own limitations and abilities to the intervention process. The job of the clinician is to use the information available to develop the best possible approach in each case. The clinician also needs to keep in mind the possibility that in focusing his or her own attention as well as that of the teacher and the child on discourse rules in the classroom, performance of these rules may improve. The process of assessment and intervention design as described here serves to raise the awareness of the participants. The teacher and the child may begin to see classroom discourse in a more systematic way.

CASE STUDY

Based on the information obtained through interviews and observation, the following program was designed for Steven. It consisted of a three-pronged approach to remediation. First, individual therapy was conducted in the therapy room. The lessons focused on following instructions and asking appropriate questions. The clinician obtained worksheets from Steven's teacher that were at Steven's performance level. These were used to provide practice in following instructions dependent only on verbal cues and on worksheet cues. The clinician deliberately constructed directions that contained these cues. Steven was also given practice in reattending following interruptions. The clinician purposely inserted asides during her instructions so that Steven was forced to shift his attention and then reattend to the task. To give Steven more experience in requesting clarification the clinician gave confusing instructions. Lack of sufficient instruction made Steven request additional information, and the clinician encouraged these requests.

In order to facilitate participation the clinician organized an intervention group made up of Steven and four other children who had been identified as reluctant communicators. Given this composition, the children in the group were forced to speak or else endure long silences. For the initial part of each session the clinician took the role of teacher and had students raise their hands to participate. The second part of the session involved peer teaching, in that the children took the role of teacher. They took turns instructing the group on a lesson topic. The child instructor was given information necessary for the performance of the task that was not available to the other children; he or she became the expert. The use of the expert notion to encourage children to interact more freely has been documented recently in classroom research (Cooper, Marquis, and Ayers-Lopez (1982).

The third aspect of the plan was discussion with Steven's teacher. The clinician reinforced the teacher for identifying Steven's problem and for her patience and acceptance of Steven's behavior. The teacher asked for suggestions, and at this point the clinician discussed her plan for Steven. After explaining the individual therapy goal of improving Steven's ability to follow instructions and ask questions, the clinician suggested that the teacher might want to monitor her instructions to Steven carefully. Presentation of all instructional content together with material related to other academic information being given before or afterwards was recommended. After discussing the goals of the miniclassroom group work, the clinician encouraged the teacher to begin to allow Steven to be the "expert" for his reading group and eventually the entire class. The teacher was enthusiastic about the program and appeared pleased with the suggestions.

Follow-up Report

Steven was enrolled in the intervention program for four months. At the conclusion of the program the teacher reported improvement in all five areas originally identified as being below average for children in Steven's class. She even reported improved speech and language skills, although these were not directly worked with during intervention. A follow-up conference three months after intervention ended revealed that Steven was continuing to improve in classroom communication skills.

The success story of Steven encourages school speech-language pathologists to become more aggressive about identifying and treating children with communication breakdown in the classroom. School is the environment in which children spend the majority of their time, and poor communication skills can severely impair their ability to develop and learn.

REFERENCES

Cazden, C., Cox, M., Dickinson, D., Steinberg, Z., and Stone, C. (1979). You all gonna hafta listen: Peer teaching in a primary classroom. In W. Collins (Ed.), *Children's language and communication.* Hillsdale, NJ: L. Erlbaum.

Cook-Gumperz, J. (1975). The child as a practical reasoner. In M. Sanches and B. Blount (Eds.), *The sociocultural dimensions of language use.* New York: Academic Press.

Cooper, C., Marquis, A., and Ayers-Lopez, S. (1982). Peer learning in the classroom: Tracing patterns and consequences of children's spontaneous interactions. In L. C. Wilkinson (Ed.), *Communicating in the classroom.* New York: Academic Press.

Corsaro, W. (1979a). Young children's conception of status and role. *Sociology of Education, 52,* 46–59.

Corsaro, W. (1979b). We're friends, right? Children's use of access rituals in a nursery school. *Language in Society, 8,* 315–336.

Corsaro, W. (1981). Entering the child's world—Research strategies for field entry data collection in a preschool setting. In J. Green and C. Wallat (Eds.), *Ethnography and language educational settings.* Norwood, NJ: Ablex.

Glaser, B., and Strauss, A. (1967). *The discovery of grounded theory: Strategies for qualitative research*. Chicago: Aldine Publishing Company.

Green, J., and Wallat, C. (1981). Mapping instructional conversations: A sociolinguistic ethnography. In J. Green and C. Wallat (Eds.), *Ethnography and language in educational settings*. Norwood, NJ: Ablex.

Green, J., and Harker, J. (1982). Gaining access to learning: Conversational, social, and cognitive demands of group participation. In L. C. Wilkinson (Ed.), *Communicating in the classroom*. New York: Academic Press.

Hymes, D. (1982). What is ethnography? In P. Gilmore and A. Glatthorn (Eds.), *Children in and out of school: Ethnography and education*. Washington, DC: Center for Applied Linguistics.

Ripich, D. (1982). An introduction to ethnographic research. *Blumberg Conference on Special Education Proceedings*. Terra Haute: Indiana State University.

Ripich, D., and Panagos, J. (1983). Accessing children's knowledge of remedial speech lessons. Paper presented at American Speech-Language-and-Hearing Association Convention, Cincinnati, OH.

Spradley, J. (1980). *Participant observation*. New York: Holt, Rinehart and Winston.

Steinberg, Z., and Cazden, C. (1979). Children as teachers—of peers and ourselves. *Theory into Practice, 18*(4), 258–267.

Wilson, S. (1977). The use of ethnographic technique in educational research. *Review of Educational Research, 47*, 245–265.

Yarrow, M., and Campbell, J. (1963). Person perception in children. *Merrill-Palmer Quarterly, 9*, 57–72.

Chapter 11

The Identification of Socially Significant Communication Needs in Older Language Impaired Children: A Case Example

J. Bruce Tomblin
Susan J. Liljegreen

Services to communicatively impaired children during the past 20 years have expanded at an impressive rate. In addition, the profile of service has broadened from a focus on primary grade children with articulatory deficits to a wide range of communication capabilities for individuals from birth to adulthood. Expansion of the overall amount of services provided to children, however, is not likely to continue for two reasons. The proportion of children in the population is declining, and the proportion of the economy devoted to education is not likely to increase. However, the foci of services provided, including content and ages served, will continue to shift.

A recent trend has been an increase in the services provided to the older school-aged child. It has been common for services in the schools to be provided within the organization and physical structure of the local school systems. Traditionally there has existed a division of educational services into elementary and high school settings and very frequently middle school or junior high school levels. Often communication intervention has ceased or been reduced noticeably as the child moves out of the elementary building.

The current focus in services for children in the adolescent age range is justified. Hall and Tomblin (1978) reported that children with what is now often referred to as specific language disorder, (Leonard, 1979) demonstrate persistent deficits in both communication capability and academic accomplishment. Aram and colleagues have also shown this pattern of persistent communication and academic deficit in language-impaired children (Aram and Nation, 1980; Aram, Ekelman, and Nation, 1984). These results lead us to view language disorders as potentially lifelong in nature and reinforces the need for expansion of clinical services to serve the communication needs of the older child.

These shifts in foci challenge us to evaluate the rationales we use to provide these services. Prutting (1982) and Tomblin (1983) have noted that in recent years we have come to identify communication disorders on statistical grounds. Thus, often children who vary one or two standard deviations from the communication skills of their chronologic or performance age-mates are judged disordered. Based on these results, children and adolescents are often placed in an intervention program directed toward reducing deviant behaviors identified by the assessment tool. Such a rationale contrasts with one that has a longer history in our field. Travis (1931) and then his students, Van Riper (1963) and Johnson (Johnson, Brown, Curtis, Edney, and Keaster, 1967), defined a communication disorder in terms of a social valuation placed on communication behavior by both the speaker and the listener.

Our current rationale in approaching the communication problems of the older child builds on the philosophy of Wendell Johnson. This view holds that individuals with communication disorders currently or in the future will face social penalties. Our purpose for intervention is to reduce the likelihood of such social penalties. This philosophy provides us with a challenge and an opportunity.

Instead of focusing on communication differences defined by test results, intervention involves assisting children and those interacting with them in finding social approval and avoiding social penalty. We believe this approach increases our options and our potential for success.

The concepts of disorder as a socially defined phenomenon and intervention as an enterprise concerned with reduction of social penalties leads to a consideration of communication as a social activity recruiting knowledge of linguistic conventions and nonlinguistic social-cognitive constructs. Concepts variously identified with discourse or pragmatic theory provide the clinical practitioner with the framework of such a socially focused perspective on communication (Prutting, 1982).

The influence of pragmatics on intervention has been most evident with young and low-functioning children (Snyder-McLean and McLean, 1978). With the nonverbal low-functioning child we have come to appreciate that communicative intents and accomplishments occur well before the child develops oral speech proficiency (Bates, 1976; Dore, 1975). This perspective points out that the normal language learners realize early that their behavior causes others to respond in regular ways. This view challenges the notion that speech must be developed first before communication will arise and contends that communication must be established as a basis from which oral communication may arise.

The application of thinking in pragmatics to the intervention of the older child, however, has been quite limited. Many of the children we see have more advanced communication capabilities and communication needs. The older child faces much greater diversity in communication settings and hence requires a greater capability to determine the type of pragmatic principles to be employed. For example, topics to be covered are more likely to involve referents to events outside of the current location and time of conversation, and also the expectations of communicative partners with regard to acceptable fulfillment of communicative roles increases with age.

Because of the complexity of both the child's communication behavior and the communication tasks, it is believed that many clinicians are not sure how to identify pragmatically and socially relevant therapy goals. Recognizing that this may be true, this chapter represents an attempt to outline a clinical process that leads the clinician to the identification of such goals for older school age children.

CLINICAL DECISIONS LEADING TO SOCIALLY RELEVANT GOALS

A major component of any clinical activity consists of a decision-making process. Different clinical approaches will contrast with respect to the kinds of decisions posed by the clinician and with the nature of the information used to make these decisions.

The clinical decisions that serve as the central focus of the approach in this chapter and thus provide its philosophical framework arise from a set of ordered questions. The answers to the prior questions influence the specific content of the following questions. The first question asks what communication events present the child with the greatest degree of social penalty. From this question we proceed to ask what are the circumstances that predict instances of success and failure in this type of communicative event or activity. Next, we ask what causal factors in the child or the setting could be changed to reduce future occurrences of failure. Finally, we are concerned with how we should proceed to accomplish these changes. This chapter will focus on the first two of these questions.

The first question above requires consideration of the settings in which the individual communicates when failure occurs and the consequences of communication failure in these settings. There are certain consequences to our asking for this information. First, we must learn about the interaction of the child and his own environment. General trait characteristics of the child that indicate that the child possesses a certain receptive or expressive level of language skill is insufficient to answer this question. These measures assume that there are single and determined ways in which children with particular trait levels (i.e., test scores) will perform in natural settings. We believe that often there are alternatives to communicative success in many settings. Instead we must either observe the child in various settings such as the classroom, cub scout meetings, or home or alternatively obtain a report from those who do participate with the child. Using both direct and indirect approaches can complement each other. By using the information gathered in these ways we should know something about the communicative situations confronting the child and the degree of success in these situations.

To answer the first question, that is, to determine what types of communicative events present the child with the greatest degree of social penalty, we must also learn something about the social penalties involved in these situations. This requires an assessment of the social values of those participating in the situation. To learn about these social values we can either ask the child-client or we can ask those in authority who interact with the child. Again, both these sources of information can be used and may complement each other. Through these reports, identification of a small number of communicative activities in which the child fails and faces social penalties is possible.

This brings us to the second question. What are the circumstances that predict instances of success or failure in the communicative event of interest? Underlying this question is the notion that the child does succeed in certain instances. If such variability exists, we are then interested in predicting this variability. In order to develop such an account it is necessary for us to recognize that communication accomplishment or failure entails complex interactions.

In predicting when breakdown is likely to occur we cannot focus on separate components. All too often, however, the temptation is to treat each component of communication as a separate entity. Duchan (1984) noted that our theories portray language (communication) as a set of components, each represented by a box. The problem is that we often assume that each box functions autonomously, and thus once we have identified a deficit in behavior it represents the locus or cause of the problem. As Duchan (1983) and Kirchner and Skarakis-Doyle (1983) note it is much more likely that we are working with a system in which various factors involved with communication interact in a dynamic fashion. When breakdown occurs, the contributing factors may be diverse and probably entail aspects of the system that extend beyond the behavioral category identified as the locus of communicative failure. Such a perspective requires that the clinician employ a theory of pragmatics that specifies the ways in which various aspects of communicative knowledge can interact. It is exactly at this point, however, that our theories of pragmatics are weak. How does variation in domains of language such as comprehension ability or phonological proficiency influence conversational participation?

Recently Hurtig, Ensrude, and Tomblin (1982) demonstrated that the repetitive questions asked by some autistic children were the product of an inability in these children to contribute additional information to the topic. The initial assumption was that these children were impaired pragmatically in their knowledge of the conditions for appropriate requesting. Thus intervention with these children focused on their requesting behavior. Ironically, their requesting ability was not the basis of the problem; rather it was their inability to add new information after receiving a response. They had learned to start a conversation with a question but were unable to add to the topic after receiving a response. As Kirchner and Skarakis-Doyle (1983) noted, in a dynamic system, breakdown in one aspect of the system (ability to continue a topic) can lead to aberrant manifestations in other aspects of the system.

The challenge for the clinician is to uncover these dynamic relationships and in doing so gain the power of at least predicting the occurrences of success or failure. If the clinician can discover the relationship between certain properties of the communicative task and the likelihood of successful accomplishment, it should then be possible to move to the final two questions, What causal factors in the child or the environment may be changed to reduce this failure and How can these changes be accomplished?

The discussion to this point has focused on the general logic of our particular clinical approach. A case example may help clarify this perspective further. In this case example the emphasis will be on addressing the first two questions. The methods employed to answer these questions are not different than those found in any rational problem-solving activity. They consist of observing the client and interviewing those who carry out daily life activities with the child. From this a particular communicative activity is selected, hypotheses are generated concerning factors associated with success and failure, and then further observations and manipulations of the communicative settings are made to evaluate these hypotheses.

CASE EXAMPLE

Subject Background

Marcia is a 12 year old girl with a long history of communication disorders. Communication intervention began when she was four years old, and she was described as having delayed syntactic and articulatory development. Later intellectual assessment using a Wechsler Intelligence Scale for Children—Revised (WISC-R) yielded a verbal IQ of 68 and performance IQ of 110. As might be expected, Marcia encountered considerable difficulties in school achievement.

At the time Marcia entered our clinic she had developed linguistic skills to the point that she was able to express most meanings needed for functional communication. Her expressive skills were marked by word-finding difficulties and frequent sentence fragments, as exemplified by the following narrative:

Adult   What did you do today?
Marcia   We went to the library...and...we got...a...books. And...and...before we to library we went on a bus...and we walk across the river.

Despite this functional level of linguistic development, Marcia was still perceived by most adults as a very poor communicator. The primary approach used to evaluate her communication difficulties in the past was the administration of various language tests. During the two years preceding our work, 17 different language tests were used, several of these two or three times. In addition, she was given several reading, visual-motor, and intelligence tests. The results of these tests showed clearly that Marcia was functioning well below age level. This poor performance was consistent with achievement test scores placing her at a second to third grade performance level.

Those working with Marcia prior to the residential program also noted that she often did not attend well to the test tasks and therapy activities. In these instances she was found to stare off and give no response or she would comment on events other than the task at hand. In fact the notion of an attention deficit was often noted as the likely cause of her poor performance on several tests.

Based on these results, her prior therapy focused on the following goals: classification and categorization, increased use of prepositions, increased use of verbs in sentences, verb tense usage, noun-verb agreement, story retelling, and sentence imitation. In addition, attention training tasks were provided in which Marcia would listen to directions on a tape and carry out the action. The therapy goals established for Marcia were typically determined by the test areas in which she performed most poorly. Clearly clinical intervention was seen as the evaluation of a set of semiautonomous skills, and then therapy was directed toward strengthening these skills. Reportedly, these efforts were somewhat successful in that her performance levels in the tasks improved. However, this success was limited. The continued evaluation efforts and the referral to our program attest to the dissatisfaction of the clinicians themselves.

Identification of Socially Relevant Therapy Goals

Our contact with Marcia occurred while she was enrolled in a residential program for children with communication problems. This program provided a setting in which we could observe her as she interacted with familiar adults in a wide range of activities. This residential program employs adults to provide 24 hour child care. These child care workers interacted with the children under their care in a wide range of settings from mealtime and bedtime to recreational activities and group discussions. Not only did these child care workers have an opportunity to observe a child in their care, they also were able to note the manner in which the children interacted with each other. In addition to the child care workers, the children also were seen for speech-language therapy in individual and group sessions by graduate students supervised by university faculty. The initial goal was to address the first question mentioned earlier: In what communicative situations does she fail and which of these are most penalizing to her?

We did not believe further standardized testing was necessary and in fact there did not seem to be any tests available that she had not already been given. Instead we chose to use the rich diversity of settings afforded us by the residential program to obtain observer reports and direct observations. Further we wanted initially to focus our efforts on locating communicative situations in which she was *either* relatively successful or unsuccessful. It was significant to note that in the prior evaluations there were a few descriptions of her interpersonal communication skills but no comments in any reports about instances in which she was successful. All too often we find ourselves searching for all the incompetencies presented to us by a child and ignore the equally, if not more, important instances of success.

The child care workers and clinicians working with Marcia all maintained logs of her communication and social behavior. Further, those working with her were asked specifically to note instances in which they believed her communication led to notable social difficulties with either them or her peers. These logs allowed us to identify certain types of communication failures noted by several different individuals. Two behaviors were quite common.

First, she often did not respond to things said to her, or if she did respond, the response was minimal and she made no effort to continue the interaction. Secondly, she complained quite often. Given the rather pervasive nature of her nonresponsiveness, we attempted to obtain more information about her conversational interactions. In meetings with the child care workers in the dormitory they confirmed that often Marcia did not respond to questions or statements directed toward her. Further, out of a list of types of communication skills that had been noted to be deficient in Marcia, her failure to respond to questions or statements of others was judged by them to be her most significant deficit. Thus this type of communicative failure became the focus of our inquiry into the next question: What conditions predict her failure to respond?

We initially suspected one of two factors that might have predicted her failure to respond. One possibility was that she did not comprehend the propositional content of questions or statements. Alternatively, it was possible that she did not understand the illocutionary force of questions . Neither of these explanations was satisfying. The latter explanation predicted that she should fail all requests because she did not understand the force of requests. The former explanation predicted that certain forms or contents of questions would be consistently misapprehended.

Neither of these predictions was found to be particularly valid. We observed numerous instances in which Marcia would respond to questions of a very similar nature to those where she had previously failed to respond. Further, these were in the same situations. Also she would, on occasion, engage in reasonable on-topic conversations, in which she was responsive to her partner's utterances (both requests and statements). In these cases she would stay with the topic. It was also noted that these successful conversations occurred with adults. She was much less successful holding a conversation with peers.

In the clinic where therapy sessions were directed by the adult around rather traditional language therapy goals, Marcia's behavior was similar to that noted by the child care workers. She was much less likely to respond to statements and requests made unless they absolutely required a response. Thus if the clinician presented the request with sufficient force she would comply. In these instances her replies were typically very minimal. Further, most of the time she spent engaged in extraneous activities such as playing with clothing or looking out the window.

Based upon our observations we hypothesized that Marcia's poorest communication performance occurred when she was asked to converse on topics with which she was not highly familiar. The best conversations were those in which she was familiar with the topic. Two discourse factors could account for this variability. Greater familiarity with a topic allowed her to have a greater command of the event relationships to be discussed in the conversation. Thus familiarity with the topic possibly increased the likelihood that she understood the relationship between the content of her conversational partner and the response she needed to provide. An alternative explanation focused on the dimension of social position in pragmatics. The topics she was most likely to excell in were those in which she was an authority in relation to the listener. Thus her position in the conversation was often a dominant one in which she was informing, and the requests made to her were genuine requests for information or assistance rather than directives and requests for compliance.

To evaluate this account we placed Marcia in a setting that maximized these factors of familiarity and status. Marcia was known to be quite capable in art and thus was given the role of art instructor, and a clinician served as her student. In this setting she selected the art project and then proceeded to instruct the adult student. Initially we found that her conversational participation was quite good; she answered questions, restated instructions in modified ways when the adult "student" feigned misunderstanding, and responded on topic. Because these sessions involved a drawing activity, there were times in which the topic shifted away from instruction in drawing. In these instances the topic shift was guided by Marcia, since we wanted the adult "student" to be nondominant in these conversations.

The adult's contact with Marcia was not limited to this instructional setting. Conversations were established in other settings. In these settings the respective roles were altered in that Marcia and the adult did not interact according to the "teacher-student" roles. In these conversations we observed the inappropriate conversational participation noted earlier—specifically that Marcia failed to respond to the conversational partner's prior utterances. These failures were found to occur on topics on which she had previously successfully conversed. However, we noted that these failures were at points where a topic was being introduced by the conversational partner, thus, at the beginnings of conversations initiated by the adult or at points of topic shift where the adult was introducing a new topic. This observation lead to what we believe is the best predictor of Marcia's conversational success and failure, topic ownership. Those instances in which Marcia was the poorest communicator were those in which she did not or could not determine the topic. Those settings in which she could and did set the topic were her best. Our earlier hypothesis regarding conversational status was in fact accurate, but incomplete. Typically the more dominant member of the conversation controls the topic and thus the factors of dominance and topic ownership will often overlap.

This account of Marcia's communicative behavior provides means of predicting Marcia's communicative success and failure that is much more powerful than the earlier explanation of poor attention. The attention explanation did not predict when Marcia would or would not succeed, only that she would be variable. In contrast, this account makes specific predictions of when she is most likely to succeed or fail.

By finding an association between topic ownership and Marcia's responsiveness to the communicative contributions of others we have addressed the second question. At this point our consideration about intervention turned to hypotheses about the types of underlying factors that might serve as a basis or cause for Marcia's difficulty in communication when she does not own the topic. In the past Marcia's variability in communication performance was explained as a product of poor attention. However, Tomblin (1983) has argued that the use of such constructs as attention for purposes of explanation is not justified. We believe that the notion of attention refers to instances in which the perceiver makes use of information appropriate to the particular setting. Thus, it can be said that Marcia's failure to respond to certain statements and requests in conversations were indeed instances of attentional failures. That is, she failed to make use of certain information for appropriate responses in the conversational task. When viewed in this manner the notion of attention no longer carries explanatory value, but rather is a restatement of the observation.

Explanatory accounts of language behavior are very difficult to achieve at this point in our study of the behavior; however, we believe that any efforts in changing behavior require assumptions about factors that contribute or cause the behavior. Since our theories of language behavior are weak with respect to causal accounts, the clinician must generate hypotheses about causal factors that are truly speculative. The validity of the hypothesis is borne out by the extent of change achieved. With respect to Marcia's difficulties, we generated the following hypotheses. Somehow Marcia had failed to learn that conversational participation includes collaboration on topics or activities introduced by others. This hypothesis was partially influenced by our observation that Marcia often failed to maintain collaboration in a group activity even when no verbal communication was involved. For instance, on group walks she would often leave the group and stray off. In discussing her behavior, both communicative and noncommunicative, with clinicians and child care workers we came to believe that Marcia had difficulties identifying or adopting the goals of a social activity when she did not generate them.

Our hypothesis concerning collaboration on topics and activities established by others then provided a tentative answer to the third question and also established the basis for addressing the final question, how to improve her performance in collaboration. Since we are focusing in this chapter on the processes of identifying therapy goals we will not discuss this issue. Our perspective on the method of intervention with this type of therapy goal, however, would be to make use of intervention approaches developed for social skills training in children (Cartledge and Milburn, 1980).

SUMMARY

This chapter has been an attempt by the authors to outline an approach to the identification of therapy goals based upon a set of basic principles.

1. At the core of communication disorder is social disvalue or penalty.
2. Pragmatic models of communication should allow us to describe a client's communication behavior in ways that are socially relevant.
3. In order to identify such goals, observations and reports of the client must be obtained from settings in which the child normally participates.
4. This information is gathered and evaluated according to a set of basic questions. These emphasize the problem-solving nature of the clinical process. The basic questions entertained were:
    a. What communication events present the child with the greatest degree of social penalty?
    b. What are the circumstances that predict instances of success and failure in this kind of communication event?
    c. What causal factors in the child or in the setting could be changed to reduce future occurrences of failure?
    d. How should we proceed to accomplish these changes?

The product of this approach should lead to the identification of those aspects of the child's communication that bring the greatest social penalties. As a result, changes brought about by clinical intervention should yield the greatest positive gain in the child's quality of life.

REFERENCES

Aram, D., Ekelman, B., and Nation, J. (1984). Preschoolers with language disorders: 10 years later. *Journal of Speech and Hearing Research, 27*, 232–244.

Aram, D. M., and Nation, J. E. (1980). Preschool language disorders and subsequent language and academic difficulties. *Journal of Communication Disorders, 13*, 159–170.

Bates, E. (1976). *Language and context: The acquisition of pragmatics.* New York: Academic Press.

Cartledge, G., and Milburn, J. (Eds.) (1980). *Teaching social skills to children.* New York: Pergamon.

Dore, J. (1975). Holophrases, speech acts and language universals. *Journal of Child Language, 2*, 21–40.

Duchan, J. (1983). Language processing and geodesic domes. In T. Gallagher and C. Prutting (Eds.), *Pragmatic assessment and intervention issues in language.* San Diego: College-Hill Press.

Hall, P., and Tomblin, J. B. (1978). A follow-up study of children with articulation and language disorders. *Journal of Speech and Hearing Disorders, 43*, 227–241.

Hurtig, R., Ensrude, S., and Tomblin, J. B. (1982). The communicative function of question production in autistic children. *Journal of Autism and Developmental Disorders, 12*, 57–69.

Johnson, W., Brown, S., Curtis, J., Edney, C., and Keaster, J. (1967). *Speech handicapped school children*. New York: Harper and Row.

Kirchner, D., and Skarakis-Doyle, E. (1983). Developmental language disorders: A theoretical perspective. In T. Gallagher and C. Prutting (Eds.), *Pragmatic assessment and intervention issues in language*. San Diego: College-Hill Press.

Leonard, L. (1979). Language impairment in children. *Merrill-Palmer Quarterly, 25*, 205–232.

Prutting, C. (1982). Pragmatics as social competence. *Journal of Speech and Hearing Disorders, 47*, 123–133.

Snyder-McLean, L., and McLean, J. (1978). Verbal information gathering strategies: the child's use of language to acquire language. *Journal of Speech and Hearing Disorders, 43*, 306–325.

Tomblin, J. B. (1983). An examination of the concept of disorder in the study of developmental language disorders. Paper presented at the Fifth Annual Wisconsin Symposium on Research in Child Language Disorders, Madison, WI.

Travis, L. E. (1931). *Speech pathology*. New York: Appleton-Century Company.

Van Riper, C. (1963). *Speech correction: Principles and methods*. Englewood Cliffs, NJ: Prentice-Hall.

Chapter 12

An Approach to Developing Conversational Competence

Jan L. Bedrosian

The development of discourse skills is currently a popular area of study in language. According to Craig (1983), during the last decade there has been a strong theoretical shift from syntactic and semantic models of child language acquisition to communicative or discourse models of language acquisition. The literature contains numerous articles describing stages of discourse development in terms of both communicative functions and conversational rules or strategies employed by normal children (e.g., Chapman, 1982; Gallagher and Prutting, 1983; Prutting, 1979; Rees, 1978).

Similarly, this theoretical shift has also been evident in the area of language disorders. Characteristics of the discourse performance of various clinical populations, including the mentally retarded (e.g., Bedrosian and Prutting, 1978; Owings and McManus, 1982; Warne, 1984), learning disabled (e.g., Bryan and Pflaum, 1978; Donahue, Pearl, and Bryan, 1980; Wiig and Semel, 1980), and autistic (e.g., Bernard-Opitz, 1982; Prizant and Duchan, 1981), have been described. Although these descriptions are essential for gaining a better understanding of these populations, the speech and language clinician is often left with the age-old question of how to use this information in developing appropriate intervention programs. In an attempt to bridge the gap between research and clinical application, the purpose of this chapter is to present methodology for systematically assessing and treating discourse skills in language-disordered children and adults.

The discourse program described in this chapter was developed within a framework of topic and conversational control, and applies only to those language-disordered individuals meeting a specific criteria. This criteria will be discussed, in addition to specific procedures for assessing topic and conversational control, categorizing communication skills, selecting appropriate intervention goals, facilitating or teaching discourse skills in both group and individual sessions, and measuring the effectiveness of intervention. Depending on individual needs, aspects of the program have been used with school-aged children as well as with mentally retarded and autistic adults.

CRITERIA FOR CLIENT SELECTION

Specification of Criteria

The assessment and intervention procedures to be discussed apply only to those individuals who meet specific criteria. Criteria for client selection are that the individual:

1. Be capable of communicating verbally as opposed to relying on only nonverbal means for expressing communicative intentions.
2. Have intelligible speech performance.
3. Be functioning at least in Piaget's preoperational period of cognitive development.
4. Have a comprehension level no lower than two and a half to three years of age in order to minimally follow the topic of conversation.
5. Have a language production level no lower than two to three years of age.

Rationale for Criteria

Information regarding developmental levels of cognition, language production, and comprehension is important for the selection of appropriate discourse goals, for grading the procedures or instructions used in teaching a specific conversational skill, and for determining the acceptability of a conversational initiation or response (Bedrosian, 1982). For example, individuals functioning at Brown Stages I or II would not be expected to use requests for repair in the form of "Can you say that again?" Other examples are provided in the discussion of specific intervention procedures.

Information specifically regarding cognitive levels of development has significance in light of the recent research examining the relationship between cognition and language (e.g., Lund and Duchan, 1983). Chapman (1981), for example, addressed several discourse skills related to the preoperational period. Because of the development of the symbolic function, the topics of the preoperational child are no longer tied to the here-and-now. The child becomes capable of initiating topics "removed in time and space from the conversations" (p. 120). Another characteristic of the child's discourse development is the increasing ability to maintain topics by providing new information. In terms of the clinical significance, preoperational-level clients who initiate topics primarily in the here-and-now or who exhibit difficulties in maintaining topics may be appropriate candidates for intervention relating to topic (Bedrosian, 1982). Chapman also stated that children, particularly those in the mid to late preoperational stages, exhibit a greater variety of discourse functions reflecting cognitive changes in their "ability to control their own behavior, to reason, to relate events to one another, and to engage in complex imaginative play" (p. 126). The variety of communicative functions exhibited by clients in later preoperational stages may provide important diagnostic information for selecting intervention goals.

In the concrete operational period, the child begins to control not only his own discourse structures but also the listener's interpretation of those structures (Bates, 1976). Bates (1976) proposed that in order for the child to simultaneously take the role of the encoder and the decoder, he must be able to perform the cognitive operation of reversibility, the ability to reverse a thought process. According to Bates, this cognitive ability is reflected conversationally in the child's use of camouflaged utterances or indirect speech acts (i.e., indirect request forms). For example, the statement, "Gosh, it's cold in here," could be interpreted as a request for the listener to close a window. Based on this relationship between cognition and discourse performance, concrete operational clients who exhibit commanding styles of interaction may be capable of modifying their commands through the use of indirect requests (Bedrosian, 1982).

Although continued research regarding the exact nature of the relationship between cognition and communication development is needed, there is currently enough evidence showing the importance of considering this relationship in clinical assessment and intervention.

PROCEDURES FOR ASSESSING DISCOURSE SKILLS

Data Collection

Procedures for assessing discourse skills involve the use of a set of conversational analysis procedures applied to data collected in a variety of communicative interactions. The choice for describing an individual's communicative performance in various interactions is based on the finding that communication abilities and styles of interaction can vary as a function of the other participants involved and the conversational setting (Ervin-Tripp, 1973).

In terms of the first contextual parameter involving the participant or communicative partner, the collection of data for the conversational program consists of an audio- or preferably videotaped recording of the client in at least two of the following interactions, each 10 minutes in length:

1. *Client-peer interaction*, with a peer or peers and the client interacting alone in a room.
2. *Client-teacher or primary caregiver interaction*, with a "significant other" adult and the client interacting together in a room.
3. *Client-clinician-peer interaction*, with the clinician examing the client's communication skills in a group setting in which there is usually an unequal number of speaking turns across participants.
4. *Client-clinician interaction*, with the clinician examining the client's ability to
   a. initiate topics during silent intervals;
   b. react to interruptions or changes of topic;
   c. maintain topics initiated by the use of declarative statements as opposed to various types of requests;
   d. attain the attention of an inattentive listener; and
   e. use repair devices when the clinician deliberately speaks unintelligibly.

Another contextual parameter important to consider in the assessment of discourse skills involves the conversational setting in which communication takes place. For adolescent and adult clients, the preferred context is a living room setting. This setting appears to be more conducive to promoting conversation than the more traditional table and chair setting (Bedrosian, 1982).

For language-disordered children, a play setting is recommended. McCune-Nicholich and Carroll (1981) and Craig (1983) discussed the importance of play in language assessments. Specifically for pragmatic assessment, play provides a "natural context for communication" (Craig, 1983, p. 116).

An important consideration in using a play setting involves physical context variables (i.e., the kinds of toys or objects present or the nature of the ongoing activity). Gallagher (1983) stated that "different toys elicit different types of communicative behavior from children" (p. 10). In a study by Wanska, Bedrosian, and Pohlman (in press), the subject matters of topic initiations in normal five year old children engaged in peer play across three different play conditions were examined, and, in fact, were found to vary as a function of the toys provided. Specifically, results indicated that the children initiated a greater frequency of memory- and future-related topics while playing with Legos than while playing with either a miniature hospital set or hospital props, which elicited greater frequencies of here-and-now as well as of fantasy-related topics. Although little research regarding the effects of physical context variables on the discourse performance of normal and language-disordered children has been conducted, the consideration of these variables in language assessment and intervention is warranted.

Data Analysis

According to Prutting and Kirchner (1983), discourse analyses can be conducted at two different levels: a molecular approach, involving a "fine grain analysis of the client's behavior"; and a molar analysis, involving a "global appraisal of the client's system" (p. 44). Both of these levels are incorporated in the conversational program. First, a molecular approach will be discussed.

Molecular Analysis. Specific procedures and coding definitions for conducting a molecular analysis are reported by Bedrosian (1982). A summary of those procedures follows.

Initially, all tape recordings from the interactions assessed are orthographically transcribed, and simultaneous utterances are bracketed together. A topic conversational analysis procedure derived from the research reported by Keenan and Schieffelin (1976) and Bloom, Rocissano, and Hood (1976), regarding topic in normal adult-child discourse, is then applied to the data. Topic is defined as the proposition or set of propositions or subject matter about which the speaker is either providing or requesting new information (Ervin-Tripp, 1973; Keenan and Schieffelin, 1976). The rationale for focusing on topic in conversation is that topic

1. Is a means through which a person can coordinate his or her conversations and actions with others, thereby fostering the development and growth of interpersonal relations.
2. Is part of what regulates or sequences a conversation.
3. Involves the initiation of communication to express needs, feelings, and ideas.
4. Requires active listening and depends on a person's comprehension level in order to maintain the flow of a conversation.

5. Provides a framework for operationalizing Grice's (1975) conversational maxim of being relevant.

Topic, therefore, offers an all encompassing framework for viewing communication skills.

For all transcripts, the turns consisting of topic initiations are coded across four areas. First, each topic initiation is coded according to the subject matter(s) (noise or sound-word play, name-calling, fantasy, here-and-now, memory-related, future-related, social routine, story-related, attention-getter) involved. The specific types of subject matters initiated in each interaction allows the determination of whether or not the client is adhering to particular sociolinguistic rules regarding topic (Ervin-Tripp, 1973). For example, name-calling might be appropriate in a peer interaction but not in an interaction involving a parent. In addition, the variety of subject matters expressed may have important implications for intervention. Second, each topic initiation is coded according to its participant orientation including self-oriented and other-oriented topics (Miller, Nunnally, and Wackman, 1975). Individuals who talk only about themselves may be experiencing difficulties in establishing relationships. Third, the communicative intent (requests for information or opinion, permission, action, or attention; tag questions; indirect requests; informatives; commands) of each topic initiation is coded. Determining the communicative intent of topic initiations may help in identifying those clients who are having difficulty in initiating and maintaining topics. For example, clients who initiate topics primarily through informatives or declarative statements may have a more difficult time in getting their topics maintained than those who initiate topics through the use of requests. Also, clients who initiate topics primarily through commands may be signaling potential interpersonal conflicts. Finally, topic initiations are coded for the presence of eye contact for purposes of attention-getting.

All other turns are coded as constituting either continuous, discontinuous, or both continuous and discontinuous discourse (Keenan and Schieffelin, 1976). Specifically, once a topic has been initiated by a participant, continuous discourse constitutes those subsequent turns that are linked in some manner to the topic that was initially introduced. The ways in which these turns are linked include: topic incorporating, subtopic, noise or sound-word play, answer question–comply with command, responses involving yes or no, incomplete responses, finish response–respond for another, emotional response, alternative, acknowledgment and request or response for repair. The types of continuous discourse turns employed by a client may offer important developmental information regarding his or her level of communicative competence (Chapman, 1981).

When a topic has been introduced and/or maintained across two or more speaking turns, discontinuous discourse constitutes a subsequent turn that is not linked in any manner to the topic at hand. The ways in which discontinuous discourse turns occur include new topic initiation, reinitiation of a topic, silent evasion of a question, evasion of a question by initiation of another topic, monologue, and consecutive topic initiations. Clients who exhibit greater frequencies of discontinuous than continuous discourse turns may be good candidates for intervention procedures regarding topic maintenance.

Both continuous and discontinuous discourse consists of a turn, by a single participant, that initially involves one or more utterances constituting continuous discourse with the previous turn, followed by one or more utterances constituting discontinuous discourse. These turns represent polite conversational transitions into new topics (Bedrosian, 1979).

Another area also analyzed is that of control. According to theory put forth by Watzlawick, Beavin, and Jackson (1967), communication involves the meeting of two or more persons who seek to define the nature of the relationship. It has been validated (J. Capella, personal communication, 1980) that two of the dimensions along which participants define the relationship are that of control, or dominance, and submission. Therefore, the dimension of control is important to consider when dealing with conversational interactions. Control in the relationship can be expressed by any one of the following means: interruptions, multiuttered questions or commands, and interrogative units (Mishler, 1975) involving chaining and arching.

An example of a coded transcription sheet is presented in Table 12-1. Following the coding procedures, the frequencies of each category for topic and control are tallied for each client across all interactions.

Molar Analysis. For those operating under strict time limitations, only specific portions of the molecular analysis could be examined depending on the individual needs of the client, or a molar analysis of the client's communication skills across interactions could be conducted. A discourse skills checklist (Bedrosian, 1983) based on the molecular analysis is provided in Table 12-2. This molar analysis also includes a section relating to observations of nonverbal behaviors.

Categorization of Communication Skills

Based on the results of the molecular or molar analysis, each client's communicative performance is categorized into general styles of interaction along dimensions of dominance or submission. Operationally defined, a dominant individual is one who (1) initiates a greater number

Table 12-1. Coded Transcription Sheet

Name: _____   Transcriber: _____

Date of Recording: _____

Situational variables: 1) Type of interaction: _____Peer_____

2) Names of Participants: _____

3) Length of Interaction: _____

4) Setting or Context: _____

KEY: xxx = unintelligible word or utterance
    ⊏ = overlapped turns
    ( ) = noises, laughter, clearing of throat, etc.
    (>2) = a silent interval that is greater than 2 seconds
    CD = continuous discourse turns
    DD = discontinuous discourse turns
    = chained or arched questions

| | Analysis | | | | | |
CD/DD	Subject Matter	Communi-cative Intent	Specific Subject Matter	Eye Contact	Speaker	Discourse
Topic Introduction	Social	Informative	Other-Related	Yes	1	Hi, Jim.
Topic Introduction	Memory-Related	Informative	Self-Related	No	1	I went on vacation and I had a good time on vacation (>2) and I had a lot of fun.
Acknowledge					2	Yeah, Betty.
Topic Incorporate					1	I went canoeing and I went lotta stuff.
Topic Introduction	Future-Related	Request Information	Other-Related	No	2	What you doing tonight, Betty?

of topics than his or her peers or primary caregiver–teacher across the interactions assessed, and (2) expresses at least one type of control (e.g., interruptions, multiuttered questions or commands).

PROCEDURES FOR TREATING DISCOURSE SKILLS

Intervention Agents

In a discussion of communicative approaches to intervention, Craig (1983) suggested a need for a variety of intervention agents so that the

Table 12-2. Discourse Skills Checklist: A Molar Analysis

Name of client: _____

Date of interaction: _____

Type of participant interaction: _____

Type of setting: _____

Length of interaction: _____

Instructions: Check the appropriate skill descriptor that follows:

	Yes	No	Sometimes	Not Applicable
I. Topic Initiations				
A. Frequency of client's topic initiations in comparison to the other participant(s): (check one)				
1. None				
2. Less than				
3. Approximately equal to				
4. More than				
B. Subject matter of topic initiations:				
1. Able to get attention of listener				
2. Repeats old topics on a daily basis				
3. Initiates new topics on a daily basis				
4. Able to greet others				
5. Able to express departures when leaving				
6. Able to make introductions				
7. Able to initiate needs				
8. Able to initiate questions:				
a. Requests for information				
b. Requests for repetition or clarification				
c. Requests for action				
d. Requests for permission				
9. Talks mostly about self				
10. Talks about the other, as well as self				
11. Talks about referents in the past				
12. Talks about referents in the future				
13. Talks about referents in the present				
14. Talks about fantasy-related referents				
15. Calls people names				
16. Uses noise or sound-word play in appropriate situations				
II. Maintaining Topics				
A. Able to keep a topic going:				
1. Responds to questions				
2. Acknowledges topic (e.g., "Uh-huh")				
3. Offers new information that is related				
4. Requests more information about a topic				
5. Able to ask requests for repetition or clarification if message is not clear				

Table continued on following page

Table 12-2 (continued)

	Yes	No	Sometimes	Not Applicable
6. Able to repeat or answer questions about what another has talked about				
7. Agrees with others				
8. Disagrees with others				
B. Not able to keep a topic going:				
1. Intentionally evades or ignores a question				
2. Initiates a topic immediately following a topic initiation by a prior speaker				
3. Engages in monologues when in a group				
III. Use of Eye Contact				
A. Able to use eye contact to designate a listener in a group when initiating a topic				
B. Uses eye contact while listening				
IV. Turn-taking				
A. Is easily interrupted				
B. Interrupts others				
C. Answers questions for others				
D. Has long speaking turns				
E. Designates turns for others in a group				
F. Sensitive to listener cues (e.g., can tell if listener is interested or bored)				
G. Excuses self when interrupting				
V. Politeness				
A. Able to make indirect requests				
B. Uses commands				
C. Uses politeness markers of "Please," "Thank you," "Excuse me"				
VI. Observation of Nonverbal Behaviors				
A. Stands or sits too close to people when talking				
B. Stands or sits too far away from people when talking				
C. Stands or sits at appropriate social distances when talking				
D. Uses nonverbal head nods to acknowledge				
E. Uses nonverbal means of getting attention to initiate a topic (e.g., taps on shoulder, points)				

client will learn appropriate style modifications associated with different listener characteristics. For clients enrolled in a public school, vocational program, or institutional setting, the initial intervention agents include the clinician and a peer group. Clients are grouped according to their styles of interaction. Each group consists of three clients, composed of both dominant and submissive individuals. The rationale for mixing styles of interaction in each group is that it will create a dynamic atmosphere for intervention. Sex, cognitive level, and language production and comprehension levels can vary within each group.

For clients enrolled in a private or university clinic setting, where it is often difficult to schedule appropriate peer groups owing to time conflicts, the initial intervention agent involves the clinician, followed later by both the clinician and primary caregiver. Although the clinician may not be a significant other, Craig (1983) suggested that the clinician may initially need to take a strong role to provide the client with "increased experience with communicative success" (p. 112).

Intervention Design

A multiple baseline design across behaviors (Hersen and Barlow, 1976) is employed for purposes of collecting intervention data. For each client, the treatment variable is applied sequentially to at least two separate communication target behaviors. Thus, while both or all behaviors are being measured simultaneously, only one is treated at a time. When criterion is met for the first behavior, the treatment variable is then applied to the second behavior.

This type of design assumes independence between or among the dependent variables involving the conversational behaviors selected for intervention. Bedrosian (1982) employed such a design in a discourse intervention program with mentally retarded adults. Results indicated a relationship between some of the discourse behaviors studied. For example, a relationship between topic initiations and interruptions was found: As interruptions decreased, so did the frequency of topic initiations. Such relationships were reported to have important implications for future clinical intervention in that larger units of discourse skills may need to be treated. Continued research regarding the independence or relationship between or among discourse behaviors is warranted.

Structure of Intervention Sessions

The structure of each 30 minute session involves an initial 5 minute period devoted to baseline measurements. During this period, the clinician refrains from initiating topics and from giving teaching instructions. The clinician does, however, respond to topics initiated by the client or clients. In addition, for interactions involving a child, the clinician does not initiate any type of play with the objects present but will respond to play initiated by the child. The remaining 25 minutes of each session are devoted to intervention.

Selection of Intervention Goals

In conducting intervention, particularly with peer groups, the initial selection of intervention goals primarily involves (1) an increase of topic initiations for submissive clients in relation to the other group participants and (2) a decrease of topic initiations for dominant clients in relation to the other group participants. The rationale for these goals was derived from the findings of Weimann (1977) demonstrating that bilateral topic control was judged to be more socially competent than unilateral topic control in interactions involving two participants. Other treatment goals for both group and individual sessions will be discussed following general teaching procedures. The criterion for intervention is based on three consecutive baseline measures with the desired communication behavior emitted.

General Teaching Procedures

General teaching procedures for facilitating discourse development include the use of instruction, modeling, role-playing, and feedback regarding performance. The procedures for teaching a specific communication skill often vary across clients, depending upon their level of development. Generally, the first procedure employed for teaching a specific communication skill is that of instruction involving the definition and discussion of the use of the skill. Clients functioning at comprehension levels of two to three years of age may not always be capable of understanding all uses of a skill. For these clients, the desired behavior is modeled. The second procedure employed involves an explanation of a role-playing task to practice the communication skill. For example, for teaching a topic initiation involving a greeting, the clinician would state: "Let's pretend that you see me first thing in the morning. What would you say to me? Now let's practice doing it." Clients operating primarily in early preoperations are not always capable of responding to a "let's pretend" discussion. Therefore, for these clients the actual situation and behavior are modeled. Emphasis is also placed on allowing the client, depending on his or her level of development, to problem solve, to think of alternative ways of expressing the same intention, to identify the behaviors involved in a new skill, to become aware of the need for and uses of a skill, and to practice the skill (Johnson, 1972). Generally, those clients functioning primarily in late preoperations are more capable of using these kinds of metacommunication skills than those operating primarily in early preoperations (Bedrosian, 1982).

Specific Teaching Procedures

Specific teaching procedures employed for various discourse goals are reported by Bedrosian (1982). A summary outline of those goals and procedures is presented in Table 12–3. The discourse goals and specific

Table 12-3.   An Outline of Discourse Goals and Teaching Procedures

Discourse Goal	Teaching Procedures
Increasing the frequency of topic initiations	1. Greetings 2. Departures 3. Ways of getting the listener's attention 4. Expression of needs 5. Initiation of requests for information 6. Initiation of requests for repair
Decreasing the frequency of topic initiations	1. Turn-taking 2. Listening skills 3. Decreasing interruptions
Increasing the frequency of other-oriented topic initiations	1. Rationale 2. Greetings and requests for information
Increasing the frequency of eye contact when initiating a topic in a group	1. Description of facial features 2. Imitation of nonverbal behaviors 3. Instruction-giving 4. Structured game 5. Nonverbal behaviors
Increasing the frequency of topic maintenance turns	1. Acknowledgement 2. Topic incorporating 3. Topic changing devices
Increasing the frequency of different subject matters of topic initiations	1. Memory-related topics 2. Future-related topics 3. Fantasy-related topics

teaching procedures follow:

Increasing the Frequency of Topic Initiations. Teaching procedures for increasing the frequency of topic initiations involve various subject matters, communicative intentions, and sociolinguistic rules:

1. *Greetings.* One subject matter involves the use of greetings.
   A. Greetings are defined to the clients as: "Hi"; "Hello"; "How are you?"; "Good morning"; and "How are things going?"
   B. Situations in which greetings are appropriate are discussed: when immediately meeting another for the first time, when seeing a familiar person for the first time that day, when walking past another in the hall, when taking a seat next to someone, and when answering the telephone. The clients are asked to contribute their ideas regarding the appropriate use of greetings.
   C. Role-playing procedures are then used to set up the situations just specified. For example, the client is asked to show how he or she would greet a friend when seeing that person for the first time that day. In instances in which the client does not spontaneously initiate a greeting, the clinician either models the

desired communication behavior or uses the phrase "What do you say when you first see someone?" in order to elicit the greeting. For children, toy telephones or puppets can be used in practicing greetings for some of the situations.

D. Situations in which greetings are not appropriate are also discussed: in the middle of a conversation; after one has already greeted a particular individual when passing strangers on the street; and when having been seated next to an individual for a period of time. The clients are again asked to contribute their ideas regarding the inappropriate use of greetings.

E. Finally, role-playing judgment tasks are used by having the client judge whether or not a greeting had been used appropriately in the various situations presented.

2. *Departures.* Procedures for teaching departures (e.g., "Goodbye"; "See you later"; "I'll be right back") are similar to those for teaching the use of greetings.

3. *Ways of getting the listener's attention.* In order to initiate a topic, the speaker must first gain the attention of the intended listener (Keenan and Schieffelin, 1976).

A. Ways of getting the listener's attention are discussed: saying the listener's name, tapping the listener on the shoulder, moving within the visual field of the listener, using a louder voice, leaning forward in the direction of the listener, and using eye contact with the intended listener when in a group of participants.

B. Role-playing procedures are employed to elicit attention-getting devices. For example: The client is instructed to give the clinician a message or an object. The clinician then moves about the room, doing various tasks, and ignores the client's attempt to deliver the message or object. This procedure usually elicits one or more attention-getting devices. In instances in which the client does not spontaneously initiate an attention-getting device or is not successful in using a particular device, the clinician either models the desired communication behavior or uses the phrase "Tell me or show me what you can do to get me to look at you" in order to elicit an attention-getting device. Similar procedures are used if the client is instructed to give an object to a peer.

4. *Expression of needs.* In order to initiate topics, a speaker often must have a need to communicate.

A. Procedures are designed to create a need for initiating. For example, in group treatment sessions, tasks are structured such that each dominant client has the necessary materials to perform or complete the tasks. The submissive client is not given the necessary task materials in order to elicit the initiation for expression of needs. These tasks include: baking cookies, drawing a poster, or putting together a jigsaw puzzle. Similar procedures can be used for individual treatment sessions. Other procedures for eliciting expression of needs involve taking clients to a restaurant, a social setting that requires the client to interact with restaurant personnel in order to eat.

B.   In each situation, a three-step elicitation procedure is used if the client does not initiate his or her needs:

1.   The client is asked if he or she has everything he or she needs for the task or situation.

2.   The client is then asked what he or she needs.

3.   If still no initiation is given, the client is then questioned directly: "Do you need (name of object needed)?"

5.   Initiation of requests for information. One communicative intent that is focused on for increasing the frequency of topic initiations involves requests for information.

A.   In order to account for differences in comprehension levels across clients in a group, the instruction "ask a question" is not employed for eliciting requests for information (Chomsky, 1969). Instead, to elicit a question regarding the client's weekend activities or feelings about a particular situation, for example, the following instructions are given: "What did (name of group participant) do over the weekend? How does (name of group participant) feel about (specify topic)? How can you find out?" If the client does not respond following this instruction, a question is modeled for him or her. For correct performance, the clinician accepts any question form corresponding to the client's syntactic level of development as long as the question is directed to the topic at hand. Various topics are used in presenting the instructions for asking questions. Often the topics are initiated by the clients themselves.

B.   A variation of this conversational procedure involves a guessing task, in which each client selects a picture of what he or she enjoys doing. The client is instructed to "Find out what (name of group participant) likes to do." Again, similar procedures can be used in individual treatment sessions.

6.   Initiation of requests for repair. Another communicative intent involves the use of requests for repair. According to Markman (1978), an individual's cognitive level is related to the extent to which

he or she can recognize not having comprehended a message. Certain procedures are designed to elicit a request for repair, specifically a request for repetition (e.g., "What?"; "Huh?"; "Could you please repeat that?"), from clients operating across various levels of cognitive development.

A. During the course of a conversation, the clinician will occasionally speak at a whisper level or deliberately mumble nonsense syllables. If the client does not spontaneously initiate a request for repetition, the following instructions are given: "What did I just say? How can you find out what I just said?" If the client still does not initiate the repair, a request form corresponding to the individual's level of syntactic development is modeled for him or her. For example, if the individual is operating between Brown Stages I and II, the request form "Say that again, please" is modeled. Individuals operating in Stages IV and V are given the request form "Can you say that again?" or "What did you say?"

B. In addition to the elicitation procedures used by the clinician, requests for repetition are also considered if any group participant has not been heard during the course of conversation. The same modeling procedures are again used in such cases.

Decreasing the Frequency of Topic Initiations. Procedures for decreasing the frequency of topic initiations involve turn-taking and listening activities as well as procedures for decreasing interruptions. The procedures are designed under the assumption that as submissive clients begin to initiate more topics, there will be less floor time for dominant clients to initiate topics. Specific procedures include:

1. *Turn-taking.*
    A. Turn-taking procedures initially involve the use of a structured card game, "Go Fish," and a board game, "Parcheesi," during which each client can talk only when it is his or her turn in the game. The order of turns among participants is established at the beginning of each game. Following a turn, the client is asked to identify the participant who has the next turn. The importance of letting each participant in the group have a turn to talk is stressed.
    B. Conversational turn-taking procedures involve the clinician designating turns among participants when conducting the procedures discussed for increasing the frequency of topic initiations.

2. *Listening skills.* Effective communication involves more than just

initiating. It also involves active listening in order to assure accuracy in understanding the message (Miller et al., 1975), to provide support for and show interest in the speaker (Egan, 1970), and to be able to maintain continuous discourse. Procedures for facilitating listening skills are as follows:

A. Each client is instructed to repeat what the previous speaker has stated before he or she can initiate a new topic (Johnson, 1972).

B. An alternative procedure involves questioning the client in regard to the content of an immediate speaker's turn in the group. The question is: "What did (*name of speaker*) just say?" If the client cannot respond, procedures for eliciting a request for repair are then implemented.

C. Various referential communication tasks (Longhurst and Reichle, 1975) are also employed.

D. Finally, the body language of a listener is discussed. A judgment task is used, requiring clients to determine the difference between an interested listener and a bored listener. An interested listener is defined as an individual who looks at the speaker, uses verbal and nonverbal acknowledgments, and sits with his or her body facing the speaker. A bored listener is defined as an individual who engages in another activity without looking at the speaker, does not use verbal or nonverbal acknowledgments, talks while the speaker is talking, turns away from the speaker, or walks out of the room during the conversation. Each client is also asked to role-play both types of listeners in response to a participant talking.

3. *Decreasing the frequency of interruptions.* Procedures for decreasing the frequency of interruptions follow.

A. An interruption is defined to the clients as "Talking when someone else is already talking."

B. Each client is asked to immediately identify his or her interruption by using the following line of questions:

1. "Who was talking just now?"
2. "What did you just do?", in order to elicit the response, "Interrupt."
3. "What do you need to do?", in order to elicit the response "Wait" or "Wait until he or she stops talking."

C. A task requiring the client to judge when a speaker has stopped talking is employed. Specifically, the client is given a message or an object to deliver to a person who is engaged in a conversation. The client is instructed to wait and to deliver the message only when the person stops talking or acknowledges the client's presence by turning towards the client. If the client interrupts the individual talking, the same line of questioning just specified is used.

D. Each client is also instructed as to what to say following an interruption. For example: "Excuse me" or "I'm sorry I interrupted."

E. Situations in which interruptions are appropriate are also discussed: in case of an emergency or when late for an appointment. The clients are asked to contribute their ideas regarding the appropriate use of interruptions.

F. Role-playing tasks are used by having the client judge whether or not an interruption has been used appropriately in the various situations presented.

G. Finally, for those clients operating at least at middle pre-operations with comparative levels of language comprehension and production, more sophisticated instructions regarding turn-taking cues specified by Weiman and Knapp (1975) are given. For example, clients are instructed to watch for the following cues used by a speaker to indicate that he or she is not ready to give up the floor:
    1. Use of coordinating conjunctions either followed by a pause or prolonged.
    2. Prolongation of words.
    3. Use of expressions like "Ahm" followed by a pause.
    4. Use of eye contact by looking up at the ceiling to indicate thinking.

    Clients are asked to deliver a message to the clinician who uses these cues while talking. The clients are instructed to wait until the clinician is done with her turn. It should be noted that in some cases decreasing interruptions can be considered as a separate goal.

Increasing the Frequency of Other-Oriented Topic Initiations. Procedures for increasing the frequency of other-oriented topic initiations are as follows:

1. The rationale for focusing on the other or for increasing the frequency of other-oriented topics is discussed with the clients: "It is important to show the other person that you are interested in him or her so that he or she will want to be your friend. So you must learn to focus on the other person by remembering to greet him or her and to find out different things about that person, instead of always just talking about yourself."

2. Procedures for teaching greetings as well as requests for information

are employed for purposes of focusing on another person. Clients are instructed to go up to individuals and use a greeting followed by a request for information before they can begin talking about themselves.

Increasing the Frequency of Eye Contact when Initiating a Topic in a Group. Procedures for increasing the frequency of eye contact when initiating a topic in a group setting can be incorporated under procedures for increasing the frequency of topic intitiations or can be employed as a separate goal. Preliminary research findings indicate a possible relationship between these two areas (Bedrosian, 1982). When teaching eye contact, it is important to consider the literature regarding normal adult usage of eye contact. According to Kendon (1965), the speaker does not maintain constant eye contact with the listener. However, when the speaker is ready to yield the floor, he or she will reestablish eye contact with the listener. In turn, the listener, who previously had been maintaining eye contact with the speaker, will then look away when attaining the floor. In addition to these rules, it is important to use eye contact when initiating a topic to one specific participant in a group, especially if one cannot remember the participant's name for purposes of obtaining his or her attention. Procedures for this goal are as follows:

1. Clients are asked to describe various features on the faces of the participants in the group. For example: color of eyes and hair, wearing of glasses, size of ears, length of hair, size of nose, smoothness of skin, or presence of freckles.
2. Each client is also instructed to imitate the nonverbal actions and facial expressions of another participant, creating a mirror-image exercise.
3. The client is then asked to give an instruction to a particular member of the group by using eye contact. The instructions are: "Tell or ask (*name of participant*) to get the (*name of object*) or to do (*name of action*). Remember to look at him (or her) to get his (or her) attention."
4. The card game, "Go Fish," is also used for purposes of requiring the client to look at a particular participant in order to get his attention to ask for a card.
5. If the client exhibits difficulty in using eye contact, he or she is instructed to turn his or her body toward the intended listener, say the name of the intended listener, look at the forehead or the top of the intended listener's head, lean toward the intended listener, or tap the shoulder of the intended listener.

Increasing the Frequency of Topic Maintenance Turns. Procedures for increasing the frequency of topic maintenance turns can include any one or more of the following continuous discourse types:

1. *Acknowledgment*. First, the use of a verbal or nonverbal acknowledgment (e.g., "Uh-huh," or a head nod) in a question-response-acknowledgment sequence can be taught. For example, clients are instructed to produce a request for information, listen to the response, and then use an acknowledgment. Such a procedure involves minimal topic maintenance skills. The client is then questioned to determine if he or she was indeed listening to the speaker's response.

2. *Topic incorporating*. Another continuous discourse type involves the use of topic incorporation. Clients are instructed to describe various aspects of a single object or issue using the phrase "What else can we say about this?" to elicit further incorporations of the topic. Procedures for topic incorporation also include teaching chaining of successive requests for information by using the phrase: "What else can you ask (*name of participant*) about (*name of topic*)?"

3. *Topic changing devices*. For those clients operating at least in late preoperations, procedures can also include teaching topic changing devices (e.g., "Oh, by the way..." or "Not to change the topic but..."). Clients are instructed to use such devices only after they have initially maintained the topic of the previous speaker's turn. This sequence results in a continuous-discontinuous turn, preventing abrupt topic changes.

Increasing the Frequency of Different Subject Matters of Topic Initiations. The final discourse goal and procedures are directed towards those clients who primarily initiate topics in the here-and-now. Procedures for increasing the frequency of different subject matters of topic initiations are discussed in terms of memory-related, future-related, and fantasy-related topics.

1. *Memory-related topics.*
   A. In order to increase the frequency of memory-related topics, clients are encouraged to talk about feelings they were having or activities they were engaged in the day before or just prior to the session. The clinician uses the phrase "Tell me or (*name of another participant*) what you did today." The client is also instructed to request similar memory-related information from other participants.
   B. Other procedures involve engaging the clients in various activities or projects, such as exercising or making posters, followed by a discussion of the events that took place. The client's level of syntactic development in terms of regular and

irregular past tense verbs is considered when determining the acceptability of the initiations.

2. *Future-related topics.* Procedures for increasing the frequency of future-related topics are similar to those involving memory-related topics.

   A. Clients are encouraged to talk about activities they will be engaged in at any point in time following the session. The clinician uses the phrase "Tell me or (*name of other participant*) what you will be doing later today." The client is also instructed to request similar future-related information from other participants.

   B. Other procedures include a discussion related to the planning of activities or projects to be done at a subsequent session. Syntactic levels of development are again considered.

3. *Fantasy-related topics.* Procedures for increasing the frequency of fantasy-related topics deal with sociodramatic play and are employed only with language-disordered children functioning at least in middle preoperations ($+$1 cognitive year). According to McCune-Nicolich and Carroll (1981), sociodramatic play involves the specification of a theme (e.g., playing house, hospital, or good guys and bad guys) and the designation of appropriate roles (e.g., mommy-daddy, doctor-patient, or Luke Skywalker–Darth Vader) to carry out the theme. Language has an important role in this type of play not only in terms of its use for initiating themes and roles but also in terms of its use for elaborating the plans of play. Research regarding the sociodramatic play skills of language-disordered children has indicated that these children spend less time in this type of play and are more initiative and concrete in their play (McCune-Nicolich and Carroll, 1981). Specific procedures for increasing the frequency of sociodramatic play in children are as follows:

   A. First, several props are made available to the clients. These props can include various hats, shirts, neckties, scarves, doctor kits, dishes, play kitchen sets, and so on.

   B. If the client does not spontaneously initiate a theme and roles, the clinician does so by using the phrases "Let's play (*name of theme*). Who do you want to be? Who should I be?"

   C. The client is then encouraged to think of ways to play out the theme. (For example: "What should we do first?") If necessary, various episodes are modeled for each theme.

   D. The clinician records the length of time used for each theme as well as the frequency of new or repeated episodes initiated by the client for each theme.

FINAL COMMENTS

This chapter describes specific procedures regarding the assessment and intervention of discourse skills in language-disordered children and adults. Although carryover procedures were not discussed, such procedures should be an integral part of any language program. Several of the conversational exercises employed in the clinical setting could also be used in the classroom or home setting.

Many speech and language clinicians have begun to incorporate discourse skills in their language intervention programs. These skills, however, are often considered as an afterthought in that a communicative framework might be employed for purposes of creating an occasional fun group activity or for teaching the generalization of previously learned grammatical rules (Culatta and Horn, 1982). This chapter suggests *beginning* intervention in a communicative context.

Focusing on discourse skills in a language intervention program does not or should not imply that other areas of language production and comprehension are overlooked. Within the context of a discourse program, the client's level of syntactic and comprehension development are considered and incorporated as an integral part of the program. For example, in terms of teaching memory- or future-related topics, the client's level of verb phrase development determines the language modeled for him or her, as well as the acceptability of an intitiation or response. Bedrosian and Willis (1984) conducted a six month discourse program focusing on memory- and future-related topics in a five year old child enrolled in a kindergarten classroom. The child was functioning in early to middle preoperations at the beginning of the program. In terms of language production, he had a mean length of utterance (MLU) in morphemes of 3.18, corresponding to Brown's Early Stage IV (Miller, 1981). Results of the program indicated not only an increase in the variety of subject matters initiated by the child but also a clinically significant increase in the child's general level of syntactic development as reflected by his final MLU of 4.20, corresponding to Brown's Late Stage V. Aspects of semantic development are also an integral part of the discourse program. For example, the vocabulary skills of a client play a major role in his or her ability to initiate and maintain a variety of conversational topics. In facilitating topic performance, then, a variety of lexical items can be modeled within a discourse framework. Word-finding difficulties can also be facilitated in this manner. It is possible, therefore, to observe changes in the overall language performance of a client by focusing on communication in a functional manner without spending long hours of syntactic or semantic drilling. Approaching language intervention from a discourse framework provides an alternative to traditional language programming.

REFERENCES

Bates, E. (1976). *Language in context: The acquisition of pragmatics.* New York: Academic Press.

Bedrosian, J. L. (1979, May). Communicative performance of mentally retarded adults—A topic analysis. Paper presented at the American Association on Mental Deficiency Convention, Miami Beach, FL.

Bedrosian, J. L. (1982). A sociolinguistic approach to communication skills: Assessment and treatment methodology for mentally retarded adults (Doctoral dissertation, University of Wisconsin, 1981). *Dissertation Abstracts International, 42,* 4338A.

Bedrosian, J. L. (1983, November). Pragmatics: Assessment and intervention methodology for language disordered children/adults. Paper presented at the American Speech-Language-Hearing Association Convention, Cincinnati, OH.

Bedrosian, J. L., and Prutting, C. A. (1978). Communicative performance of mentally retarded adults in four conversational settings. *Journal of Speech and Hearing Research, 21,* 79–95.

Bedrosian, J. L., and Willis, T. L. (1984, November). Effects of intervention on a school-aged child's topic performance. Paper presented at the American Speech-Language-Hearing Association Convention, San Francisco, CA.

Bernard-Opitz, V. (1982). Pragmatic analysis of communicative behavior of an autistic child. *Journal of Speech and Hearing Disorders, 47,* 99–108.

Bloom, L., Rocissano, L., and Hood, L. (1976). Adult-child discourse: Developmental interaction between information processing and linguistic knowledge. *Cognitive Psychology, 8,* 521–552.

Bryan, T., and Pflaum, S. (1978). Linguistic, cognitive and social analyses of learning disabled children's interactions. *Learning Disability Quarterly, 1,* 70–79.

Chapman, R. S. (1981). Computing child's mean length of utterance in morphemes. In J. F. Miller (Ed.), *Assessing language production in children: Experimental procedures.* Baltimore, MD: University Park Press.

Chapman, R. S. (1982). Issues in child language acquisition. In N. J. Lass, L. V. McReynolds, J. L. Northern, and D. E. Yoder (Eds.), *Speech, language, and hearing: Volume 1, Normal processes.* Philadelphia: W. B. Saunders.

Chomsky, C. S. (1969). *The acquisition of syntax in children from 5 to 10.* Cambridge, MA: MIT Press.

Craig, H. K. (1983). Applications of pragmatic language models for intervention. In T. M. Gallagher and C. A. Prutting (Eds.), *Pragmatic assessment and intervention issues in language.* San Diego: College-Hill Press.

Culatta, B., and Horn, D. (1982). A program for achieving generalization of grammatical rules to spontaneous discourse. *Journal of Speech and Hearing Disorders, 47,* 174–180.

Donahue, M., Pearl, R., and Bryan, T. (1980). Learning disabled children's conversational competence: Responses to inadequate messages. *Applied Psycholinguistics, 1,* 387–403.

Egan, G. (1970). *Encounter group processes for interpersonal growth.* Belmont, CA: Brooks/Cole Publishing.

Ervin-Tripp, S. M. (1973). *Language acquisition and communicative choice.* Stanford, CA: Stanford University Press.

Gallagher, T. M. (1983). Pre-assessment: A procedure for accommodating language use variability. In T. M. Gallagher and C. A. Prutting (Eds.), *Pragmatic assessment and intervention issues in language*. San Diego: College-Hill Press.

Gallagher, T. M., and Prutting, C. A. (1983). *Pragmatic assessment and intervention issues in language*. San Diego: College-Hill Press.

Grice, H. P. (1975). Logic and conversation. In P. Cole and J. L. Morgan (Eds.), *Syntax and semantics: Speech acts*. New York: Academic Press.

Hersen, M., and Barlow, D. H. (1976). *Single case experimental designs: Strategies for studying behavior change*. New York: Pergamon Press.

Johnson, D. W. (1972). *Reaching out: Interpersonal effectiveness and self-actualization*. Englewood Cliffs, NJ: Prentice-Hall.

Keenan, E. O., and Schieffelin, B. B. (1976). Topic as a discourse notion: A study of topic in the conversation of children and adults. In C. N. Li (Ed.), *Subject and topic*. New York: Academic Press.

Kendon, A. (1965). Some functions of gaze direction in social interaction. Unpublished report to the Science Research Council.

Longhurst, T. M., and Reichle, J. E. (1975). The applied communication game: A comment on Muma's "Communication game: Dump and play." *Journal of Speech and Hearing Disorders, 40*, 315–319.

Lund, N. J., and Duchan, J. R. (1983). *Assessing children's language in naturalistic contexts*. Englewood Cliffs, NJ: Prentice-Hall.

McCune-Nicholich, L., and Carroll, S. (1981). Development of symbolic play: Implications for the language specialist. *Topics in Language Disorders, 2*, 1–16.

Markman, E. M. (1978, October). Comprehension monitoring. Paper presented to the Conference on Children's Oral Communication Skills, University of Wisconsin-Madison, Madison.

Miller, J. F. (1981). *Assessing children's language production: Experimental procedures*. Baltimore, MD: University Park Press.

Miller, S., Nunnally, E. W., and Wackman, D. B. (1975). *Alive and aware: How to improve your relationship through better communication*. Minneapolis, MN: Interpersonal Communication Program.

Mishler, E. (1975). Studies in dialogue and discourse: II. Types of discourse initiated by and sustained through questioning. *Journal of Psycholinguistic Research, 4*, 99–121.

Owings, N., and McManus, M. (1982). Analysis of communication function use by adult mentally retarded clients in three residential settings. Paper presented at the 106th annual meeting of the American Association on Mental Deficiency, Boston.

Prizant, B., and Duchan, J. (1981). The function of immediate echolalia in autistic children. *Journal of Speech and Hearing Disorders, 46*, 241–249.

Prutting, C. A. (1979). Process / pra̯, ses\ n: The action of moving forward progressively from one point to another on the way to completion. *Journal of Speech and Hearing Disorders, 44*, 3–30.

Prutting, C. A., and Kirchner, D. M. (1983). Applied pragmatics. In T. M. Gallagher and C. A. Prutting (Eds.), *Pragmatic assessment and intervention issues in language*. San Diego: College-Hill.

Rees, N. S. (1978). Pragmatics of language: Applications to normal and disordered language development. In R. L. Schiefelbusch (Ed.), *Bases of language intervention*. Baltimore: University Park Press.

Wanska, S. K., Bedrosian, J. L., and Pohlman, J. (1984). Effects of play conditions on the topic performance of preschool children. Unpublished manuscript, Kansas State University, Manhattan.

Warne, D. (1984). Turntaking repair and topic maintenance abilities in mentally retarded adults. Unpublished master's thesis, Kansas State University, Manhattan.

Watzlawick, P., Beavin, J. H., and Jackson, D. D. (1967). *Pragmatics of human communication*. New York: W. W. Norton and Company.

Weimann, J. M. (1977). Explication and test of a model of communicative competence. *Human Communication Research, 3*, 195–313.

Weimann, J. M., and Knapp, M. L. (1975, Spring). Turn-taking in conversations. *Journal of Communication*, pp. 75–92.

Wiig, E. H., and Semel, E. M. (1980). *Language assessment and intervention for the learning disabled*. Columbus, OH: Charles E. Merrill.

PART V

SUMMARY

Chapter 13

Some Conclusions About School Talk

Danielle N. Ripich
Francesca M. Spinelli

The contents of this book demonstrate a tremendous growth of our knowledge base in communication problems in children as well as an expansion in our role as school speech-language pathologists. In the past the narrowly defined parameters of speech and language intervention did not include much more than articulation and linguistic rule training in the context of a small therapy room. However, the image of the school speech-language pathologist sitting in a room behind the boiler with a child and a pack of *s* cards has become dated (Koenig, 1984). In addition to the therapy room, school clinicians presently work within regular and special classrooms and learning resource centers. They work with children whose physical and mental disabilities range from mild to severe. This expansion of therapy settings and services has come about as a result of changes in education in this country and a broadening of perspectives within speech-language pathology.

In the late 1960s and the early 1970s public schools began to be held responsible for the education of all children from birth to adulthood who lived within their district. Prior to this time schools educated normal children from 5 through 18 years of age. The needs of most of the children discussed in this book were not addressed by local school systems. The redefinition of the population to be educated in the public schools dramatically altered the case load of school speech-language pathologists. They were suddenly confronted with children of all ages who were mentally retarded, hearing impaired, learning disabled, multilingual, and communicatively impaired at more severe levels than previously seen in this setting.

During this same period, the field of speech-language pathology underwent a dramatic phase of growth. Numbers of speech-language pathologists increased; but, perhaps more importantly, the field began to broaden the scope of services delivered. School case loads shifted from primarily articulation training to include syntax and semantic intervention. More recently, research into the pragmatics of language and discourse features of communication has generated an even greater expansion of services. This latest expansion is the focus of the book.

Although numerous issues were raised by the authors, four issues with important implications for children's communication in school predominated. The first issue was the ability of communicatively impaired children to participate in classroom discourse. The second issue was the source of discourse variation; some children's discourse rule sets are deviant, and others appear to be valid but different from typical school discourse. The third issue was the need to include discourse as a communicative skill area for assessment and intervention in children who demonstrate problems in interaction. Finally the fourth issue is one that has not been previously addressed. It centers around the expectations placed on children by parents, teachers, and children themselves to perform at a particular level of discourse competence. The following discussion examines each of these issues and draws implications for education.

CLASSROOM DISCOURSE

Communicatively impaired children are, by and large, passive participants in conversation at school. This statement, or a variation of it, was reiterated across several chapters in this volume. Bloome and Knott (Chapter 4) explain why school discourse rules make children more passive. Even though children are participants in the construction of lessons, they are often merely expected to act as cooperative responders. Asking questions slows the progress of the lesson and is viewed as obstructing learning. This passivity interferes with children's full and active participation in teaching-learning exchanges. For example, teachers are notoriously indirect (Donahue, Chapter 6) so that their messages may be confusing for children to follow. Children often request clarification from their teachers. However, because communicatively impaired children are not aggressive interacters, they may not seek clarification but instead try to guess the teacher's meaning from other cues. It is easy to see how this pattern leads to confusion and interferes with gaining accurate academic information in the classroom. In their passivity, these children do not make requests, bid for turns, or challenge other speakers. Steven, the child in the case study in Chapter 10 (on ethnographic assessment and intervention), typifies this kind of passive classroom communication style.

Children's covert conversations, often involving questions about the instruction that is taking place, are one example of how children circumvent the strictures of classroom discourse. For communicatively impaired children, however, this and other strategies for enriching their communication experience are not always possible. Most interactions of communicatively impaired children occur with teachers. Normally achieving (NA) peers reportedly avoid conversations with communicatively impaired children, effectively cutting off this avenue of interaction. The avoidance may result from a number of problems. Donahue speculates that communicating with learning disabled (LD) children may be too much work for the normal child, as LD children are not adept conversational partners and do not easily modify their interaction to fit a particular context. This places a large share of the communication burden on the LD child's conversational partner. Using Donahue's analogy, conversing with an LD child is like playing tennis with a weak opponent: The stronger player has to work especially hard to keep the ball in play. For most peers it is not worth the extra effort required.

For the same reason, perhaps, hearing impaired children are not selected as conversational partners by hearing students. Because the hearing impaired child responds poorly to some conversation, he or she is perceived as a passive communicator and consequently is not a highly desirable partner for interaction. Griffith, Johnson, and Dastoli (Chapter 8) discuss the problems hearing impaired children experience in participating in group conversations in and out of the classroom. Following shifts in speakers are reportedly the most difficult obstacle encountered by these children, with almost half of them stating that they often feel left out of group interaction. This isolation probably creates an even greater distancing and passivity on the part of the hearing impaired and is analogous to Donahue's discussion of the "poor-get-poorer" phenomenon. In other words, feeling left out causes the hearing impaired or LD child to withdraw even further. Mainstreamed hearing impaired children appear to suffer the most from this lack of peer interaction. Self-contained classrooms offer hearing impaired children more interaction opportunities.

Mentally retarded children in mainstreamed classrooms are similarly avoided, so their best opportunity for being communicative also occurs in the special classroom setting. In fact, according to Calculator (Chapter 7), the special classroom may provide the optimum opportunity for these children to interact. However, this opportunity is not without limitations. The other students are likely to be impaired communicators as well so that there is no one with strong skills to compensate for the discourse problems that occur. The home environment may be the poorest setting for communication. In contrast to Terrell's (Chapter 2) and Tattershall and Creaghead's (Chapter 3) descriptions of a rich conversational home environment for normally developing children, residential homes for several retarded children are often highly restrictive in communication opportunities. Here, similar to Bloome and Knott's observation of teachers' attitudes, conversation is seen by caregivers as interfering with the "real work" (e.g., getting children dressed, fed, and so on). Children are rewarded for being passive, quiet, and cooperative. When these children are in school, teachers may encourage communication. However, unless mentally retarded children are directly motivated they will probably remain in their previously more rewarded, passive condition.

In summary, communicatively impaired children interact more with teachers than peers. Often teachers, aware of the importance of developing good communication in these children, encourage conversation. However, this conversation is frequently highly routinized talk that places children in a passive responder conversational role so that their interaction is limited in variety.

DIFFERENCE AND DEVIANCE IN SCHOOL DISCOURSE

Clearly, some children have difficulty mastering classroom discourse roles. Iglesias (Chapter 5) as well as Bloome and Knott (Chapter 4) discussed the mismatch between home and school experienced by culturally diverse children. These children are faced with a dual problem. First, they must learn to distinguish, then selectively use, differing sets of discourse rules. The correct choice takes into account the setting and the participants in the interaction.

Like culturally diverse students, children with communication impairments experience difficulty mastering classroom discourse rules. Several of the chapters documented that hearing impaired, cognitively impaired, language disordered, and learning disabled children's deficiencies in knowledge and use of discourse rules can interfere with classroom learning. The interpretation could be made that the children's deficits were the underlying cause of the problem. To some extent this is true. Griffith and colleagues point out that hearing impaired children are at a disadvantage because they cannot utilize all available communication cues and thus do not receive all conversational information. Bedrosian (Chapter 12) notes that particular cognitive abilities may be requisite for certain kinds of discourse mastery. For example, topics beyond the present time and space will not be raised by children operating in the here-and-now. In addition, Donahue as well as Ripich and Spinelli suggest that learning and language disabled children may experience difficulty in conversation because of linguistic and social deficits. Clearly, deficits in abilities related to the acquisition of discourse rules result in discourse problems.

However, a recurring point was made that impaired abilities, requisite or associated, are insufficient to explain all discourse problems. The problems also result from conflicts between different but valid sets of rules. As Donahue, Griffith and coworkers, and Iglesias point out, communicatively impaired children often demonstrate mastery of highly complex sets of social interaction rules. However, their discourse rule set may not match appropriate classroom rules. This mismatch, along with their other communication problems, makes these children appear to be very poor classroom communicators (Donahue, Bloome and Knott, and Ripich and Spinelli).

Donahue makes the point that children who leave the classroom to receive special assistance miss classroom events and thus have a reduced shared background with the other students. She also notes that these children have limited opportunity to fill in the gaps because of reduced peer and teacher interaction. These children do not experience the same "school" as do NA peers. This mismatch is compounded by the use of different discourse rules in the resource room (Donahue), therapy room (Ripich and Spinelli), and special education room (Calculator and Griffith et al.). Students in these contexts may be juggling multiple sets of sometimes contradictory rules. This need to use multiple rules may make them appear to be less socially competent than they actually are.

Thus it appears that while communicatively impaired children may have deficits that interfere with their ability to interact effectively, they are also operating with a different set or sets of discourse rules reinforced by the school. Donahue refers to this latter phenomenon as the "newcomer hypothesis." She suggests that based on teacher reinforcement and inappropriate generalization of rules used in other contexts, disabled children have developed a different set of interactional norms. This, in conjunction with their limited shared experience due to absences from the classroom, makes them in effect "newcomers" in that setting. Unfortunately, they are not newcomers and do not have the assistance and understanding afforded to new members of the classroom. It appears, then, that children with disorders share much with culturally diverse children, who too, are not necessarily deficient but are operating under a set of different rules (Iglesias).

ASSESSMENT AND INTERVENTION

The third issue focuses on viewing communication breakdown in a broad perspective. Tomblin and Liljegreen (Chapter 11) point out that even with in-depth formal assessment of a child's speech and language skills, information relating to the underlying communication problem can be missed because the focus is too narrow. They suggest that clinicians should view communication breakdown as a socially defined phenomena and direct their intervention process to target those behaviors that carry the greatest social penalty. In case of a particular child for example, poor topic maintenance may be a greater problem than phonologic errors, but because of the orientation of speech-language pathologists, intervention might be focused on phonology, with the discourse area of topic maintenance improvement relegated to the phonology "carryover" phase of each lesson.

Ripich and Spinelli's approach supports the notion of including information regarding social penalties as part of assessment. They rely on social judgments of classroom teachers and students in conjunction with the clinician's validating observations to determine the disorder and goals of remediation. In this assessment and intervention process the entire system, including intrapersonal and interpersonal factors, is examined. The previous focus of assessment and intervention on intrapersonal aspects of communication, that is, syntax, phonology, and so on, failed to take into account the nature of communication as an interpersonal event.

Tomblin and Liljegreen point out that a comprehensive approach is critical; breakdown can occur at any point in the system and a breakdown affects all other points. It becomes clear how problems in one area can affect other areas that can have consequences on even different communication areas. For example, a child with poor syntactic and semantic skills may cause a teacher to encourage the child to talk more to obtain practice using corrected linguistic forms. In conjunction with this, however, the child learns a discourse rule that says it is acceptable to talk extensively and to interrupt at times that other children cannot. The child is then using a rule that may cause others to view him as an inappropriate communicator.

In summary, children must know the rules of classroom discourse in order to have access to the content of lessons. Authors in this volume are advocating teaching appropriate discourse rule use as an integral part of communication intervention. Approaches that are designed to incorporate discourse rule competency as part of the intervention system provide the communicatively impaired child with the best opportunity to succeed in school.

DISCOURSE EXPECTATIONS

The final issue centers around expectations of parents,' teachers,' and children's conversations with communicatively impaired children. Terrell describes the developing communication abilities of children and points out that parents constantly adjust their conversational expectations for a child based on the child's utterances. Linguistic elements such as utterance length and phonologic complexity are markers that signal the level of language ability the child has reached. Discourse abilities may be more subtle and difficult to observe and as such more difficult to adjust for. We are only beginning to define discourse features, and it seems reasonable that we may be less adept at matching discourse expectations for children's performance to their actual competency.

Tattershall and Creaghead, through their interviews, culled information regarding communication expectations at home and in school. Their findings suggest that as children move through the education process, the teachers' expectation levels increase. This is supported by Iglesias's contention that bilingual kindergarten children's errors are often attributed to language problems, but by third grade these same children are thought to be poor learners if they make these same errors.

Donahue, Calculator, Griffith and colleagues, Iglesias, and Spinelli and Ripich (in their chapter comparing the classroom and the therapy room) discuss the issue of teachers' different conversational rules when interacting with communicatively impaired children. Teachers may wittingly or unwittingly reinforce different discourse rules in children according to academic ability, as in Eder's (1982) report on differing rules for interruptions in high- and low-level reading groups. Teachers also appear to vary in interaction patterns according to their perception of children's communication competence (Iglesias). Furthermore, as Griffith and colleagues and Calculator suggest, some teachers may have lower expectations for disordered children and thus not motivate them to attain their potential discourse competence.

There is evidence that classroom interaction is often too complex for communicatively impaired children, but perhaps just as often the interaction is made too simple. Needs are anticipated so that no genuine request behavior is required of the children. Calculator discusses this overcompensation by teachers of mentally retarded children. Griffith and coworkers point out that hearing teachers ask lower-level cognitive questions of hearing impaired students than do deaf teachers. We can speculate that the hearing teachers view these children as deficient and so underestimate their communicative and cognitive reasoning abilities. There is evidence to suggest that this discourse mismatch, of either too complex or too simple an interaction, is experienced by communicatively impaired children frequently.

The expectations of the children themselves may also hamper interaction. Communicatively impaired children may fear being misunderstood or misunderstanding to such an extent that they avoid interaction (Griffith et al.). We can speculate that the anxiety generated by these avoidances has a negative impact on the ability of these children to concentrate and learn in classrooms. The problems surrounding discourse expectations encountered by communicatively impaired children is a critical area for future research.

CONCLUSION

In reaching conclusions about school talk we followed a circuitous path that led us from home and residential treatment settings to regular and special classrooms, resource rooms, and therapy rooms. In the process we gained an appreciation for the variations and complexities of the discourse rules that children must acquire. If we are to help children along the path to discourse competence, we need a clear understanding of the difficulties they encounter. This book is designed to serve as a signpost pointing the direction we must take.

REFERENCES

Eder, D. (1982). Differences in communicative styles across ability groups. In L. C. Wilkinson (Ed.), *Communicating in the classroom*. New York: Academic Press.

Koenig, L. (1984). Lecture presented at Clinical Practicum Meeting at Case Western Reserve University, Cleveland, OH.

Author Index

Subject Index